A History of
Modern Philosophy

A History of
Modern Philosophy

By Mariano Fazio & Daniel Gamarra

 Scepter

This is a translation of *Historia de la filosofía III: Filosofía moderna*,
copyright © 2014 Mariano Fazio and Daniel Gamarra,
Ediciones Palabra, S.A., Madrid, Spain.

English translation, copyright © 2017 Scepter Publishers, Inc.

Published by Scepter Publishers, Inc.
info@scepterpublishers.org
www.scepterpublishers.org
800-322-8773
New York

Translated by Cesar Magsino, Ph.D.
Text and cover by Christina Aquilina

Library of Congress Cataloging-in-Publication Data

Names: Fazio, Mariano. | Gamarra, Daniel, 1952–2015, author.
Title: A history of modern philosophy / Mariano Fazio and Daniel Gamarra.
Other titles: Historia de la filosofía. 3, filosofía moderna. English
Description: 1 edition. | New York : Scepter Publishers, 2017. |
"This is a translation of Historia de la filosofía III: filosofía moderna " 2014
Mariano Fazio and Daniel Gamarra, Ediciones Palabra, S.A., Madrid, Spain.
English translation, copyright " 2017 by Scepter Publishers, Inc." |
Includes index.
Identifiers: LCCN 2017013787 (print) | LCCN 2017023017 (ebook) |
ISBN 9781594172809 (ebook) | ISBN 9781594172793 (pbk. : alk. paper)
Subjects: LCSH: Philosophy, Modern—History.
Classification: LCC B795 (ebook) | LCC B795 .F3913 2017 (print) |
DDC 190—dc23
LC record available at https://lccn.loc.gov/2017013787

ISBN
Paperback: 9781594172793
eBook: 9781594172809

Printed in the United States of America.

CONTENTS

FOREWORD

Having already published our *History of Contemporary Philosophy*, Scepter Publishers now welcomes our *History of Modern Philosophy*, published a few years ago in Italian and in Spanish, then edited by the authors for this English edition.

While working on this new edition, my co-author Prof. Daniel Gamarra was called to the House of the Father, where I am sure he shares my joy to see this short book translated into the noble language of Shakespeare.

We would like to thank the translator, Cesar Magsino PhD, for his magnificent work, as well as Joseph Keefe PhD; John Boles and Jotham Njoroge for their help in the editing process.

Rome, May 6, 2016

INTRODUCTION

A ll historical disciplines need periodization, and so does the history of philosophy. Yet while dividing history into periods or eras allows us to neatly order historical themes and events, it could also create an overly rigid structure that ends up obscuring the continuity of history as it actually happened. Thus at the start of a study on Modern Philosophy, it is only fitting to remind the readers that we are not dealing with an absolutely defined period that began and ended at exact moments.

If we take a look at the periodization of history in general, we see that the start of the Modern Age usually falls between the middle and the end of the fifteenth century. The two most significant dates that mark the start of the new era are 1453, the fall of Constantinople, and 1492, the discovery of America. At the same time, it is reasonable to think that neither the first nor the second event occurred by chance, but that these were preceded by long periods of preparation, without which such events would not have taken place. Moreover, the very process that led up to a specific event provides the essential elements for comprehending its significance.

On the other hand, historians usually indicate the beginning of Modern Philosophy around the year 1620, when Descartes began his philosophical activity. There is a large and notable difference between this date and that which general history uses to mark the beginning of the Modern Era. If we take the year 1453 as the beginning of the Modern Age, then the difference is more than a century and a half. At the same time, we have to ask whether before Descartes there had not been a philosophy worthy of the name "modern." Putting the question more clearly: is modern philosophy a completely Cartesian invention? The history of philosophy is not an island: it is no exception among other historical disciplines. Just as in general history, in the field of philosophy, the facts—all ideas, currents of thought, philosophers—are always preceded by periods of preparation, by earlier events that predisposed their emergence in history. Even the very beginning of philosophy in ancient Greece was prepared by social conditions, cultural peculiarities, and by pre-philosophical speculation more religious and poetic in character.

To say that there are preparations, predispositions, and continuities in history is not the same as saying that there is an evolution, in the progressive sense of the word. Newer philosophical systems are not necessarily better or worse than their antecedents. Rather, each philosophical system is a better or worse development of the only true antecedents of philosophy, the human intellect and human freedom. In itself, the history of philosophy is not a process of constant and necessary progress.

Having affirmed, therefore, the continuity in the history of philosophy, we can now devote ourselves to the intended topic of this *History of Modern Philosophy*. We shall begin with the fifteenth century. In those years, very close to the Middle Ages, Renaissance philosophy was developing, although it had already begun to differentiate itself from the medieval worldview. The continuities and ruptures between the two historical periods, the traditional past and the emerging modern world, are particularly evident. Philosophical traditions and novelties, modern propositions, and reception of the ancient heritage, all mark the rhythm of this period in which modern philosophy begins to emerge. In the sixteenth century, we witness on the one hand, a skeptical inclination, and on the other hand, a renewed vigor for the scholastic philosophy of the medieval tradition.

The elements that we have just mentioned form part of the background of Descartes, but they constitute a cultural and speculative scenario that is already modern. Descartes may stand out as the founder of a new philosophy, but he is not isolated from tradition. His philosophy has its historical roots, and among his own contemporaries he found his critics. It is sometimes considered, however, that modern philosophy—to be worthy of its name—is the one that adequately responded to the rationalist project inaugurated by the French philosopher. It is true that such a project's unity of interests and main line of thought evidently manifested a new era. It is also true that Descartes and Bacon, fathers of rationalism and empiricism respectively, were clearly aware that they heralded a new philosophical period. But it must also be said, without a doubt, that the philosophy of the seventeenth century has Renaissance and Scholastic roots. But while rooted in history, modern thought was not merely the mature blossoming of older traditions; it truly generated its own cultural and speculative fruits.

Science, especially Physics, also began to emerge in the cultural and philosophical panorama of the seventeenth century. Copernicus, Kepler, and Galileo are to science what Descartes is for modern philosophy: creators, and not mere innovators or supporters. But modern science was not born only unto itself. From a theoretical point of view, the modern sciences posed new and difficult problems for philosophy.

Rationalism, empiricism, and modern science are the interweaving threads that constitute the fabric of this new cultural era. Man's consciousness of his capabilities, of the power of his freedom, and of his ingenuity increased as he entered the modern age. The maturity of this awareness will become the central category of the modern age—and consequently of our own: the category of autonomy. Man feels free to think as he wants; he feels free to judge visible and invisible reality, society and institutions, science, art, and religion. The so-called Age of Enlightenment shows the extremity of this accentuation of autonomy, understood primarily as an autonomy of reason, and which in turn is antagonistic toward tradition.

Modern philosophy is not the same thing as the Enlightenment, although the Enlightenment sprung up within modernity as a new cultural movement. From a philosophical point of view, the Enlightenment is part of modern philosophy, but this is not to say that it is its exclusive expression. On the contrary, there are some expressions of modern philosophy, not pertaining to the Enlightenment, which will have profound influence in the future. Moreover, the harshest criticisms of the Enlightenment would also come from within the currents of modern philosophy. Thus it is necessary to distinguish, with historical rigor, between the modern philosophy that preceded the Enlightenment, and the modern philosophy that blossomed under the influence of this new cultural phenomenon.

Kant dominated the last part of the eighteenth century. His philosophy represents, in a sense, the final act of the Enlightenment. In it, Enlightenment thought becomes conscious of its own limits. The philosopher from Königsberg stands out for rethinking the philosophical and cultural issues of an era, and bequeathing his own system of thought which later philosophers would be compelled to take into consideration.

The itinerary of this *History of Modern Philosophy* aims to present this rich and complex period in a fairly linear fashion, relying on the most representative authors, and briefly analyzing and expounding upon their thoughts. This text, therefore, is an introduction, bringing the reader into contact with the philosophical thought of an era. Despite the book's introductory nature, the authors have sought to present the complexity of the period under examination. A schematic representation of history will always seem simplistic. The pages that follow are schematic only as to their form; there are elements in the text that are starting points for readers who wish to delve into some of the arguments discussed in these pages.

This book is divided into five parts. The first is devoted to the most important events of Renaissance philosophy. The second is dedicated to rationalism, and the third to empiricism. These parts, in turn, are further divided into chapters where we analyze the important works of philosophers from these two schools. The fourth part takes up the study of the Enlightenment, and the last part is devoted to Kant's transcendental philosophy. The book concludes with a general synthesis, which offers a brief overview of the last decades of the eighteenth century, introducing early criticism of the Enlightenment made by the philosophers of the romantic period.

The distinction between modern philosophy and contemporary philosophy is essentially didactic. Continuities between the two periods are much more numerous than their divergences. Although this continuity is especially noticeable in German Idealism, the authors have chosen not to deal with this important philosophical current for pedagogical reasons. Those who are interested in the topic can complete their study by reading our *A History of Contemporary Philosophy: Nineteenth and Twentieth Centuries* (Mariano Fazio and Francisco Fernández Labastida).

PART ONE
THE RENAISSANCE

1.1 GENERAL CHARACTERISTICS OF THE RENAISSANCE

The term Renaissance designates a series of cultural processes that took place in the fifteenth and sixteenth centuries, but whose first signs can already be found in the fourteenth century. Perhaps the distinguishing characteristic of the Renaissance spirit is a return to the classical culture. The arrival of Greek humanists in Italy favored the studies of Greco-Roman antiquity. The meticulous analysis of the sources and the effort to understand the texts in their historical context gave life to this revival of the classical culture.

During the Middle Ages, scholastic theology used many classical sources as instruments for giving a systematic exposition of the faith. But in the Renaissance, the focus was assessing the very sources themselves: philological, rhetorical, and linguistic studies brought Plato, Aristotle, the Stoics, and Cicero back to academic interest. Humanists emulated Greco-Latin eloquence, surpassing the decline of the low-medieval stylistics.

A similar process took place in the visual arts. Using ancient Mediterranean architecture, paintings, and sculptures as examples for models, many Italian artists gave a classical reminiscence to their work throughout Europe. It suffices to mention the names of Leonardo, Michelangelo, Raphael, Botticelli, and Titian, to understand the importance of the Renaissance in the emerging modern world.

The reawakening of interest in the origins of European civilization also manifested itself in a renewed impulse to study the

origins of Christianity. During the Renaissance, numerous edi-
tions of Sacred Scripture were published that sought to replicate
the original text of the Bible more accurately than that which
was offered by the traditional Vulgate edition, which was considered to be riddled with errors. At the same time, the Dutch
humanist Erasmus of Rotterdam and other authors began to
write about the Fathers of the Church, who were revered as the
most authoritative testimony of early Christian life

In the scientific field, during these years of change, the
astronomical discoveries of Copernicus, Tycho Brahe, and
Kepler introduced cosmological theories that later modified
the world's understanding of the universe. However, their
new vision would take years to gain popular acceptance. In
turn, major technological advances were made in navigation,
military art, mining, etc., in such a way that although these
advancements relied on medieval inventions, they were considered very advanced for their period and paved the way for a
more sustained revolutionary and technological development
in the seventeenth century.

It is not possible to detail everything in these pages. The
Renaissance has many diverse facets, and it is not feasible to
sufficiently address the effects that such a movement exerted
on modern consciousness. But a cursory analysis might give
the following first impression: the Renaissance rediscovered
the classical world in its radical anthropocentrism, in sharp
contrast to the theocentric medieval Christian tradition. From
the fifteenth century onward, the transcendent vision of life
was abandoned for a new focus on the intrinsic value of natural things. Obviously, this brief description may be accused
of being simplistic; a more thorough and precise analysis of
events would be necessary.

In the field of the arts, the Renaissance witnessed a prolifer-
ation of a secular aesthetic, involving mythological themes and
sensual representations, as well as an exaltation of the Christian faith through buildings, paintings, sculptures, and musi-
cal compositions. In fact, renaissance architects combined both

tendencies when they utilized materials of classical ruins when constructing the most important churches of Christian Rome. The common element among the several artistic expressions of the Renaissance is an appreciation of nature, embodied in new techniques that gave a predominate role to the human body and that used the laws of perspective to reproduce artistic space. It ought to be mentioned that this common appreciation of creation and earthly life is not necessarily opposed to a transcendent vision of human existence. In defending the predominance of the sense of sight, Leonardo da Vinci (1425–1519) nicely coined a characteristic of Modernity when he said that "the eye is the most dignified of the senses," giving primacy to what the eyes can see and observe for themselves, over what the ears can hear from authorities of tradition.

The Renaissance inclination to return to the sources of Christian life, namely Sacred Scripture and the Fathers, did not imply an out-and-out criticism of religion as such, but rather a yearning for a purification of Christian living that identified and purged elements of superstition and merely human customs that had settled in over the centuries. The philological studies of Lorenzo Valla, for example, disproved the "Donation of Constantine," which allegedly was a decree of the Emperor that bequeathed all of Constantine's temporal powers over central Italy to the Pope, as a medieval invention devoid of historical foundation. Sometimes the humanists were driven by mere academic interest, but in many cases too, philological studies were motivated by a sincere desire for moral reformation, as with the works of Thomas More, Juan Luis Vives, and, to some extent, Erasmus of Rotterdam.

The reassessment of the classical age at times presented a temptation to "overcome" Christianity, offering models such as the stoic-epicurean life, as in the case of libertinism. But that same reassessment also opened a possibility of presenting Christianity as the culmination of what is truly human, as that which perfects and completes the deficiencies of man understood in a classical view.

The intellectuals of the Renaissance had a lively awareness that a new era was being inaugurated. Giorgio Vasari (1511–1574), painter and art historian, was the first to use the term "modern" in reference to the new styles in painting, architecture, and sculpture, as a way of saying that they had excelled even beyond the classics. Francis Bacon spoke of a "third period" after the Ancient Period and the Middle Ages, stating that "this third era exceeds by far the cultural heritage of Greece and Rome."[1] In 1559, Mathias Quadt also declared that "what in the past was assimilable only to a few and selected followers is now comprehended by ordinary, mediocre people, with modest instruction. There will come a day when all the secrets of nature will be accessible to the human mind."[2] In the same period, Jean Fernel praised "our era, which sees the arts and sciences triumphantly reborn after twelve centuries of neglect."[3] Thus came into being the self-referential concept of modernity, with its affirmation of human capacities, and pitted against the previous period, which they labeled as Gothic and barbarian.

We will now discuss the specific philosophical elements of this period.

1.2 RENAISSANCE AND PLATONIC PHILOSOPHY

In the first half of the fifteenth century, the Turks at the gates of Byzantium threatened the survival of the Eastern Empire. The imperial capital did eventually fall in 1453. Before that happened, many educated people fled Byzantium to escape the Turkish threat, seeking more peaceful lands for their cultural and intellectual life.

Many of these Greek authors and teachers disembarked on the banks of the Arno and settled in Florence. The intellectual

---

1. Francis Bacon, The Works of Francis Bacon: *Essays or Counsels Civil & Moral with Other Writings* (London: George Newnes, 1902), 433.

2. John Hale, La civiltà del Rinascimento in Europa: 1450–1620 (Milano: Mondadori, 1994), 600.

3. Hale, 601.

migration of so many Greeks to the Tuscan capital inspired a great interest in recreating the classical culture, and eventually led to the founding of the Platonic Academy in that city. There in this Academy Renaissance philosophy developed. Thus the Renaissance, as a historical-cultural phenomenon, found its focal point in Italy and its foundation in Florence.

The history of the Greek presence in Florence begins with the humanist chancellor of the Florentine Republic, Coluccio Salutati (1331–1406), who appointed Emmanuel Crisolora as the city's first professor of Greek. The successor of Salutati, Leonardo Bruni (1374–1444), translated some of Plato's dialogues as well as two of Aristotle's works, *Ethics* and *Politics*. Subsequently, Bruni wrote a book on ethical doctrine based on various ancient authors, entitled *Isagogicum moralis disciplina*.

After the works of Leonardo Bruni, Platonism reemerged in Florence, partly under the influence of Greek theologians that had come to the city for the upcoming Church Council. The first major figure from the philosophical point of view, who arrived in Florence in 1438, was Giorgio Gemiste Plethon (1355–1450).

Plethon was a Neo-Platonic philosopher, who recognized the importance of Aristotle, but did not hold back from being critical of his philosophy. Some of Plethon's contemporaries have noted some degree of exaggeration in his criticism.

He also proposed a global cultural reform of a Platonic character, which included philosophy and religion, politics and morality. He wanted this reform to be institutionally imposed through the Church and the State, both of which in their own turn would also be subject to spiritual and political reform.

Plethon developed some anthropological themes commonly held by most Florentine Platonic philosophers, but in particular, he developed the view of man as a microcosm: a kind of limit and horizon between the material and the spiritual.

Giovanni Argyropoulo (†1486) is less significant in Renaissance philosophy than Plethon. Nevertheless, he is a good representative of the Hellenizing trends of the milieu. Most notably, Argyropoulo translated St. Thomas's *De ente et essentia* into Greek. He shared Plethon's interest in a synthesis between Neoplatonist philosophy, culture, and faith. Both Plethon and Argyropoulo represent a convinced anti-Aristotelianism, characteristic of the time, which dismissed Aristotle as a mere naturalist whose ideas clashed with the humanistic interests proposed by Platonic philosophy.

From a cultural point of view, Basil Bessarion (1403–1478) is known for his philosophical writings. A priest and later a bishop, he became a disciple of Plethon while living in Florence from 1438 to 1452. As a cleric, Bessarion manifested a deep concern for the unity of the Church, while as a philosopher and theologian, he is known for synthesizing theology and Neoplatonic philosophy.

Undoubtedly, the presence of the Greek intellectuals in Florence was a catalyst for Bessarion's ideal of unity within the Church. Indeed, he dedicated his many years in the Tuscan city to ease the opposition between the Greek Platonists and the Latin Aristotelians, an intellectual and theological conflict that jeopardized the possible reunion of the Churches of the East and the West. To foster that unity, he wrote a philosophical book called *Adversus calumniatorem Platonis*, which defended the philosophy of Plethon against the attacks of the Aristotelian Giorgio di Trebizonda (1396–1486), but which adopted a tone of mediation between the two, and not as a direct attack on Aristotelianism.

Some years after the Council of Florence in 1459, Cosimo de Medici, inspired and enthused by the Greek presence and influence in his city, founded the Platonic Academy. Among the theologians, philosophers, doctors, writers and clerics at the Academy, the most famous was undoubtedly Marsilio Ficino, whom Cosimo summoned from Bologna to Florence to cultivate and promote the humanities there. Giannozzo Manetti (1396–1459) and Leone Battista Alberti (1404–1472) also members of the Academy, were known for contributing to the development of fifteenth-century Florentine culture.

The century's most important philosophy was cultivated by Marsilio Ficino, Giovanni Pico de Mirandola, and above all, Nicholas of Cusa. Though Cusa was neither a member of the Academy, nor even well known in Florence, he was well versed and active in the philosophical and theological world of his time, and his philosophical writings would eventually influence other countries such as France. Chronologically Nicholas of Cusa came before Marsilio Ficino and Giovanni Pico, but we will discuss his ideas last, as a synthesis of Platonism in the 1400s.

Marsilio Ficino (1433–1499). A fairly prolific writer with a distinctly Neoplatonic inspiration, Ficino was also well versed in Aristotelian and medieval philosophy, especially that of Thomas Aquinas. He translated many literary and philosophical works of classical Greece, including, most importantly, Plato's Dialogues.

Two of his early works, *De laudibus philosophiae* and more famously *Institutionis Platonicae*, define him as a neo-Platonist. In 1457, though, after writing *De amore divino* and *Liber de voluptate*, he temporarily abandoned philosophy, and went to Bologna to study medicine.

Not long thereafter, Cosimo de Medici invited him to Florence to work at the Academy as a professor of Greek. It was during this period that he translated Plato's *Orphic Hymns and Letters*, Iamblichus' *De secta pythagorica*, and Theophilus of Smyrna's *Mathematica*. In 1469 he began his most prolific period of contribution to philosophy, when he translated the *Symposium*, the *Philebus*, the *Parmenides*, and *Timaeus*. A few years later, in 1474, he published his own works *De religione christiana* and his most important work, *Theologia Platonica*. Later he wrote commentaries on Plotinus' *Phaedrus* and *Enneads*. His translations are remarkable for their rigorous accuracy based on the wording, yet despite this, he managed to preserve the spontaneity and literary beauty in the original texts.

At age 40, Ficino was ordained a priest. Like Bessarion and Nicholas of Cusa, his major concern was the conversion of non-Christians and the unity of the Church, especially

with respect to the possible reunion with the Greek Orthodox
Church. Ficino was greatly influenced by neo-platonic philosophy and Plotinus. He conceptualized God as the Supreme
Beauty and the Highest Good, and attempted to address central
questions of Platonic philosophy. But it mattered to him greatly
that the basic tenets of his philosophy agree with Scripture,
such as when he drew parallels between the question of platonic reminiscence and Paul's discussion of the natural knowledge of God from Paul's Epistle to the Romans.

His most important work, as was said, is the *Theologia Platonica*. In this book, Ficino proposed that the world is sorted
into categories, which are subdivided into strata according to
varying degrees of perfection in beings. This idea was known as
universal harmony. According to this theory, there is a scale of
being by which reality increases in perfection, from material to
spiritual existence: the material world, beasts, man, angels, then
at the apex of being is God: pure Unity, absolute Simplicity. This
model of gradual participation in spiritual existence was typical
of Renaissance philosophy. It was also their way of addressing
the difficult platonic question regarding the dialectic between
unity of principle and multiplicity of things in the world.

In the *Theologia* Ficino also highlighted the situation of man
as a being between two worlds: a material creature with a spiritual nature, he straddles the upper limit of the material world
and the lower limit of the spiritual world. In this perspective, he
approaches the old dispute about the soul's spiritual and immortal nature. Earlier philosophers had denied the soul's immortality, some in absolute terms, while others (such as certain
members of Padua's Aristotelian school) in a more nuanced way.

Behind this question lies a metaphysical, epistemological,
and ethical problem. If the soul is mortal, or if its immortality
cannot be proved, whether implicitly or explicitly, the ability to
grasp intellectually a metaphysical reality becomes tenuous or
impossible.

In fact, in the times of Ficino, metaphysics suffered a deep
crisis, best demonstrated by this question about the soul's

immortality. Ficino was convinced that the soul is immortal and can be known to be so. The *Theologia Platonica* is, in this sense, an encyclopedic compendium of valid arguments supporting this thesis, including selections from Thomas Aquinas' *Summa contra gentiles*, with which Ficino was very familiar. Ficino realized the importance and the repercussions of the issue, whether in the speculative or ethical field, in a cultural time when man was believed to be the center of creation. Many accusations of naturalism have been directed at Renaissance philosophy and culture. Given the metaphysical crisis and responses produced during the Renaissance, such accusations are not entirely unfounded.

Ficino's efforts at resolving the metaphysical crisis are not an isolated case. But the balance between humanism, metaphysics, and faith found in his philosophy will change significantly in the next century.

Giovanni Pico della Mirandola (1463–1494). Pico is the most famous and important disciple of Marsilio Ficino. He had a proficient knowledge of Greek and Hebrew, having been exposed to Hellenic thought and Sacred Scriptures in their original languages. Just like his teacher, his philosophical preferences are Neoplatonic. One of Pico's main goals was to harmonize Hellenism and Jewish religious thought, which would result in a Christian Platonism. Pseudo-Dionysius also influenced Pico's philosophy, especially in the area of negative theology.

Though Pico was uncommonly well-versed in Greek and Arab philosophy as well as in Scriptures, his early death left few contributions as an author. Among his more important works is the *De concordantia Platonis et Aristotelis*, which reflects the tendency of many authors of the Florentine Academy to observe more continuity than division between the two Greek thinkers. Pico's *De ente et uno* followed the same line of interpretation, in which he proposed a balanced agreement between Plato and Aristotle. However, though many of Pico's contemporaries advocated for that harmony, at the same time these very authors were in fact anti-Aristotelian.

According to Pico, God is the One who is beyond being; God is in all things and comprehends them all. Plotinus was the father of this idea, and Ficino had introduced it into Renaissance philosophy. By the time Pico wrote his book, Nicolas of Cusa had also further developed the idea. Along with this thesis about God, Pico tackled the question of the degrees of being: God is the Being who transcends all the degrees of being.

But in claiming that God comprehends all things, Pico did not intend to defend a kind of pantheism. Rather, he simply attempted to conceptualize the presence of God in the world. He believed that the finite perfection of creatures is a participation in the Supreme Divine Being, though not through a pantheistic identification with him.

God is nevertheless unreachable. The hyper-transcendence of the One with respect to being makes the divine unity indivisible in itself. For man, God is ineffable because he is beyond his intelligence. Thus for Pico, God is simultaneously darkness, life, and wisdom.

According to Pico, the world is an orderly, harmonious system organized according to levels of reality and perfection. God created the world so that man could contemplate it and admire its greatness and beauty. Having been created by God, the world finds in him the foundation of its order and harmony; further, God created the universe to be contemplated, reflecting the metaphysical goodness of creation.

Man is therefore in a world that is good with respect to its foundation and its structure. As a created material being with an angelic-like spirit, straddling the boundary between the physical and spiritual worlds, man can contemplate and share in this created goodness. But the way he sees the world is not a pure contemplation, because he can also act upon the world with his freedom. By developing culture, art, politics, etc., man in effect constructs a world for himself.

Man will discover and imitate the ideals according to where he sets his sights, whether to what is higher or to what is lower. In the first case he can be reborn in the degree of the highest things and direct himself towards the divine, while the other will lead him to degenerate into lower things of this world. Thus, man as microcosm and as a free being may rise or fall in perfection, but always as a result of a free choice. With this point, Pico argued against the determinism of astrology, which denied freedom in favor of a human existence absolutely determined by the motions of heavenly bodies.

In his book *In astrologiam libri XII*, Pico distinguished three orders in the world: the sublunary world common to man and animals, the celestial corresponding to the stars, and the supra-celestial of angelic creatures.

Man, according to Pico, is superior to everything in the sublunary world because he can participate fully in divine things. By virtue of this participation, he has access to the supra-celestial world. The celestial world is a rational system, not a magical one. It has its own laws, but they do not determine human freedom.

***Nicholas of Cusa (1401–1464)*.** Nicholas of Cusa dealt with many metaphysical and anthropological questions in a more profound and original way than did the Florentine Neoplatonists. He straddled two worlds: the disappearing medieval world, and the awakening modern one. Though the philosophy of Nicholas of Cusa is rooted in earlier medieval traditions, it is a new system of thought, a modern philosophy.

Nicholas of Cusa takes his name from his place of birth, Kues, sometimes also called Krebs or Kryfts. Kues is a small town on the Moselle River. He was born there in 1401. In 1416 he moved from his village to nearby Heidelberg to study. From 1417 to 1423 he studied in Padua, where he obtained a doctorate in canon law. In 1426 he became a priest and moved to Koblenz. Some years later in 1432, he would participate in the Council of Basel. About that time, he wrote *De concordantia catholica* (1433–1434), in which he defended the theory of conciliarism, which he would subsequently abandon. He was very much in touch with the Renaissance intellectual world, taking an interest in many theological, philosophical, and ecclesiastical problems.

Among them, we find his concern for the union of the Roman Catholic Church with the Greek Orthodox Church. In fact, some years later, he would be one of the promoters of the Council of Florence, in which the Orthodox and Roman Churches reunited, though only for a short time.

In 1448 he was appointed cardinal, and in 1450, archbishop of Bressannone (Brixen). A year later he was appointed papal legate to Germany. Until his death in Todi in 1464, he held positions in the Church.

His philosophical and theological writings are abundant. Among his most important treatises are *De docta ignorantia* and *De coniecturis* (1440); *Apologia doctae ignorantiae* (1449); *De visione Dei* (1453); *Tetralogus de non aliud* (1462), *De venatione sapientiae* and *De ludo globi beryllo* (1463); and *De apex theoriae* (1464).

He wrote numerous theological writings, sermons, and scientific works, particularly in mathematics. Based upon his sources, the thought of Nicholas of Cusa was influenced by Meister Eckhart, Scotus Eriugena, Pseudo-Dionysius, and Plotinus, and in certain matters he was also inspired by St. Augustine.

If we are to look for followers, however, or authors with analogous philosophical ideas, we must wait for the later, more developed modern philosophies of Leibniz, Malebranche, Hegel, and Schelling.

In Nicholas of Cusa, we observe a close relation between metaphysical and anthropological ideas and practical life. The concept of harmony, often appearing in his writings, and the great theme of God as *coincidentia oppositorum*, reflect to some extent his political and ecclesiastical ideas.

He considered the Church and the Empire as unities amidst multiplicity, and he saw the institution of the papacy as the expression of the Church's essential unity. His political thought was founded upon a harmony between church and state, a topic pertaining to the question of the unity with the Orthodox

Church, a question that was ever more strongly felt as the Council of Florence approached.

Nicholas of Cusa's metaphysical speculation was very deep. He developed a metaphysics of God's names and a metaphysics of the presence of God in the world. We will briefly discuss his opinion on the knowledge of God and the manifestation of God in the world.

Using a neoplatonic framework with great originality, Nicholas of Cusa developed the concept of *coincidentia oppositorum*, which claims that unity of contraries and opposites is fully achieved in God, while in creatures we find multiplicity and distinction. God transcends the order of creatures, and therefore also the order of distinctions and oppositions. Similarly, insofar as God is infinite act, in him there is no distinction between essence and existence, which is found in creatures. Nicholas of Cusa spoke of God as both the maximum and minimum, that is, as opposites that are united. He also referred to God as the *complicatio oppositorum et eorum coincidentia*.

In *De docta ignorantia*, Nicholas of Cusa addressed the problem of the metaphysical limit of knowledge, in other words, the problem of the knowledge of God. Following the neoplatonic tradition, he emphasized the *via negativa* by which we can get to know God. Since man's knowledge is limited, positive knowledge of God is defined as ignorance. This is not to say that man knows nothing, but in the situation in which the intellect is faced with an infinite reality, which is clearly not an empirical object, man can at least know this: that he does not know.

In this sense, we are speaking of someone that recognizes his ignorance when he is faced with the transcendent Being. But the transcendent Being is also Wisdom itself, thus such ignorance is also "learned."

Human knowledge is also discursive, and is guided by the principle of non-contradiction, which states that two conflicting premises cannot both be true with respect to the same subject. But since God is the *coincidentia oppositorum*, the highest unity in which all is one, human knowledge cannot fully coincide with the essence of God. The human mind is like a polygon inscribed in a circle, which represents God's essence. The sides of the polygon can approach the diameter, but cannot be superimposed, because they will never completely coincide.

Thus, coinciding of opposites in God is identity, while for men the knowledge of God as the coinciding of opposites is conjecture. Conjecture is not only characteristic of human knowledge about the essence of God. It is a general characteristic with respect to knowing any reality: the human process of knowing is conjectural.

Nicholas of Cusa spoke of three types of knowledge: the sensible, the rational, and that proper of the intellect itself, which is distinguished from reason by virtue of its unifying function. Purely positive knowledge is sensible knowledge, while rational knowledge proceeds by means of the dialectic affirmation-negation. The oppositions of reason are, in turn, denied by the intellect, so that intelligence can reach a certain knowledge of the *coincidentia oppositorum*. Nicholas of Cusa believed that in this act of *intellectus*, by denying oppositions, we achieve a unity, a synthesis.

Faced with the ability of the intellectus to achieve synthesis, language becomes insufficient, since it is merely an instrument of reason. There exists, however, a linguistic tool to overcome such an obstacle: the analogical and symbolic use of language. This linguistic thesis is explicit and repeatedly appears in the works of Nicholas of Cusa.

Symbolic language is particularly suitable for the knowledge of God. God is *Posse Ipsum* — power Himself. He belongs to a realm that is absolutely transcendent. In this regard, negative knowledge of God recognizes that the finite intellect cannot receive the light that emanates so brightly from God. However, as far as God is revealed through creatures, creatures are signs of God, and human knowledge finds in them a manifestation of the light of divine transcendence.

Nicholas of Cusa's discussion of the relationship between God and the world is not easy; it is harder still to interpret his work when he does not provide all his logical steps. Some authors have even seen some pantheistic tendencies in his thinking. But let us look at the main elements.

God is the source of all things, which, in turn, teach us something about God. Though creatures are various and limited, they can witness to God because they are all created by the Being who is essentially one. God, Unity itself, created the multiplicity that manifests his Unity. Nicholas of Cusa referred to God as *omnia complicans* insofar as all things are in him, and *omnia explicans*, insofar as he is in everything.

For Nicholas of Cusa, the world is a theophany, that is, a contraction of the divine: the universe is the *maximum contractum* that exists through, or rather, because of, the *absolutum maximum*, namely God Himself.

Insofar as the world is a manifestation of God, Nicholas boldly referred to the world as *quasi Deus Creatus*, like a created God. He made a radical claim about the presence of God in the created world and the procession of the created world from God. The movement of "coming out of God" and "manifesting God" reflects the dependence of the world on God, while simultaneously asserting a distinction between God and the world. God is not identified as the things through which he is manifested, because the creature is distinct from the Creator, though creatures find their origin in him.

Besides the anthropological questions already studied, we can also address Nicholas of Cusa's definition of man as a synthesis and microcosm in which matter, organic life, sensitive animal life, and spiritual life are united. Man is, strictly speaking, a small world that has a soul. Man is a perfect world, even though he is a small part of the big world.

And so again, in man we find the problem of *coincidentia oppositorum*. Both matter and the soul—vegetative and spiritual life—subsist in man. However, differing from God, man in himself is finite; opposites do not coincide in a synthesis and absolute maximum, although the human mind is a sort of *implicatio* that condenses everything into a unity.

The human mind is, therefore, the image of God, except in the fact that God is a unity with the original *coincidentia*, while in man the *coincidentia* is secondary, insofar as man assimilates all things in his unity through knowledge. Knowledge passes through three stages: the senses, reason, and intellect. Nicholas of Cusa calls reason and intellect the *mens* of man. The concept of *mens* is closely related to another concept of *mensura*.

Reason, in fact, is measured; it judges by evaluations. The intellect, meanwhile, being unity, gives reason the measuring standard by which to assess. And since unity is the source of all numbers, number relationships that govern the movement of things are the expression of divine unity that is actualized in the universe.

1.3 RENAISSANCE AND ARISTOTELIAN PHILOSOPHY

Parallel to the development of Neoplatonism during the Renaissance, there was also a renewal of Aristotelian philosophy. While many fifteenth-century authors used Neoplatonism for the service of Christianity in the reform of society and man, Aristotelianism gave rise to a naturalistic trend in Renaissance philosophy at the end of the fifteenth and during the sixteenth centuries.

Naturalism is not only found in Renaissance Aristotelianism. There has also been an anti-Aristotelian naturalism more rhetorical and ethical in character. Fifteenth-century anti-Aristotelian naturalists criticized Aristotle's alleged inability to express transcendence (which is why Christian philosophers generally preferred Platonism). During the sixteenth century, however, anti-Aristotelianism especially disagreed with the Aristotelian interpretation of nature.

Aristotelianism had first come to the West in the twelfth and thirteenth centuries, having been preserved, studied, and interpreted by Arab and Jewish philosophers. By the fifteenth and sixteenth centuries, Aristotelianism was considered a medieval tradition, having been welcomed and absorbed by scholastic philosophy. But in the fifteenth century, Aristotelianism arrived for a second time to Western Europe, and this time, directly from Greece, unadapted by Jewish, Arab, or Scholastic influence. Greek intellectuals fleeing the Turkish threat brought a purely Greek Aristotelianism with them, which Renaissance Italians welcomed as more genuine than the Jewish or medieval renditions. Medieval Aristotelianism maintained its influence in the Renaissance, though, considering that the anti-Aristotelian movement came about in reaction against a particular interpretation of medieval Aristotelianism by Alexander of Aphrodisias.

Of the many topics that Aristotle had addressed, Renaissance Aristotelianism limited its study to logic, epistemology, and physics. Humanists had claimed for themselves the other topics that Aristotle had studied—ethics, politics, rhetoric, and poetry—but they tended to criticize Aristotelianism. Renaissance Aristotelianism was thus only a partial development of the whole corpus of Aristotle's philosophical work. Those few branches of Renaissance Aristotelianism generally conformed themselves to century-old questions about empirical science and to the same topics that scholastic Aristotelians had discussed in the fourteenth century.

It is true, though, that the school of Padua scholars modernized and developed the methodology of logic and physics, bestowing greater importance on direct experience and reasoning applied to facts.

The two most famous Greek Aristotelians among the arrivals from Greece were Giorgio of Trebizond (1396–1486) and Giorgio Scholarios (1405–1472). In Italy, the non-Arabized Aristotle was received with special fervor by the Venetian Hermolaus Barbarus (1453–1493), though it was in Padua and Bologna where Renaissance Aristotelianism found a suitable home for its development.

The most important author among the Aristotelians, although he came after this first phase of Aristotelian philosophy, was

Pietro Pomponazzi (1462–1525), born in Mantua and professor at Padua and Bologna. His framework for interpreting Aristotle's philosophy was anti-Averroist, having been influenced by Alexander of Aphrodisias' Aristotelianism.

Averroism affirmed the thesis that all men shared a single intellect, an idea known as the unity of intellect. This theory had been discussed in the thirteenth century, but newfound supporters of the fifteenth- and sixteenth-century Renaissance caused the issue to resurface, with a different resolution this time.

Pomponazzi published his most important work *De immortalitate animae* in 1516. The book was received with criticism from Averroists and Thomist Aristotelians, among them Agostino Nifo.

Pomponazzi's main thesis actually contradicted Aristotle. He taught that the soul, being the form of an organic body, does not survive when the body dies. The fact that the intellect does not use the body to conceive universal concepts is no proof that the form of the body can have a life independent of the body. Neither did Pomponazzi consider the immortality of the soul as a necessary foundation of morality, since virtue is its own reward in this life, and vice its own punishment—an idea coming from the ethical doctrines of Stoicism. Nevertheless, Pomponazzi professed belief in the immortality of the soul because it is revealed in Sacred Scriptures. His double opinion on the issue confines the soul's mortality to being an object of the epistemological order, meaning that it cannot be proven even though we know it to be true by faith.

This same mindset is found in his *De fato, libero arbitrio et praedestinatione*, which was published posthumously. In this book, Pomponazzi accepted the existence of freedom only because it was a teaching of the Church. In philosophy, on the other hand, he could not devise an argument that reconciled free will and divine providence. He therefore asserted that the events in this world, including human acts, are necessary. He preferred to believe in providence, so he sacrificed freedom to necessity.

Like other authors of Renaissance naturalism, Pomponazzi admitted that magic was a way of escaping necessity. But beliefs such as these impede any faithful interpretation of Aristotle.

Despite the determined efforts of supporters, late Renaissance Aristotelianism, with its implausible interpretation of nature, disappeared in the seventeenth century with Galileo and the arrival of modern science. A separate school of scholastic Aristotelianism also arose in the fifteenth and sixteenth centuries, resurrecting the medieval scholastic tradition to address the philosophical questions of the times.

1.4 RENAISSANCE SCHOLASTICISM

a) The Situation

Scholasticism is not often mentioned in the context of Renaissance philosophy. The Renaissance was a new era with new ways of thinking. Scholasticism, however, is often considered an artifact of the Middle Ages, a kind of timeless and motionless philosophy.

In some respects, this is true. Scholastics of the fifteenth century faced different philosophical and theological questions than those that had occupied scholastics of the thirteenth century. Later scholastics retained some methodology of early Scholasticism, while abandoning others. They preserved the method of *disputatio,* though they replaced Peter Lombard's *Liber sententiarum* with the commentaries and *summae* of the great authors of the thirteenth and fourteenth centuries, such as Thomas Aquinas, Albertus Magnus, Duns Scotus, and Ockham. Later scholasticism also took an interest in modern science, marked by a flowering of studies of logic, gnoseology, and epistemology.

While fifteenth-century Scholasticism cannot quite be considered Renaissance philosophy, the Scholasticism of the sixteenth-century scholar certainly was, while retaining the essential characteristics of the scholastic tradition.

Sixteenth-century scholastics mainly dealt with two new problematic questions of the time. First, the discovery of America raised questions about the natural law, political philosophy, and anthropology. Second, scholastic authors of this period engaged the European culture of the time in their studies of humanism, the Renaissance mind, and religious issues generated by the Protestant Reformation.

Late Renaissance scholasticism of the sixteenth century manifested a new force, whose Spanish and Portuguese authors would have a profound historical and cultural influence on later modern philosophy. Great authors throughout the seventeenth century would review their work in the fields of metaphysics, epistemology, and philosophy of law.

Also of note, the end of the sixteenth century witnessed the appearance of manuals for the first time. The first was a metaphysical treatise of Francisco Suarez, called *Disputationes metaphysicae*, which was well known throughout European universities.

The two authors that defined this new period of scholasticism were Thomas de Vio (1468–1534), better known as Cardinal Cajetan (i.e. native of Gaeta), who authored an important commentary on Thomas Aquinas's *De ente et essentia* and *Summa Theologiae*; and Francisco de Vitoria (1483–1546), founder of the School of Salamanca, father of international law, and reformer of political philosophy. He was also outstanding for his commentary on Aquinas's *Summa Theologiae* and for his revolutionary methods in university education. It was he who introduced the method of direct commentaries on the works of St. Thomas in the Spanish classrooms.

b) Francisco de Vitoria (1483–1546)

The Spanish Dominican was educated in Paris and then a professor in Valladolid and Salamanca. His bold and independent thinking permitted him to use Thomas Aquinas's legal-philosophical principles to develop an authentic secularization of medieval theocracy. He was inclined to affirm the distinction between the natural and the supernatural order, aware of the consequent relative autonomy of temporal affairs.

His teachings are primarily known through the *relecciones*, that is, lectures delivered in the Salamanca classrooms. The most interesting *relecciones* are entitled *De potestate civili* (1528); *De Indis prior* (1538); and *De Indis posterior sed de iuris belli* (1539).

Adhering to the teachings of Aquinas, Francisco de Vitoria distinguished the natural from the supernatural order:

"The natural order is proper to human nature as such, regardless of its elevation to the order of grace. Man is simply considered a being created by God in his image and likeness, endowed with a material body and a spiritual and immortal soul. In this sense, every man, by virtue of his being, whether Christian or not, possesses a set of fundamental rights inherent to his person. The supernatural order corresponds to man as a being elevated by grace to a state superior to the human nature, which was restored by the redemption of Jesus Christ. These are different orders, which are not mutually exclusive nor contradictory, but complementary."[4]

The distinction between the natural and supernatural orders was an important tool for dealing with the questions posed by the discovery of America. Further, de Vitoria wanted to snuff a lingering medieval current that attempted to justify control of things in the natural order according to standards for the supernatural.

Francisco de Vitoria accepts the teleological view of the universe belonging to the Aristotelian-Thomistic tradition, describing it as "a formidable philosophical argument that sheds light on all problems."[5] Teaching that the final cause is the first and the most important of all causes, Francisco de Vitoria observed that human nature also has a teleological-ontological

---

4. Guillermo Fraile, *Historia de la Filosofía Española* (Madrid: Biblioteca de Autores Cristianos, 1971), 287.

5. Francisco de Vitoria, *De potestate civili*, 152–153. We have used the version of Teófilo Urdanoz and Francisco de Vitoria. *Relecciones teológicas* (Madrid: Biblioteca de Autores Cristianos, 1960).

constitution. The teleology of man allows him to establish for himself a final end in the natural order: the possession of God, and natural rights proper to all men by virtue of their common humanity that will allow them to reach their ultimate goal.

Thus for Francisco de Vitoria, every human—whether Christian or gentile, European or barbarian—has the right to life, bodily integrity, cultural instruction, and religious freedom. He based the latter freedom on Aquinas's principle that *voluntatis est credere,* that the act of faith, to believe, is a free action, besides being a gift from God. These natural rights are not undermined by infidelity or by personal sins, whatever they may be, since *ea enim quae sunt naturalia homini, neque subtrahuntur, neque dantur homini per peccatum* (what is natural for man is neither removed from man nor given to him by sin).[6]

Francisco de Vitoria's analysis of human nature brought him to the conclusion that man is social by nature. We read in his *De potestate civili* that "Human societies have been constituted in order for man to help each other bear the burdens of life; and since the civil society, among all other societies, is that in which men satisfy their needs in the most comfortable way, it follows that this community establishes completely natural relationships, absolutely in keeping with nature."[7]

He believed that political authority is justified by the common good, which is the aim of civil society, an aim that requires the coordination of individual wills. All power has its remote origin in God, but the material cause is, "by natural and divine right, the very republic, which is competent to govern itself, [to] manage and direct all its powers to the common good."[8] A political community entrusts power to a governor, though the endowment of this originating power need not be a result of the unanimous wills of the members of the community: "it is

---

6. Summa Theologica, I. q.98, a.2.

7. Francisco de Vitoria, *De potestate civili*, 155–156.

8. Vitoria, *De potestate civili*, 159.

enough, then, that the majority agrees for a lawful thing to be done."[9] But political power is not absolute; it is limited by natural law and by the state's own laws. When a governor infringes upon these limitations, his power becomes illegitimate, and the political community can depose him.

Though the teachings of Francisco de Vitoria are perfectly true to the Aristotelian-Thomist tradition, his more systematized structure and original presentation distinguish him as a "modern" thinker compared to his medieval predecessors. But the Spanish Dominican's greatest contribution to political philosophy is the concept of a "Community of Nations" or a "Universal Community," which he applied to the case of the Americas.

According to Fraile, Francisco de Vitoria, "with his legal theories, gave the deathblow to the medieval illusion, a bit amorphous and inorganic, of the universal empire and of theocratic imperialism. But he replaced it with a concept of the universal community to which all men belong by virtue of their social nature, which is previous to and superior to the division of nations."[10] Indeed, well before Grotius, Vitoria understood the need to create an international juridical order based on an international law of peoples ("law of nations is that which natural reason establishes among all nations"). Common human nature demands a universal common good. Individual nations must work together to attain that end, in the same way that members of the political community ought to foster the common good of their own nation or state.

Much of his internationalist theory arose in the context of the American problem. He devoted two *Relecciones De Indis* to the discussion. Particularly the first *relección*, he affirms the human personhood of American Indians, their capability to self-control, and their essential freedom from being coerced to convert. And using rational arguments, he demonstrated the

9. Vitoria, *De potestate civili*, 179.
10. Fraile, *Historia de la Filosofía Española*, 297–8.

invalidity of the Pope's donation of the Americas to the Catholic Monarchs.

A modern and Christian world was ushered in by Francisco de Vitoria and the school of Salamanca; modern, because they recognized autonomy in temporal matters, and Christian, because they recognized both the dignity of the person as being in the image of God as well as the universal call to faith and grace. Francisco de Vitoria's *Relectio de indis* had a new way of thinking about the relation of the natural and supernatural orders, particularly between spiritual and temporal power. He supplanted the historical concretions of medieval theocracy by proposing a secularization that establishes the legitimate autonomy of the temporal order without severing the roots that unite the temporal to the transcendent order. Francisco de Vitoria's *Relectio de indis* is one of the doors through which we pass from the medieval to the modern world.[11]

There were other authors of great influence from the University of Salamanca. Two of the most known are Domingo de Soto (1494–1560), who wrote commentaries on Aristotle and St. Thomas, and Melchor Cano (1509–1560), who wrote the celebrated work *De locis theologicis*.

Coimbra University was another important center of renaissance scholasticism. Some teachers of this university published a philosophy course known as the *Cursus Conimbricensis*. One of the teachers, Pedro de Fonseca (1548–1599), was especially well known for his commentary on Aristotle's *Metaphysics* and his *Institutiones dialecticae*.

Another professor of Coimbra, Luis de Molina (1535–1600), defended free will against Luther's theses in his work *Concordia liberi arbitrii cum gratiae donis, divina praescientia, providentia, praedestinatione et reportatione*, published in Lisbon in 1589. The philosophical difficulty centered on whether the infinite wisdom and freedom of God could be compatible with the freedom of man. Molina tried to reconcile human and divine freedom

---

11. See Mariano Fazio, *Francisco de Vitoria: Cristianismo y modernidad* (Buenos Aires: Ediciones Ciudad Argentina, 1998).

by maintaining that God possesses knowledge of all possible future determinations of human freedom. He proposed that special knowledge of God, which he called *scientia media*, was an intermediate knowledge between God's direct vision and his knowledge of possibilities that remain as possibilities. Throughout the seventeenth century, a large number of courses (*cursus*) following the framework of Thomistic philosophy appeared. Among the more important ones were the *Cursus philosophicus* and *Cursus theologicus* of John of St. Thomas (1585–1644) and Juan de Lugo (1583–1660), and the *Cursus philosophicus* of Francisco Soares, published in Coimbra in 1651.

c) Francisco Suarez (1548–1617)

Francisco Suarez was the most important author of the last period of the second scholasticism. His works include a commentary on the *Summa Theologiae* of Thomas Aquinas, which contains philosophical and theological points that Suarez developed during his many years teaching in Spain and Portugal. In 1612, he published (with some revisions in 1616) some writings on natural law and ethics entitled *De legibus*, which was a commentary on the *De anima* of Aristotle.

But Suarez is mostly known for his *Disputationes metaphysicae*, published in 1597. The *Disputationes* are presented as a gloss to the *Metaphysics* of Aristotle, but from the first page it is clear that his book was more of a systematic exposition than a commentary.

In this sense, the *Disputationes* introduced a novelty in philosophical literature, especially scholasticism. Having abandoned the medieval form of commentary and disputation, Suarez wrote a treatise on metaphysics, which was a clear attempt at systematization. His constant concern for the order of the topics and the connection between them produced a text that would serve as a framework for later scholastic philosophy and modern rationalism.

Suarez proposed an organic system of metaphysics that was constituted independently of theology, but that theologians might still find useful. This marks another novelty, breaking with the approach of the great medieval *summae* and commentators. In this sense, Suarez's philosophical attitude is already modern, though he was very much aware of his medieval and Renaissance philosophical heritage.

Suarez was a philosopher of vast erudition. His main sources are Aristotle, Thomas Aquinas, Duns Scotus, and William of Ockham, along with other thirteenth-century authors and fourteenth- and fifteenth-century nominalists. At the same time, he was very familiar with Renaissance philosophy with all its new interests and tensions.

One of the most important philosophical discussions of scholasticism was that of the distinction between essence and being. Suarez made this discussion one of the focuses of his philosophical work—not that it was the sole topic of his *Disputatio metaphysicae*, but it did have a central systematic position.

Suarez carefully defined the concept of essence as that which is most radical and intimate to any reality. Essence is thus what is expressed in a definition, the set of constitutive marks of a thing. According to Suarez, the essence is the first principle, the core of reality, ontologically prior to being itself. He thinks that the question on the distinction between essence and being originates from a reflection on essence, and can only be answered based on the ontological characteristics of the essence.

Existence, which is Suárez's usual way of referring to being, is something added to the essence. Once the essence is defined, it can exist, in such a way that the existence is external to the essence as considered by itself. Existence does not add anything more or anything specific to the thing from the point of view of the essence. If reality is what is expressed in the definition, what really counts in the order of knowledge is the essence, not existence, which does not specify anything to what the thing is.

Moreover, according to Suarez, essence is unchanged whether in the state of existence or in the state of possibility.

In fact, between the essence that truly exists and the possible essence, there is no difference in definition. Possible man and the real man are defined by the same concept; the difference is existential, not essential.

Therefore, if essence is the heart of reality, what should an essence be like for it to exist? Or more broadly: why can an essence exist? It must be assured, according to Suarez, that the essence is complete. An essence must not be contradictory to itself, meaning that all of the fundamental, identifying characteristics that compose an essence should be compatible with the others. An essence structured in this way can exist.

The intrinsic possibility of essence constitutes both the definition of the thing and the condition of the thing's existence. Suarez thus includes possibility in the concept of reality by insisting that anything that is not contradictory is real. A possible essence is no different from an essence in a concrete existing thing, since anything, even existence, that were to be added to the concrete existing thing would be merely accidental with respect to what the essence is in itself.

From this comes the distinction between *actual reality* and *possible reality*, which differ by the fact of existence, and not according to essential contents. This, of course, assumes that the essence is possible, meaning that is has no internally self-contradicting properties.

Before Suarez, being was considered the primary metaphysical concept, through which reality is defined. Metaphysics, according to the classic authors, studies *ens in quantum ens*, being as being. But Suarez maintains that being is the primary and fundamental essence, the most general and indeterminate quality. In this sense, Suarez interpreted the object of metaphysics differently than did the tradition that inspired him. But if the first being is the most generic essence, this is certainly not an existing being but the general essence, and thus also is the most general concept. Suarez reassigns the proper object of metaphysics from being to the most general concept. He explains that the most general concept is the objective concept, which is the object itself that is known, rather than the formal concept, which is the psychological act of knowing something.

The problem with Suarez's approach is that his metaphysics studies the concept of being rather than the real being. Although it is true that the objective concept is the thing known, and not just the psychological act of knowing, still it must be affirmed that whatever is known is not independent of the act of knowing. So what Suarez recommends is a metaphysics based on the being that is known and not the real being, a science of concepts and knowledge about concepts.

By giving a new centrality to essence as something independent of the act of being, Suarez created a situation in which the essence is that which is most real, with that reality measured according to the internal non-contradiction of the essence. It does not matter whether the essence is actual (existing) or possible (not existing); what matters is that the essence simply not be contradictory with itself. But this precisely identifies essence with concept. Thus, for Suárez, the act of being is the most general essence, a non-contradictory concept, but distinct from reality itself.

In this way, the metaphysics of Suarez took a decisive step towards modern rationalism. In that school, essences will grow in importance, especially from a systematic point of view, while metaphysical considerations of being and existence will fade out. It is not merely a coincidence that Leibniz was inspired by Suarez's metaphysics after reading his *Disputationes metaphysicae*, nor that Wolff's definition of existence would preserve Suarez's concept of possibility.

1.5 Between Stoicism and Epicureanism

Accompanying the development of the second scholasticism, particularly during the second half of the sixteenth century, was a reappearance of philosophical skepticism, which reemphasized ethical doctrines inspired by Stoicism and Epicureanism.

Gianfrancesco Pico della Mirandola (1469–1533), nephew of Giovanni, was the first of this philosophical revival, having been influenced by the skepticism of Sextus Empiricus. Dissatisfied with philosophical explanations about the world and man, Gianfrancesco proposed fideism as the only means of arriving at the truth. A notable contemporary in this skepticist trend was Agrippa of Nettesheim (1486–1535). Some years later in France came Henri Estienne (1522–1598) who published the *Outlines of Pyrrhonism*, and G. Hervet (1499–1584) who published the works of Sextus Empiricus, while in Germany Justus Lipsius (1547–1606) spread stoicism as far as the Netherlands with his *Manductio ad stoicam philosophiam* and *Physiologia stoicorum*.

However, the best representative of Pyrrhic stoicism is the writer Michel de Montaigne (1535–1592). His best known work, written between 1580 and 1588, is the *Essais* (*Essays*). Montaigne resurfaced the great classical questions of skepticism, such as the mistrust of the subjectivity of sense experience, and the intellect's inability to arrive at absolute truth. Constantly changing reality, according to Montaigne, prevents us from possessing certain truth.

But at the same time, Montaigne respected faith as a source of truth, so much so that he rejected all forms of atheism, which he considered contrary to nature. Even so, he denied the possibility of a natural knowledge of God, asserting that knowledge of God comes through grace and faith, classifying his opinion as fideist.

For Montaigne, the fundamental aim of philosophy is the attainment of happiness. In this regard, philosophy is a way of life that grants wisdom by showing the way to live happily. But in order to be wise, one must drop the pretension of knowing the truth as it might be found in an ideal situation, because ideal situations do not exist. What man does know, however, is himself, albeit not in an absolute and unchanging way. He knows himself in the continuous flow of variations of life, such that what is useful and good here and now might not be so later. In a way, wisdom is the culmination of practical sense, which knows how to capture whatever happiness that can be taken from each particular moment. Philosophy—and the life lived according to philosophy—is, ultimately, the art of living, which finds its realization in loving life. But that love of life does not extend to the negative and painful moments, only to the happy circumstances that allow the enjoyment of each fleeting moment.

Montaigne's thought featured certain Stoic and Epicurean elements, which, he proposed, are means to wisdom and consequently to happiness. Wisdom and happiness, however, can only be attained in a limited manner, according to each man and the knowledge he has of himself. This knowledge lacks any pretension of possessing an essential knowledge of human nature—Montaigne categorically rejected the scholastic thesis and methods—though this empirical knowledge can be the means to a peaceful and cultured existence.

He preached an attitude of acceptance toward the social order and traditional religion, for the sake of peace and tranquility. Religion is not based on reason, but springs from obedience to the commands of moral conscience. Later developments of skepticism, especially those of the first half of the seventeenth century that, as we shall see, were inspired by Montaigne, rejected his reflections on religion and focused on the Epicurean elements of his philosophy.

In Montaigne's intellectual circle was another skeptic, Pierre Charron (1541–1603), author of Les Trois Vérités, in which he argued against atheism, and De la sagesse, his most famous book, which was published in 1601. Charron shared Montaigne's theory of the subjectivity and limitation of human knowledge. He maintained that true wisdom respects and actualizes the moral ideal, which is independent of dogmatically expressed religion. Charron did not oppose religion, but he stressed that it belongs to the domain where human nature is autonomous in determining its happiness.

The skepticism of the sixteenth-century Renaissance has a certain conformist and peaceful character, which will be drastically transformed in the early seventeenth century. Cultural, ethical, and philosophical libertinism, which will be discussed in the second part of this course, will be inspired by Montaigne's and Charron's skepticism, but it will be more critical of society, religion, and philosophy as sources of wisdom. The more radical critiques will attempt to suppress all forms of religious faith, favoring instead a new ethic based solely on knowledge of human nature. Atheism will be the key feature of the new skepticism, which the great seventeenth-century philosophers will oppose.

Sources

Leon Battista Alberti, *Opere volgari* (Bari: Laterza, 1960).

Nicholas de Cusa, *Scritti filosofici: a cura di Giovanni Santinello* (Bologna: Zanichelli, 1965–1980).

Marsilio Ficino, *Teologia Platonica: a cura di Michele Schiavone* (Bologna: Zanichelli, 1965).

Michel de Montaigne and Albert Thibaudet, *Essais* (Bruges: Gallimard, 1950).

Giovanni Pico della Mirandola and Eugenio Garin, *De hominis dignitate, Heptaplus, De ente et uno* (Firenze: Vallecchi, 1942).

Pietro Pomponazzi, *Trattato sull'immortalità dell'anima* (Roma: Galilei, 1914).

Francisco Suárez and Antoine Théophile Duval, *Opera omnia* (Paris: Apud Ludovicum Vivès Bibliopolam Editorem, 1859)

Teófilo Urdanoz and Francisco de Vitoria. *Relecciones teológicas* (Madrid: Biblioteca de Autores Cristianos, 1960.

PART TWO
RATIONALISM

2.1 GENERAL CHARACTERISTICS

Having studied Renaissance philosophy and all the characterizing elements that distinguish it from the philosophy of the Middle Ages, we now enter into the classical period of modern philosophy. René Descartes is often considered the first modern philosopher, the founder of a new philosophical method. Though this opinion is substantially true, it ought to be qualified. As discussed earlier, there are two centuries before Descartes in which what is commonly understood as modern philosophy still has not yet begun, yet during which, medieval philosophy has already ceased to exist.

This chapter will cover two centuries that defined and shaped the philosophical and cultural spheres of the world today. This important historical period begins with Descartes and Francis Bacon. The seventeenth and eighteenth centuries witnessed gradual differentiation and growing complexity in the main lines of philosophical thought.

The philosophy of this period can be organized into four elements: rationalist philosophy, empiricist philosophy, the birth of modern science, and the Enlightenment. Within each of these elements are diverse characteristics that make each difficult to categorize under a single, simple label. This should be kept in consideration to avoid an overly partial or linear overview of this period.

Modern philosophy is characterized as making the subject and subjectivity its center of reflection and interest. This perspective or central thesis would never be abandoned by modern philosophy. As the world advanced into modernity, this idea was repeatedly made more explicit, from which were derived many unprecedented cultural and philosophical implications in Western culture. In fact, the rationalism of continental Europe and the empiricism of the British philosophers share the radical philosophical perspective that begins with the subject.

The common root of rationalism and empiricism, nevertheless, does not reduce them to being mere philosophies of the subject, nor are they merely two aspects of the same philosophy. Rationalism and empiricism are distinct in their theoretical developments, interests, and the subsequent theses that derived from each of the two philosophies. But, it is true that in the eighteenth century, both schools were merged by the remarkably profound and speculative synthesis of Kant.

The seventeenth century is the century of Descartes and Bacon, but also of Galileo. The importance that modern science had in this century made it a hallmark of the period. The discovery of the mathematical method as applied to the natural sciences is especially representative of the zeitgeist. Rationalist philosophy mainly developed according to a systematic framework, hence assuming many characteristics similar to those of the mathematical method. For its part, empiricist investigation emphasized the use of data obtained by observation. The mathematical method and empirical observation are also featured in empirical science which additionally employs systems and experience. Thus in this century, the dialogue between philosophy and science reached a remarkable intensity, with a constant exchange of theses about the natural world and human knowledge.

Various philosophers expressed another element of the philosophy of this period: an interest in religion. It is just as difficult for theology as for history, philosophy, and culture, to pinpoint a moment in time when the Middle Ages stopped and modernity started. It is much easier to describe the continuity between the two eras. However, while medieval theological interests did not disappear with the advent of modernity, certainly there was a notable change of perspective.

Authors such as Descartes, Pascal, Malebranche, Spinoza, and Leibniz addressed questions about God with remarkable depth and an important speculative expression.

English empiricism, in general, being less metaphysical, dealt with the question of God less frequently and from a different perspective. Other cultural movements, such as libertinism and some currents of the Enlightenment, will qualify themselves as atheist. But certainly modern philosophy should not be identified *tout court* with libertinism or the atheism of some currents of the Enlightenment.

Modern philosophy also brought great developments to political philosophy. A central notion that appears in various authors is the social contract. This concept expresses the search for a dynamic principle for the organization of society, as well as embodies an anthropology that maintains a generally individualistic perception of man, reflecting the modern awareness of human autonomy.

In this period, modern states became stronger. Revolutions brought absolute monarchies to an end, yielding to the first forms of modern democracies, which were marked by a tendency toward individualism. Tolerance was an important question in the developments of the social contract theory, stemming from political-religious strife between various religions on the European continent. Up until the beginning of the sixteenth century, the only religion in Western Europe was Catholicism. But after the Lutheran and Calvinist reforms and the Anglican schism, coexistence with differing religious beliefs became a problem. Wars of religion created a political situation that led some thinkers to propose tolerance as a means toward peaceful coexistence.

The following chapters will focus on continental rationalism and British empiricism. Both schools share the knowing subject as their center of philosophical speculation, a characteristic that makes them distinctly modern, even though the topic has held constant throughout the history of Western Philosophy.

Continental rationalism and British empiricism differ in metaphysics and epistemology, though the two schools certainly overlap at times. Hobbes, for example, widely uses the method of Galileo, and Locke and Berkeley were respectfully influenced by Descartes and Malebranche.

While rationalism's metaphysics is largely related to the great traditions of ancient and medieval metaphysics, as a new attempt to understand man, the world, and God, it is more than just a simple continuation. The Cartesian starting point—the *cogito*—is also a metaphysical perspective. Descartes' work, together with that of Malebranche, Spinoza, and Leibniz, will lead to the Cartesian framework becoming the common platform of philosophy. The rationalist metaphysical inquiry is characterized by the pursuit of certainty, expression of clear and distinct ideas, and problems deriving from the separation of extended substance and the thinker.

In addition to all this, we must add that Descartes—together with others that came before him in the sixteenth century—is the spiritual creator of the system that will affect all modern metaphysics. Some of the basic concepts of their philosophical system to which later philosophers returned for further exploration include truth being defined as logical coherence, the mathematical deductive method, clarity and distinction, and unity. These creators of the modernist system also are marked by a certain contempt and alienation from sense experience. Rationalist metaphysics is more deductive and less observing, more interested in accurate and precise definitions than in a description of real phenomenon.

Empiricism, however, was more interested in gnoseological questions than in questions of classical metaphysics, although it shares with rationalism the search for certainty. The first question for the empiricist philosopher is not of being, but of how one can come to the knowledge of reality starting with experience. This enquiry about the human experience of knowing and affectivity was conducted with great analytical spirit. Empiricist philosophy was always tied to a type of sense experience, following its theory that every idea always ought to be based on sense data. The empirical approach dismissed any metaphysical dimension of intellectual acts, considering abstractions to be mere products of the imagination, separated from experience. Instead, empiricists maintained that ideas are images, representations, or reflections of sensible phenomena, of particular things. Universality—empiricists would rather speak of generality—is a quality of names or of terms, but not of ideas or concepts. These claims of empiricism reflect several underlying principles of nominalism.

Logically, the empirical method cannot be the same as that of rationalism. Instead of mathematical deduction, empiricism argues that induction is the preferable scientific and philosophical method. If rationalism has a clear systematic spirit, empiricism has an analytical spirit of observing experience and its epistemological presuppositions.

Empiricism undertook the task of judging man's cognitive ability from a reductionist conception of the same cognitive experience. This attempt was a theoretical possibility that Kant eventually took on as his project. For its part, metaphysical rationalism, as opposed to empiricism, presupposed that the human cognitive capacity can attain objective truth by following the deductive method, without calling rationality itself into question. This theoretical position earned the name of *metaphysical dogmatism*.

The artificiality of rationalist systems, the lack of contact with sensory experience, the propensity to follow arbitrary definitions rather than the reality presented by the senses, will all be the subject of criticism by the Enlightenment philosophers. Above all, Condillac and Voltaire would accuse rationalism of being an imaginary and artificial construction. The eighteenth-century Enlightenment in general followed British empiricist philosophy. Empiricism, though, led to a form of skepticism, which denied that metaphysics could be the ultimate knowledge of reality, dismissed the science of theology as a contradiction, and converted objective morality to a hedonistic and utilitarian ethics.

a) Erudite Libertinism

To complete these introductory pages on rationalist and empiricist philosophy, it is necessary to mention a phenomenon that took place chronologically in the first half of the seventeenth century, although its influence extended up through the eighteenth century. This phenomenon is libertinism, which includes some philosophers who, while drawing from philosophical ideas of the Renaissance, were clearly already modern thinkers. They have been credited with being a "skeptic obstacle" for rationalist philosophers. The libertines arguably can be said to be antecedents of the Enlightenment who lacked the rationalist and empiricist traditions.

Erudite libertinism is partly the legacy of sixteenth-century skeptic philosophy, which the libertines considered their main influence. Though the libertines did not adequately develop a real philosophy or system, they are mostly known for their critical attitude towards philosophical and cultural traditions. As their activities made headway, the libertines would become known as "freethinkers," the name that was used for them at the height of the Enlightenment.

They were widely influential. Spurred on by the skepticism of Michel de Montaigne and Pierre Charron, they returned to some theories of Renaissance naturalistic philosophy. At the same time, they would become a target of criticism for many seventeenth-century philosophers, such as Descartes, Pascal, Malebranche, and Spinoza, who in various ways opposed the often extreme positions of the freethinkers.

The geographical discoveries had their own influence on the libertine mind. Among the abundant seventeenth-century literature on the newly discovered peoples was spread the myth of the *noble savage*, which claimed the existence of individuals who lived in a state of pure nature, enjoying original goodness and innocence. The libertines developed their own thesis connected to the idea of the noble savage, claiming that moral precepts come from a natural morality that does not pertain to any particular religion.

Their analysis of human nature is strictly historical, rejecting any anthropological or metaphysical perspective. In fact, the libertines did not have any metaphysical beliefs whatsoever; their explicitly critical opinion of metaphysics can earn them the anachronistic categorization as historicists. Their deep skepticism and their reasoning about the state of nature intensified their belief in the fittingness of the demise of religion. They insisted that morality is not based on religious truths, but on an innate sense of natural goodness. They charged religion, even the very idea of God, with creating divisions among men. Ultimately, they accused morality and religion of making men forget what is good about human nature in itself, citing the wars of religion to demonstrate the legitimacy of their anti-religious convictions.

Following upon the premises just mentioned, as an antidote to religion, atheism is the natural state of man and the morally superior position that safeguards the original natural values of man. Hence, natural morality constitutes the true religion, being a kind of natural knowledge within the reach of reason alone. Philosophy should thus become the true religion, since it is founded on nature, which is truly universal, and not on a particular dogmatic creed.

The spirit of libertinism is crystallized by the concepts of the *honnête homme*, the honest man, and the *esprit écarté*, the free spirit, who live by natural truths and are guided only by reason. With reason at the helm, men would come to a fundamental consensus, which would generate genuine critical universality by which everything could be judged without the *prejudices* of a moral value or a religious absolute.

Libertinism in this period attained a certain degree of development. Though inspired by the philosophy of Charron, Montaigne, and Renaissance naturalism, it was not until the seventeenth century that the libertines produced their main representatives. At the end of the century, particularly with the work of Pierre Bayle, libertinism became the immediate antecedent of the Enlightenment. Libertinism ran parallel with continental rationalism, British empiricism, and Pascal, continuing into the Enlightenment of the eighteenth century.

It should be added that neither rationalist nor empiricist philosophers were entirely free of certain libertine ideas. The chronological sequence of how the different philosophies influenced the other is not entirely clear, but nevertheless the close relation between philosophy, libertinism and Enlightenment help give historical perspective.

Among the principle libertines, the first to mention is Cyrano de Bergerac (1619–1655), a playwright famous for his *Le pedant joué* written in 1645 and *La mort d' Agrippine* of 1654. Before writing plays, though, he had written two philosophical novels, *Les états et l'empire de la lune* and *Les états et l'empire du soleil*. Cyrano was a rationalist and a naturalist who believed that the entire universe is a great living being internally structured with atoms. The universe is autonomous, being uninfluenced by God, and the source of its own movements. His ethical theories are related to Epicureanism, especially to the school of Lucretius.

Another important libertine, equally influenced by the Epicureans, was François La Mothe Le Vayer (1588–1672). Le Vayer was tutor to the brother of Louis XIV and author of the *Dialogues made in Imitation of the Ancients* and *On the Virtue of Pagans*. He is considered a disciple of Montaigne. Epicurean and Stoic tendencies coexist in his works. In the last years of his life, and after a long period working with Richelieu, he resumed his activity as a writer and composed *Skeptic Soliloquies*, which was later considered a kind of manifesto of the freethinkers.

Gabriel Naudé (1600–1653) is another important libertine, author of *Considérations politiques sur les coups d'état*. Dismissing religions as mere instruments of political power, he opposed any religious manifestation, whether it be a true religion or just a demonstration of magic. "The fear of God," wrote Naudé, "separation from the world, and all unimaginable sciences are useless for keeping man at his duty."

The remaining notable representatives of erudite libertinism are Elia Deodato, Guy de la Brosse, and Gabriel Foigny. Negative responses to libertinism took several forms. Pascal profoundly and comprehensively criticized all kinds of libertinism. Descartes, however, took their skepticist opinion into consideration that sure knowledge of the truth is impossible. Meanwhile, finding himself in the strongly libertine environment of the Netherlands, Spinoza dedicated much of his philosophy disputing libertine doctrines.

Although rationalists and libertines agreed upon the critical capacity of reason, rationalists rejected libertine skepticism, especially when it came to knowledge of the truth. On this topic the libertines sided with a purely empirical approach to knowledge, manifesting a certain continuity between libertinism, empiricism, and the Enlightenment. Pierre Bayle (1647–1706) in particular is a link between libertinism and the Enlightenment. He is often considered the first philosopher of the Enlightenment, even though his philosophy is certainly an enlightenment that has not yet reached maturity. Bayle synthesized into an articulate philosophy what the libertines had only expressed as undertones in a style more literary than philosophical. Bayle was a prolific writer and teacher in France and especially in the Netherlands. He is the author of the *Historical-Critical Dictionary*, published in 1697, which consists of articles in which Bayle examined philosophical and cultural concepts from ancient and modern thought. It is a direct antecedent of Diderot and D'Alembert's *Encyclopedia*.

Bayle was a critic of religion and natural theology, and had a largely skeptical and disenchanted vision of history. In fact, the *Dictionary* proposed historical facts about the various topics and authors without having a pre-established philosophical or historical system to follow. Rather, Bayle's intention was precisely the opposite: he wanted to debunk the idea that there could be any plan or wisdom behind history. His concern was setting down the historical facts as such, making him a precursor of the modern historical method. Bayle's fundamental ideas do not belong to the realm of metaphysics. He criticized tradition, history, and knowledge, not so much in order to reveal the truth, but rather to discover falsehood and deceptions. For his efforts to spread a critical attitude lacking deep convictions and without care about the truth, Bayle can be counted among the skeptical thinkers: "human reason is too weak to reach the truth; it is a principle of destruction and not construction, it only serves to create doubt, to make us turn right and left making any dispute endless."[12]

* * *

Having finished the overview of the seventeenth and eighteenth centuries, it is time to study individual philosophers of those periods. In the following pages we present the major metaphysical systems of continental rationalism as developed by Descartes, Malebranche, Spinoza, and Leibniz. Pascal and Vico receive separate chapters, in which their philosophical principles are presented as a reaction against Cartesian rationalism.

2.2 RENÉ DESCARTES (1596–1650)

a) Life and Works

Descartes was born in La Haye, in Touraine, on March 31, 1596. He studied at the Jesuit college of La Flèche until 1614, and in 1616 he obtained a degree in law at Poitiers. Dissatisfied with the training he had received in the classroom, he decided to enlist in the army of Maurice of Nassau shortly before the Thirty Years War. His military life took him to the Netherlands, where he met Isaac Beeckman, a mathematician to whom he dedicated his first book, *Compendium of Music*.

In 1619 Descartes moved to Germany, where he served in the army of Maximilian of Bavaria. On the night of November

---

12. Pierre Bayle, *Dictionnaire historique et critique*, II (Rotterdom: 1697), s.v. "maniquées."

10, Descartes had three dreams that he interpreted as a calling from heaven to a personal mission in the field of knowledge. In the dreams he had seen the mathematical method as a path leading to the foundation of knowledge. Descartes published the fundamental principles of the new method in *Regulae ad directionem ingenii* (1628–1629).

About this time, Descartes traveled to Italy and France, where he befriended Mersenne and Cardinal Bérulle. He moved to Holland in 1628, desiring to live alone, where he lived until a year before his death. From 1630 until 1633, he worked on his *Treatise on the World and on Man* that was published posthumously. In 1637, he published three essays on meteors, the *Dioptrique* and *Géometrie*. These were preceded by *A Discourse on Method*, which would become his most famous work, and which would mark what is widely considered the true beginning of modern philosophy. A few years later in 1641, he published *Meditationes de prima philosophia*. In 1644, he published his *Principia Philosophiae*, which was an attempt to give a systematic explanation of his philosophical and scientific thought. Descartes wanted this book to become a handbook for teaching in schools. In 1649, he wrote the *Passions of the Soul*, developing a psychology upon which to base his definitive morals, though Descartes never ended up writing on that subject. A year later, in 1650, he traveled to Sweden at the invitation of Queen Christina, with whom he kept up a correspondence about philosophy. In Stockholm, on February 11, 1650, Descartes succumbed to pneumonia and died.

b) The Cartesian Project

The magnitude of Descartes' intellectual aspirations embraced all of reality: metaphysics, physics, anthropology, and morality had a place in his system. Having begun his intellectual life with reflections on mathematics and geometry rather than on philosophy, Descartes' whole philosophical system would correspondingly follow a geometric-mathematical method. One of the defining features of the Cartesian world is the concept of the unity of science. Descartes affirmed this unity although it contrasted with Aristotelian thought, basing his reasoning uniquely on the mathematical method. Such a method would become for Descartes a requirement of the faculty of knowing, which always seeks certainty and evidence. These categories of certainty and evidence are two other key elements of the Cartesian project, which can be characterized as a search for the unity of knowledge through irrefutable evidence. The pursuit of certainty and evidence manifests a Cartesian attitude in dialectical opposition to the largely scholastic philosophy of his time, which, timid with uncertainty about its own propositions, lacked a compelling theoretical synthesis suited to the mentality of the new modern man. The lack of certainty, as we have seen, had led to various forms of skepticism, such as that created by Montaigne. According to Gilson, Cartesian philosophy was, in this sense, a desperate attempt to break free from the skepticism of Montaigne and his disciples.

In contrast to his dissatisfaction with the state of his philosophical world, Descartes noted that mathematical sciences and geometry possessed the unconditional certainties that he so fervently sought. He deemed the method employed by these sciences the most suitable for achieving certain knowledge in any field of study.

The *one* science for Descartes is also a *total* science. Defining philosophy as love of wisdom, he compared it to a tree whose roots are metaphysics, whose trunk is physics, and whose branches are medicine, mechanics, and morals. The fruits are in the branches, but cannot be enjoyed without passing through the roots and the trunk. This image graphically expresses his opinion that philosophy has a practical purpose. The Cartesian project is, above all, practical—the goal of life being "to advance the search for the truth." The purpose of this search is not merely contemplative, but is a kind of knowledge where "the intellect shows the will in all circumstances the choice that should be made." In a famous text of his *Discourse on Method*, Descartes explained the practical purpose of philosophy in another way: to "make us masters and lords of nature."

Although it was previously stated that Descartes shared the idea of a systematic spirit, such an idea is present in his work only implicitly. Formal organizations of ideas and principles do not appear in such a systematic way as they would appear later in the rationalism of Leibniz and Wolff. In this sense, Descartes is only an initiator, never having fully adopted the method of systematic knowledge. He did, though, provide the methodological foundations for it, as well as describe the locus and nature of the principle of evidence—in clear and distinct ideas—which will enable further development of philosophy as a system.

c) The Method

The Method is one of the central themes of Descartes' philosophy. According to his mental categories, the method is the safe path that leads to perfect knowledge. All perfect knowledge is a science, which in turn can be defined as certain and evident knowledge.

In Descartes' opinion, the only science of his day that had certainty and evidence was mathematics. Following in Galileo's footsteps, Descartes believed that the mathematical method reveals the intrinsic structure of reality. The rules that govern that reality are also the system and expression of an order in which ideas are inter-connected. Descartes' primary thesis asserts the fundamental unity of all sciences and, consequently, that there must exist a single and universal method for all the sciences. Such a method should facilitate the use of reason so that all knowledge will consist of clear and evident ideas. In his *Discourse on Method*, Descartes proposed four simple, universal rules of methodology in the form of general statements. These fundamental propositions defined his method, and he frequently formulated those principles in other ways to give a more exact explanation of his method. The cornerstone of his four methodological principles is the question about evidence, which in turn leads to another equally fundamental question about clear and distinct ideas. Let us analyze the rules of the *Discourse*.

The first rule says: "Do not accept anything as true unless I clearly knew it as such, that is, I must carefully avoid haste and prejudice, and not include in my judgments anything that is not presented clearly and distinctly to my intelligence, so that I may exclude any possibility of doubt."[13] This rule has to do with evidence and to the clear and distinct ideas that result from evidence.

Descartes gives the name of 'intuition' to the intellectual act of acquiring evidence. Intuition is "neither the fluctuating testimony of the senses nor the deceptive judgment of an imagination that composes things badly, but rather the conceptual act of the pure and attentive mind, a conceptual act so easy and so distinct that no doubt whatsoever can remain about what we are understanding. Or stated differently, 'intuition' is the indubitable conceptual act of the pure and attentive mind, that comes from the light of reason alone, and is more certain than the very same deduction because it is more simple."[14] For Descartes, the problem of doubt is intrinsically related to the question of evidence: one must overcome doubt in order to achieve certainty or clarity. His ideas took on a methodical form of systematic doubt, which, simply stated, means doubt everything until you get to the evidence.

The second rule of the *Discourse* concerns analysis: "Divide each problem under examination into as many parts as possible and as might be necessary in order to resolve it adequately."[15] Dissecting the compound into its simpler elements helps the intellect avoid ambiguities. Descartes wanted certain knowledge, which in his opinion could only come from the simplest elements of reality. Arriving at certainty requires simple,

13. René Descartes, *Discourse on Method*, 2.

14. René Descartes, *Regulae ad directionem ingenii*, 3.

15. Descartes, *Discourse on Method*, 2

undeniably true ideas, which are produced through intuition, and count as evidence.

The third rule set forth by Descartes is: "I must direct my thoughts with order, beginning with the simplest objects and the easiest to learn, and to ascend slowly, gradually, to the knowledge of the more complex things, assigning a certain order in thought to those things that do not naturally stand in a relation of antecedence or sequence."[16] This rule has to do with synthesis. Once a complicated thing has been broken down into its simple elements, those elements ought to be reconstructed. The synthesis of ideas will thus begin with simple elements—self-evident principles—that do not depend on each other, and then proceed to relative and dependent elements.

The fourth and final rule of the *Discourse* prescribed: "in every case, to make enumerations so complete and reviews so general so as to be sure that nothing was omitted."[17] Enumerations assure that an analysis is complete, while reviews assure that a synthesis is correct. This rule prevents the haste and prejudice that Descartes mentioned in the first rule, as well as manifests the meticulosity of one's mental operations.

The development of the entire Cartesian philosophy can be found in a nutshell in Descartes' method. The method regulates the objects of knowledge without depending on them. Truth, for Descartes, depends completely on the part of the thinking subject, since the truth is confirmed by the certainty with which it is possessed. The subject imposes its conditions on the object, consisting of clear and distinct ideas that satisfy the conditions for evidence.

d) Methodical Doubt and the Cogito

At this point, it is necessary to justify the very rules of the method. In other words, an initial certainty must be formulated

16. Descartes, *Discourse on Method*, 2.
17. Descartes, *Discourse on Method*, 2.

that acts as a foundation for the rules of the method. Descartes' first step toward formulating this initial certainty is doubt. Doubting allows the thinking subject to criticize and reject all opinions and all uncertain or obscure ideas that are little more than mere prejudices, in order to build the whole edifice of philosophy on entirely new and sure foundations.

Cartesian doubt is not a skeptical doubt. In the first place, it is methodical, with the goal of finding a solid foundation for knowledge, while skeptics simply profess a wholesale epistemological doubt. Descartes' method of doubt is also universal, meaning that he doubts any obscure idea that may have even the slightest chance of being false. Finally, doubt is voluntary; to doubt depends directly on the will to doubt.

Resulting from the universal methodological doubt arises the first and undeniable evidence: the thinking subject is a reality and the object of an immediate intuition: *cogito, ergo sum.* The subject overcomes doubt through the evidence of his own thinking. The action of thinking is evidence, a self-evident truth, that presupposes a subject in existence in order to do the thinking. Thus the subject's thinking is evidence of the thinking subject's being: 'I think' and 'I am' are on the same level of self-evident truth, that together allow the subject to definitely overcome universal doubt.

One can and should doubt everything—God, heaven, the body, external reality—but one cannot doubt that, when thinking about all those things, he is a thinking substance. The *cogito* can withstand even a very crafty hypothesis in which all of reality could be dismissed as being some kind of illusion conjured up in our heads by some higher power to fool us into believing false experiences of a world which does not actually exist—even then, the *cogito* at least provides complete and direct certainty of one's own thinking.

What therefore is the *cogito*? What is its ontological status? The *cogito* is an intellectual intuition, a first evidence. It is not reasoning or a syllogism. It is the recognition of the subject's own existence by a simple act of mental vision.

There is, therefore, an inextricable link between thought and being: thinking manifests being, that is, the *cogito*—I think—manifests the *sum*—I am—the subjective existence. Thus, the evidence of thought is also subjective evidence of existence. The ego is evident in thinking.

In a way, on the topic of the *cogito*, Descartes coincides with St. Augustine, who also defended the *cogito*. There is, however, a big difference between the two authors. Descartes' *cogito* is inseparably part of the philosophical method, which for Descartes is the foundation of doing philosophy. The active position of the *cogito* in the method makes it impossible to develop a proper philosophy of the *cogito*, independent of the method.

e) Subject and Thought

The *cogito*, as already seen, is not an abstraction, but a subject or, rather, an act of the subject: it is I who thinks. Descartes described the subject as follows: "I am a substance whose essence or nature is to think, and in order to exist, there is no need of any place, or to be dependent on any material thing."[18] Having identified a being in the "I," Descartes characterized the self as a thinking substance, a *res cogitans*, distinct from the body, which is *res extensa*. He distinguishes between a general concept of thought and the first evidence provided by the pure *cogitare*. Thought can be broadly interpreted as anything that one can be conscious of, such as imaginations or feelings, while the act of pure *cogitare* as an intrinsic clarity of thinking is evidence of subjectivity. Sensitivity and imagination, meanwhile, are functions of the mind and the body; but insofar as they depend on the body—the *res extensa*—they do not get involved with the intellectual intuition of the *res cogitans*. The essence of mind is thought; thought is the mind's fundamental attribute. Observing that the soul cannot be conceptually separated from the activity of thinking, Descartes asserts that the soul is thought itself. Thus Descartes reduces man, considered in himself, to be

18. Descartes, *Discourse on Method*, 4.

essentially *res cogitans* and not *res extensa*. By this thesis, Descartes threatens the substantial unity of the body and soul of man—a unity that gives such richness to human activity.

Descartes presents the will as a core element and foundation of Cartesian philosophy. The will carries out the methodical doubt. By doubting everything, the subject can clearly manifest his free will. While his intelligence may be limited to knowing only a few things clearly and distinctly, the will in itself has no limits. The will has a certain absoluteness which directs actions, following an internal spontaneity with respect to the clearly conceived object. The Cartesian system thus takes on a voluntaristic interpretation: the *cogito, ergo sum* resolves the subjective dynamism of doubt, which was born from a desire to doubt. Subjectivity is characterized by the *cogito*, as the source of its clarity, and by the *volo*, as the drive behind its activity.

f) The Existence and Nature of God

While the *cogito* is the first evidence, the second idea in the Cartesian system is God. Descartes started with the *cogito* and later came to the idea of God, who is the guarantor of the truth generated by clear and distinct knowledge coming from evidence. Descartes attributes an important role to God in his system: "Every certainty and truth of science depends on the knowledge of the true God, such that, until I know him, I cannot perfectly know anything else."[19]

Cartesian doubt embraced both the idea and the very existence of God. Descartes thought that the resolution of doubt through the *cogito* is not sufficiently definitive to ensure the existence of the world and eternal truths. God, however, could guarantee it. So for Descartes, the existence of God is crucial to the universal overcoming of doubt.

Arnauld, a seventeenth-century French logician, criticized Descartes for attributing the function of guarantor to God. Descartes, he says, can only be sure that God exists because he

---

19. Descartes, *Meditations on First Philosophy*, 5.

perceives that truth clearly and evidently. But before having the certainty that God exists, he ought to be certain that whatever he perceives clearly and distinctly is true. In the end, says Arnauld, Descartes must determine whether the *cogito* is the true principle of philosophy, or whether it is subordinate to God.

1) Proofs of God's Existence.

In a famous text of his third *Metaphysical meditation*, Descartes distinguished between the formal reality and the objective reality of ideas. The formal reality is the actual reality of something; thus the formal reality of an idea would be a particular mode of thought. In this sense, all ideas are the same since each idea receives its formal being in thought. Objective reality, on the other hand, is the content of an idea. The diversity of ideas lies in their content: the idea of God is not the same as the idea of fire. The objective reality of an idea has a certain consistency independent of the activity of the thinking subject. Because the objective reality does not depend on the thinking subject, it requires a cause—the formal reality—that contains that reality not only objectively, but also formally or really. Thus, Descartes says, "for an idea to contain some objective reality rather than another, it should certainly have received it from some cause, which must possess at least as much formal reality as the idea contains objective reality."[20]

Keeping in mind the distinction between formal reality and objective reality, Descartes examined whether there is something in the idea of God that does not proceed from the thinking subject.

1. *God: the idea of the perfect and infinite being.* Descartes' first argument for the existence of God considers how it is possible that a finite and imperfect subject can have an idea of perfection and infinity. Man recognizes that

---

20. Descartes, *Meditations on First Philosophy*, 5.

the limited nature in himself conflicts with the infinity and perfection he knows in God. How is it possible, Descartes asked, to see oneself as imperfect without first having the idea of a more perfect being? The same act of thinking by which one doubts and desires yields the idea of a perfect being, which then makes one able to know his own finitude.

A subject can have an idea of substance, since he himself is a substance. But how can a finite being have an idea of an infinite substance unless that idea were placed in him by some infinite substance? Therefore, God must exist. He is the necessary cause of the idea of God in man.

2. *The contingency of self.* Descartes said that "if I were independent of everyone else, and if I were the creator of my being, certainly I would not doubt at all, and I would not have any more desires and I would not lack any perfection: for I would have given myself all the perfections of which I have any idea, and so I would be God."[21] In a sense, this argument is an explanation of the first proof, but it adds a new concept that Descartes himself will later develop and predicate of God, namely, that he is the cause of his own being. Descartes affirmed that just as he is not infinite and therefore does not have all perfections, the being that has all perfections must, by the fact that it has all perfections, be the cause of itself and therefore necessarily exist.

3. *The ontological argument.* Descartes' third proof is also his most famous. Though the argument has certain similarities with St. Anselm's, it is not the same. He begins with the idea of a supremely perfect being. Man has a clear and distinct idea of God, just as clearly and

21. Descartes, *Meditations on First Philosophy*, 3.

distinctly as he understands that three angles are equal to two right angles in a triangle. But upon considering the idea of a triangle we do not arrive at its existence. However, if one examines the idea of an omniscient, omnipotent, and extremely perfect being, one realizes in one's intuition that God exists. The idea of God includes his existence: "thus, the mere fact that our knowledge perceives that necessary and eternal existence is contained in the idea of the being that is supremely perfect, we must certainly conclude that this supremely perfect being exists."[22]

2) The Cartesian God.

Having examined the evidence for God's existence, it is now possible to proceed to the main features of Cartesian natural theology.

First, the idea of God is innate. It is the stamp that the architect imprinted in his work. Every man is born with the idea of God. The image and likeness of God are manifested especially in the will, with its nearly infinite breadth.

Secondly, God is *causa sui*. Descartes sustains that the principle of causality is universal and has a distinctly epistemological mark. The universal principle should be applicable to all reality, created or uncreated, even to God himself. But God, having no previous cause outside of himself, is therefore the cause of himself.

The interpretation of this concept is not easy because it is not a simple contradiction in terms. Descartes realized that a cause must precede its effect. But to understand his point, the issue should be understood from the perspective of potency taking precedence over act in God: the infinite potency of God causes itself, even though this cause is neither temporary nor does it presume God's non-existence prior to the time of causation. Descartes wished to indicate

---

22. Descartes, *Principles of Philosophy*, 1.14.

that the power of God is certainly the cause of creation, but also that it is power in itself. Thus, the universality of causality has no exceptions.

The epistemological character of the principle of causality comes from the Cartesian equivalence of cause and reason. In fact, Descartes spoke of *causa sive ratio*. This way of thinking draw parallels between causality and reasons given in argumentative discussion. God is not only the cause of the world and of himself, but he is also what gives reason to the world and to himself. With the expression *causa sui*, Descartes meant that God's ultimate reason for being resides in himself.

Descartes also admitted the existence of eternal truths in God, following the Augustinian tradition, which also influenced other modern thinkers. Descartes' view is somewhat voluntaristic when he asserts that God established certain eternal truths simply by an act of the divine will. But he tempers that voluntarism by proposing other truths established by divine reason, such as the impossibility of God's non-existence, or the impossibility of the existence of a deceptive God. In Descartes' view, the eternal truths that depend on the divine reason give stability to the created world.

A final characteristic of Descartes' natural theology is the notion of continuous creation, which he preferred to the concept of conservation. Descartes proposed that God conserves the world by a succession of creative acts, instantaneously multiplied and put into effect. To make it easier to understand the world's dependence on the divine power as creation rather than as conservation, Descartes had a particular interpretation of time as a succession of disconnected moments.

g) The Corporeal World; The Soul and the Body

1) The Existence of Bodies

Once Descartes had established the existence of the self and of God, he then addressed the question of the world's existence. The outside world is the first truth annulled by methodical doubt; so it is up to Descartes to now rigorously establish its existence. It is not possible to have clear and distinct ideas about the material world, precisely because it is material and, consequently, perceptible only by the senses. There is one clear and distinct idea about the natural world, though, which is an exception: the idea of extension. Extension is the essence of material things; the material world is *res extensa*. This innate idea is the cause of all the other qualities that can be perceived.

In addition to the clear and distinct idea of extension, man experiences sensations that incline him to accept the probability of the existence of the corporeal world, since those sensations impel the subject that experiences them to seek their cause. Further, God gave to human subjects "a very strong inclination to believe that the sensations I receive come from corporeal things, such that I do not see how God could be released from the charge of deception if these sensations were product of causes other than the corporeal things."[23]

At this point, it is neither possible to accept the testimony of the senses rashly, nor to doubt them completely. The senses produce a clear and distinct concept of extension, whereas the other qualities that they perceive, such as color, taste, weight, and sound, are secondary and subjective. It would ignore the rules of the method to admit that things known confusedly have an objectivity comparable

23. Descartes, *Meditations on First Philosophy*, 6.

to clear and distinct ideas. Hence, material bodies are substantially *res extensa*.

For Descartes, substance is "the thing that exists so that it does not need anything else to exist."[24] The distinguishing character of substantiality is therefore independence. God alone, then, can be substance in an absolute manner, since all other substances depend on him. Descartes' criterion of truth is that one ought to have clear and distinct knowledge. A clear and distinct idea of extension or of thought, then, must necessarily correspond to a real external substance or a complete thinking and independent substance, since "all that we conceive in a clear and distinct way are true."[25] To further defend the existence of the corporeal world, Descartes had recourse to God, who cannot deceive. God is truthful and guarantees the truth of man's sensations and his inclination to apprehend the reality of the outside world.

2) *The Soul and the Body*

The essence of the soul is to think. It is possible to imagine the soul without the body. It is also possible to imagine the body without the soul. Consequently, Descartes says that the soul and body are two different substances, thought (*res cogitans*) and extension (*res extensa*).

Descartes admitted the evident fact that man experiences sensations that involve both the soul and body. Sometimes Descartes spoke of the substantial union of man's body and soul, but that was more in recognition of an undeniable experience rather than offering rational explanation. Descartes stated that "For the same reason that one can conclude that a body is attached to our mind much more closely than all other bodies, we can also see that pain and

---

24. Descartes, *Principles of Philosophy*, 1.51.
25. Descartes, *Discourse on Method*, 4.

other sensations come to us unexpectedly, and the mind recognizes the fact that such feelings do not come from itself nor even can they belong to the mind for the simple reason that it is a thinking substance, but rather because it is connected to something else that is extended and mobile, which we call the human body."[26]

Descartes' concept of independent substance conflicts with his attribution of substantiality to the both the *res cogitans* and the *res extensa*. In fact, the logic of Cartesian dualism is considered an unsolvable problem. Cartesian dualism is the most onerous legacy Descartes bequeathed to the philosophers that came immediately after him. Spinoza tried to resolve the problem through the idea of "one substance"; Malebranche through the theory of occasionalism; Leibniz through the idea of pre-established harmony. The Cartesian criterion of substantiality, the lack of an analogical use of knowledge, and the criterion of clarity and distinction as a qualification for all valid knowledge led to this dualism of *res cogitans-res extensa*. It is likely to remain an intractable problem in continental rationalism. Descartes himself had to make an unconvincing attempt to explain the unity of man. He claimed that the union of body and soul resided in a small organ of the body, the pineal gland.

The lack of unity between the *res cogitans* and *res extensa* produced an anthropological question that was to last for centuries: the division in man created by the separation of the two substances left human acts and activity with an unsatisfactory explanation; the split needed to be solved.

---

26. Descartes, *Principles of Philosophy*, 2.2.

h) Cartesian Physics

Physics is a rational science. Physics experiments produce clear, certain, and proven results when subjected to reason.

Descartes claimed that the principles of physics derive from the laws that God inscribed in the world. But since his purposes are impenetrable, it would be rash to investigate final causes whether in nature or in general. Instead, physicists should limit themselves to studying efficient causes, identifying relations of cause and effect between natural phenomena.

Matter, as characterized by Descartes, is merely extension. The shape and movement of matter also belong to the order of extension. From this perspective, qualities are subjective impressions, while simultaneously they are caused by variations in movements. According to Descartes, the universe is a vast mechanism. Although all bodies are made of the same material, differences of motion between their parts account for the differences in solid, liquid and gaseous states. Descartes reduces movement and qualitative changes to modifications of the bodily dimensions. Furthermore, Descartes denies the existence of empty space in his universe, claiming that all bodies are contiguous.

i) Morality

1) Provisional Morals

Descartes treats morality in the same way that he deals with the other parts of his philosophy: it has a definite, secure place, and is developed analytically. For Descartes, moral philosophy could only be substantiated after dealing with metaphysical and physical topics of his system.

But while the moment to study morality in a solid and definitive manner has not yet arrived in the history of philosophy, Descartes formulated some principles for an ethics of behavior that would help man not lose his way toward his final goal. This first formulation of morality has been named provisional morals.

Even though the adjective 'provisional' suggests something transient, Descartes believed that there are elements in this morality that can help construct definitive morals. In the *Discourse on Method* he spoke of three provisional moral rules:

1. "Obey the laws and customs of my country, faithfully observe the religion in which God gave me the grace to be educated from childhood, be ruled in any other thing according to the most moderate opinions that are commonly accepted and practiced by most sensible people with whom I have lived, and be far from any excess."[27] The author, who aspired to live in a state of happiness, gave priority to his practical sense over a true anthropological foundation of ethics.

2. "The second maxim is to be as firm and decisive in my actions as I could, and to follow even the most doubtful opinions, once I had adopted them, with no less constancy than if they had been quite certain."[28] This rule emphasized the priority of the will over doubt. As a criterion of morality, a firm will enjoys more validity than the judgment that doubts or compares conflicting moral principles.

3. "My third maxim was to try always to master myself rather than fortune, and to change my desires rather than the order of the world, and generally to get used to believing that there is nothing that is entirely within our power except our own thoughts."[29] The will is the only thing that he can freely determine. Thus, one ought to make "virtue out of necessity,"[30] which is realized in not wanting anything that the intelligence does not present as possible.

27. Descartes, *Discourse on Method*, 3.
28. Descartes, *Discourse on Method*, 3.
29. Descartes, *Discourse on Method*, 3.
30. Descartes, *Discourse on Method*, 3.

Having set out the rules of provisional morality, Descartes goes on to give a general criterion as the basic and fundamental rule of the same rules. The most important moral task for the French philosopher is "to use my entire life to cultivate reason and to make progress as far as possible in the knowledge of the truth, using the method I prescribed."[31] Here we find a point of contact between the cognitive realm of rational certainty and the moral dimension of human existence. For Descartes, happiness—the fulfillment of what it means to be human—would be obtained mainly in the order of knowledge, since knowledge itself is a good, and man cannot discern what is the true good without a precise knowledge of what can make him happy.

2) Definitive Morals

Although Descartes never got around to explicitly formulating a set of definitive morals, there are certain elements in his moral philosophy that can be labeled as such. At the end of his life, Descartes emphasized the secular character of morals, which led him to think that this world and this life is the best for man. He thought that morality has the highest scientific status, since it is the highest degree of wisdom. In order to learn how to lead a moral life, it must be remembered, first, that God exists and that all things depend on Him; then, that the nature of the soul is nobler than that of the body; and finally, one must be aware of the greatness of the universe.

Another element worth noting is that all individuals need other people, since each person is a part of the state, society, and family. It is therefore necessary to prefer the interests of the whole—the state, society, or family—to one own interests.

---

31. Descartes, *Discourse on Method*, 3.

In characterizing Descartes' definitive morals, one could also include parts of his treatise on the passions of the soul, in which he referred to the dominion that the soul ought to have over the body's passions. Passions are good, but their misplaced or excessive indulgence ought to be avoided. The highest virtue that reveals the noble inner reality, in Descartes' opinion, is generosity, which he defines as the good use of free will.

Notwithstanding the above mentioned elements, Descartes never systematically developed his definitive morals, thus we must be content with outlining some of its possible integral elements.

* * *

The philosophy of Descartes is the first historical expression of an intellectual position that would become prevalent in the history of modern philosophy. Unlike previous philosophers, Descartes chose subjectivity as the starting point of philosophical reflection, and found in it the constitutive principle of philosophical evidence. For him, clarity and distinction were the criteria of truth that simultaneously created a style of thought, a method of reasoning, and a new definition of subjectivity.

Insofar as it is a first principle of evidence, the *cogito* is defined as self-transparency, as a reality completely clear to reason. But this dimension of the subject should be compared with other elements that, having accepted this definition of subjectivity and rationality, will turn out to be heterogeneous. Although the *cogito* provides the reality of the '*sum*,' the 'I am,' the first evidence of one's subjective existence, reality still remains in an almost unattainable place. Realities can only be accepted in principle if they are clear, distinct, self-evident ideas. The limitations of this thesis immediately make themselves apparent, especially on an anthropological level. Corporality becomes an obstacle to describing the unity of man, even though Descartes in fact had to accept it. In the field of ethics, Descartes formulated his thought in a fragmentary way. Subsequent rationalist philosophy would develop ethics starting from his anthropological and methodological assumptions. The Cartesian method, in which mathematical-geometrical elements are very present, would play a decisive role in later developments of experimental science, anthropology, and ethics, as well as rationalist metaphysics.

2.3 BLAISE PASCAL (1623–1662)

a) Life and Works

Pascal's philosophical environment simultaneously confronted him with Cartesian rationalism on the one hand, with its assertion that certainty can be achieved through reason, and the popular skepticism of Montaigne on the other. This situation defined the dramatic character of his thought and his profound and fundamental criticism of rationalist and skeptic reasoning.

Pascal was born in Clermont-Ferrand on June 19, 1623. He was the son of a civil servant. His mother died three years after his birth. Blaise did not enjoy good health: his weak physical constitution, in fact, led to his early death at the age of 39.

Pascal spent his childhood and adolescence in Paris. Soon he proved to be a child prodigy, especially in the fields of mathematics and geometry. He came in contact with illustrious mathematicians and physicists, among which was Mersenne, an acquaintance of Descartes. At 16 years of age, he invented an arithmetic machine and published *A Treatise on Conic Sections*. In 1636, Pascal became involved with Jansenism, though he did not completely adhere to its doctrine. Three years later, he moved to Rouen in Normandy. The death of his father in 1651 left a deep impression on him. During these years, he continued dedicating himself to scientific research. In 1653, his sister Jacqueline entered the Jansenist convent of Port-Royal.

On the night of November 23, 1654, Pascal experienced a kind of ecstasy: he felt that God rested his hand on him. Pascal saw this event as a manifestation of divine grace. As a result of this religious experience, Blaise wrote the *Mémorial*, which he kept with him until his death in a paper sewn to his clothes. It reads:

The year of grace 1654.
Monday, 23 November, feast of St. Clement, pope and martyr,
    and others in the martyrology.
Vigil of St. Chrysogonus, martyr, and others.
From about half past ten at night until about half past midnight.

   FIRE.
   God of Abraham, God of Isaac, God of Jacob,
   not of the philosophers and of the learned.
   Certitude. Certitude. Feeling. Joy. Peace.
   God of Jesus Christ.
   My God and your God.
   Your God will be my God.
   Forgetfulness of the world and of everything, except of God.
   He is only found by the ways taught in the Gospel.
   Grandeur of the human soul.
   Righteous Father, the world has not known you, but I have
       known you.
   Joy, joy, tears of joy.
   I have departed from him:
   They have forsaken me, the fount of living water.
   My God, will you leave me?
   Let me not be separated from him forever.
   This is eternal life, that they know you, the one true God,
       and the one that you sent, Jesus Christ.
   Jesus Christ.
   Jesus Christ.

I left him; I fled him, renounced him, crucified him.
Let me never be separated from him.
He is only kept securely by the ways taught in the Gospel:
Renunciation, total and sweet.
Complete submission to Jesus Christ and to my director.
Eternally in joy for a day of trial on the earth.
May I not forget your words. Amen.

Since then, the philosophy of Pascal took on a religious character; his critique of rationalism became more explicit and penetrating; his innermost concerns became focused on knowledge and eternal life.

Between 1656 and 1657, he wrote the *Lettres écrites à un provincial par un de ses amis,* in defense of the Jansenists. The last two letters were written after the Church had condemned the ideas contained in Jansen's *Augustinus.*

Despite his interest in religion, reinforced by his inner experience, he did not abandon scientific research. Pascal furthered mathematics, providing the basis for infinitesimal calculus. His weak physical constitution and his increasingly frequent illnesses limited him during these years.

He began to write *Les Pensées* in 1657, by which he wanted to convert infidels to Christianity. He left his short thoughts and sentences to posterity in that book, though he intended to do more with it, using *Les Pensées* as the basis of a future Apology, which he never finished. Until his death he was working in this apologetic task.

In 1661, due to his worsening health, he definitely abandoned the disputes concerning the Jansenism of Port-Royal. He died on August 19, 1662, full of religious sentiments and with desires of passing on to eternal life. In 1670 the first edition of the *Pensées* was published, as directed by his nephew Etienne Perier, who also wrote the preface.

b) General Characteristics of Pascal's Thought

Pascal's work is a supreme effort to replace abstract philosophy with a philosophy of life that is capable of making man face the big questions of his concrete existence: God, freedom, death, and eternal life. At the same time, Pascal's work cannot be separated from the life of its author. In his works he expressed his personal position and definitive attitude in the ambit of his own concrete existence.

His initial rationalism and later criticism of rationalism as well as his religious conversion are the essential keys for the adequate interpretation of his work. From November 1654, Pascal felt inside that he was chosen by the Lord, and consequently he absolutized contrasts and radicalized his philosophical positions, particularly in his consideration of the dramatic dimension of human existence, marked by finitude, yet faced with the infinity, eternity, and immensity of God.

At the center of his philosophy is morality: man must discover what his true good is. The answers that other philosophers had given to this problem—here Pascal was mostly thinking of Montaigne—manifest a great relativism. All goods presented by philosophers are partial. Philosophy is not capable of solving this existential question; a sure answer can only come from faith and religion. Philosophy is merely a propaedeutic to faith, and morals rest on the immortality of the soul and the existence of God as fundamental principles.

Pascal often referred to the "madness" of the human sciences and philosophy. He thought that men ought to humble themselves, since getting to know the true God is not a speculative matter but a practical and moral one. However, man can never know God completely. Pascal's God is the *"Deus absconditus.* Since God has hidden himself, every religion that does not affirm that God is hidden is not true, and every religion that does not explain this does not instruct. Our [Catholic] religion does all this: *vere tu es Deus absconditus* (Is 45:14)."[32]

---

32. Blaise Pascal, *Pensées*, 585.

c) The Types of Knowledge; Reason and the Heart

Perhaps the most famous phrase of Pascal—and a good summary of his position on Cartesian rationalism—is the following: "The heart has its reasons of which reason knows nothing." Reason must recognize that there are many things that exceed it. If one does not understand this, then his reason is very weak.

Pascal claimed that there are essentially two types of knowledge: that which depends on memory and that which depends on reasoning. The first type is a historical knowledge governed by the principle of authority. Theology is an example of this type of knowledge. The second is a dogmatic knowledge, governed by physical experience or mathematical-geometric reasoning. This knowledge has no relation to authority, as it is based on experience or on the laws of reasoning. In these scientific matters, Pascal recommended following modern authors, who abandoned the method of authority and adopted the experimental and mathematical method.

But there is a third kind of knowledge, neither governed by experience alone nor by reason alone: this third knowledge is the knowledge of the heart, which apprehends the first principles. Pascal thinks that the heart is a kind of intellectual instinct that opposes and precedes the discursive processes of reason. But the heart is also the organ of religious certainty and of the love of God. "It is the heart and not reason that feels God. And this is faith: God who is sensible to the heart and not to reason."[33] The heart has an original character that links the intellectual with the volitional, and becomes a point of contact between man and God, with truth, and with the first principles.

---

33. Pascal, *Pensées*, 278.

d) The Project of an Apology of Christianity

Les Pensées was a monumental work, but unfortunately it was incomplete. In it, Pascal dealt with the major questions about human existence: fundamentally, the finite condition of man and the infinity to which he is simultaneously directed. As has been said earlier, Pascal intended to use *Les Pensées* as the starting material for a work of Christian apology, which would have presented faith as the solution to the deepest longings of the human heart, whose fulfillment is only found in God. In the misery and finitude of man there is a longing for the infinite, for the greatness and freedom that man can only find in personal union with God.

As part of this apology, Pascal systematized the concepts of knowledge and the good into an anthropology that would, in general, contradict both Cartesian philosophy and ethical skepticism. His new anthropology proposed that man is miserable and great at the same time, a reed, but a reed that thinks.[34] He is a worm of the earth, yet, at the same time, the glory of the universe. Man is miserable because original sin left its mark on human nature. But the desires for infinite greatness reveal in man a state previous to the state of sin, an age of innocence, from which man had fallen. This idea manifests a certain continuity with the philosophy of Platonic reminiscence and anticipates some of Kierkegaard's musings.

Pascal argues that there are three kinds of men: those who do not seek God; those who seek God but cannot find him; and those who have found God. The first kind, representing the libertines, are irrational and only seek to foolishly amuse themselves. The second kind, representing the wise rationalists, are unhappy in their rationalism. The third kind are filled with happiness. The skeptical philosophies of Pyrrho and Montaigne show the weakness of the human spirit.

Since nature does not provide definitive proofs of God's existence, man must place his bet on the truth of Christianity

---

34. See Pascal, *Pensées*, 347.

in order to reach the reality of God, true wisdom, and genuine good. The bet neither proves the existence of God nor the truth of Christianity, but it prepares the way for faith. Pascal explained that the wager consists of a necessary choice between the existence or non-existence of God. Being a necessary question, "you must wager. It is not optional. You are obliged. Which will you choose then? Let us see. Since you must choose, let us see which interests you least. You have two things to lose, the true and the good; and two things to stake, your reason and your will, your knowledge and your happiness; and your nature has two things to shun, error and misery. Your reason is no more shocked in choosing one rather than the other, since you must of necessity choose. This is one point settled. But your happiness? Let us weigh the gain and the loss in wagering that God is. Let us estimate these two chances. If you gain, you gain all; if you lose, you lose nothing. Wager, then, without hesitation that He is."[35]

Betting on the existence of God means living according to Christianity. Christian activity itself with the existential fulfillment that it brings will provide conviction of the truth of its teachings.

e) Faith and Reason

There are different interpretations of the *Pensées* of Pascal, because its propositions are ambiguous and, above all, because as a work it is incomplete. Some historians accuse it of fideism, rightly indicating elements that suggest this. But Pascal's fideism is different. Without outrightly rejecting reason, he thought that philosophical problems find their ultimate response in the realm of theology and faith. The purpose of the *Pensées* is not to convince, but rather to guide one to conversion; the purpose of the work transcends the limits of simple philosophy.

Other interpreters claim the *Pensées* is some kind of Pascalian skepticism. However, the texts that appear skeptical can be easily interpreted as mere anti-rationalist arguments meant to defend the faith.

_____

35. See Pascal, *Pensées*, 233.

Christianity, according to Pascal, does not deny reason, but rather assumes it. It seems, however, that there is no room in his philosophy for a natural theology, at least in the line of a medieval Aristotelian philosophy. Pascal's philosophy is rooted in the Augustinian tradition, which prefers careful considerations of interiority to more naturalistic arguments. Pascal maintains that when man faces God, he must say *credo* and not *scio*, although this belief simultaneously a kind of knowledge, just not of a rationalist type.

* * *

The characteristics of Pascal's thought are many and are defined in relation to the various problems posed by his contemporaries. If, on the one hand, Pascal reacted against Cartesian rationalism, he shared with Descartes a deep anti-skeptical attitude. His criticism of skeptical rationality as well as of rationalism are based on a vision of man understood as a finite being that simultaneously is capable of transcending his finitude and the limits set by the world. This transcendence has metaphysical and religious connotations that are difficult to separate. As such, Pascal's anthropology must be read from the horizon formed between the finitude and the greatness of man. Man's greatness comes, on the one hand, from his freedom and his intellect's inherent ability to transcend the world, and on the other hand, from man's capacity to be united to God, waiting for a life that, although higher, does no harm to human nature.

2.4 Nicolas Malebranche (1638–1715)

a) Life and Works

Malebranche was born in Paris in 1638. He studied philosophy at the college of La Marche, and then theology at the Sorbonne University. In 1660 he entered the Congregation of the Oratory, one of whose members was Cardinal Bérulle. There he studied Augustinian and Cartesian philosophy in depth. In

1664 he was ordained a priest. At this time he read, with much benefit, the *Treatise on the World and Man*, published after the death of Descartes.

Malebranche published *The Search after Truth* in 1668, continued by a series of publications over the following years; in 1676, *Christian Conversations*; in 1678, *Elucidations on the Search after Truth*; in 1680, *Treatise on Nature and Grace* (in a polemic with Arnauld); in 1683, *Christian and Metaphysical Meditations*; in 1684, the *Treatise on Ethics*; in 1688, *Dialogues on Metaphysics and Religion*, considered his most systematic work; in 1692, *Laws of Communication and Movement*; in 1697, the *Treatise on the Love of God*, in which he intervened in the pure love controversy of Bossuet and Fénelon.

He was appointed member of the Academy of Sciences in 1699. In 1708, he wrote *Dialogue between a Christian philosopher and a Chinese philosopher* about the existence and the nature of God. And in the year of his death, he published his *Reflections on Physical Pre-motion*.

Malebranche enjoyed great fame in life, partly due to his frequent interventions in the doctrinal controversies of his time. With Malebranche, after a hiatus with Pascal, we again take up the thread of continental rationalism.

Though his philosophy bears its own distinguishing characteristics, Malebranche was much inspired by Cartesian philosophy and is, in a certain sense, its continuation. Malebranche consolidated a well-defined line of rationalist philosophy, while also preserving a profoundly Christian view of man and a creationist view of the world. The Oratorian wanted to fill a theoretical space that Descartes opened but never resolved: the question of how finite substances and the causality of God interact in the movements of nature and in human actions.

While the rationalism of Malebranche's time, originating with Descartes, had not yet bloomed into the Enlightenment, libertinism had certainly spread in intellectual circles, and the encyclopedia, especially with the work of Pierre Bayle, had already debuted in some first renditions at the end of the seventeenth century. Malebranche, though, never saw the consolidation of the Enlightenment.

b) Philosophy and Theology

Malebranche wanted to build a Christian philosophy. He was of the opinion that metaphysics and theology share the same object, but begin from different starting points. In order to arrive at the truth, one must assent to faith as much as to evidence. Concurring with Augustine's phrase *"nisi credideritis, non intelligetis,"* Malebranche believed that the principles of philosophy find their ultimate foundation in faith. The sources of Christian philosophy, therefore, are reason and revelation. As we shall see, his philosophy tended to rationalize dogma and use the virtue of faith to resolve philosophical problems.

The French philosopher rejected Aristotelianism, believing that Descartes had discovered more in thirty years than had all the other philosophers of history. With respect to his rejection of Aristotelianism, it would be more precise to say that he rejected the Aristotelianism of his day, and particularly that of his teachers, since he never really studied original Aristotelianism in depth. Malebranche tended toward novelty in philosophy, but toward antiquity in theology. He wrote: "In matters of theology, we venerate what is ancient because we love the truth, and the truth is found in antiquity. In philosophical matters we should, on the contrary, and for the same reason, love novelty, and precisely because we must always love and seek the truth. But at the same time, reason does not allow us to believe more the word of these new philosophers than that of the ancients. Reason demands that we examine their thoughts with care and that we accept them only when we have no reason to doubt."[36] There is evident influence of Descartes in this statement.

---

36. Nicolas Malebranche, *The Search after Truth*, 2.2.5.

c) Theory of Ideas

Malebranche's theory of knowledge was highly influenced by the Cartesian system, which gave primacy of place, as we have seen, to certain and evident knowledge, which is the only true knowledge. The senses, on the other hand, are unreliable and do not give true knowledge of reality, though they may be useful for the conservation of our bodies. They perceive secondary qualities that, instead of belonging to the things themselves, are just subjective modifications of the spirit: "When it gets hot, we are not fools at all to believe that you feel hot. But we are fools if we think that the heat you feel is outside the soul that feels it."[37]

Being a good Cartesian, Malebranche argued that true knowledge is spiritual, rational, and ideal in nature. In other words, true knowledge is clear and distinct. And so, "we must attribute to each thing what is conceived clearly and what is contained in the idea that represents it."[38] To get to know material reality, Malebranche thought, man should not turn to the senses, but to the clear and distinct idea of extension, which is the essence of material reality. Therefore, to have knowledge of the truth, one must silence the imagination, a false and enslaving faculty.

Malebranche presented a special theory of knowledge, at which he arrived after criticizing the gnoseology of Aristotle, the empiricists, and Cartesian innate ideas. Malebranche's theory revolved around four possible forms of knowledge:

1) First, some things can be known by themselves, not needing any idea to act as a mediator between the thing and the knower. It is in this mode of direct and intuitive knowledge that man knows God, who is the only one that works directly in the spirit of man.

37. Malebranche, *The Search after Truth*, 1.5.
38. Malebranche, *The Search after Truth*, 3.2.

2) Second, knowledge of corporeal things takes place through the mediation of ideas. Malebranche uses complicated reasoning to explain this theory, and so it is best left to him in his own words: "We do not perceive objects that are outside of us by themselves. We see the sun, the stars, and an infinity of things outside of us, but it is unlikely that the soul leaves the body and goes, so to speak, to take a walk through the heavens to contemplate the heavenly bodies. Ergo, the soul does not see them by themselves. The immediate object of our mind when we see the sun, for example, is not the sun but something that is intimately connected to our soul, and that is what I call idea. By this word, therefore, I understand the immediate object or what is closest to the spirit when I perceive an object." The idea, therefore, is not the Aristotelian-Thomistic *species*, through which man knows things. The idea, as defined by Malebranche, already has an ontological reality in itself: man can know ideas, not things. This concept will become clearer in his writings about the vision of the ideas in God.

3) Third, man knows things through his consciousness or inner sense that are not distinct from his spirit. Malebranche explains this concept: "we do not know the soul through the idea of the soul, nor do we see it in God, but we know it through our consciousness,"[39] that is, "about our soul we only know what we perceive as happening in us."[40] This kind of knowledge, therefore, is not a clear and distinct knowledge, but rather a knowledge by inner experience.

4) The fourth kind of knowledge is assumptions, which are produced by comparing different things with each other.

---

39. Malebranche, *The Search after Truth*, 3.2.7.
40. Malebranche, *The Search after Truth*, 3.2.7.

d) Vision in God

In addition to the direct and intuitive knowledge—without the mediation of ideas—by which humans can understand God, the immediate object of our mind is the ideas. When faced with ideas, the soul is passive: it only receives what is given to it. A new question arises here about how ideas come to the soul, and what constitutes such ideas for Malebranche. In line with the Augustinian tradition, the French philosopher asserts that the ideas are eternal and necessary, and have a certain ontological consistency.

Malebranche excluded the possibility that ideas originate from the soul, and he also denied their innate character. Moreover, like a good rationalist, he thinks that attaining the universal concept of a thing through abstraction from sense data is impossible. The only possible solution that Malebranche gave to explain the knowledge of ideas is the theory of *vision of ideas in God*—which conveniently corresponds with reason and demonstrates the soul's dependence on God.

Malebranche claimed that God does not use difficult paths to do what can be done simply, because he never acts unreasonably. God has in himself the ideas of the things he has created. The human soul, being united intimately and immediately with God through a natural, necessary, and absolutely essential relationship, sees the works of God directly in God. The place of the spirit is in God Himself.

The ideas that man sees in God are independent and eternal, infinite and necessary. But the vision of God itself is not absolute; the spirit sees the essence of God only in relation to the creatures that it sees in God. "In our opinion, we see God when we see the eternal truths, not because these truths are God, but because the ideas on which these truths depend are in God."[41]

---

41. Malebranche, *The Search after Truth*, 3.2.6.

The theoretical foundations of the vision in God of Malebranche can be summarized in the following points:

a) The rejection—Cartesian in origin—of the Aristotelian species as the medium through which knowledge is obtained;

b) The passive nature of the intellect as a merely receptive faculty;

c) The distinction—also Cartesian in origin—of soul and body as two independent or autonomous substances;

d) Clear and distinct ideas as a source of true and evident knowledge;

e) The consideration of God as the only force that can illuminate both the essence of things and our intelligence.

Given the above, it is easy to understand why Malebranche's system has no need of a proof, strictly speaking, for the existence of God. "If you think of God, you come to realize that he cannot be deprived of existence. Other beings, even if they are known, may not exist: we can see their essence without their existence, their idea without their existence. But we cannot see the essence of the infinite being without its existence, the idea of being without being. Being in fact has no idea to represent it; it does not have an archetype that contains all its intelligible reality. It is the archetype of itself, and in itself it includes the archetype of all beings."[42]

If this were a philosophical proof, Malebranche would be proposing two premises as the basis of why knowledge itself is possible: first, an idea of the infinite being is present in the intellect, and second, the human intellect is present in God. While the idea of the infinite being may be limited by the finite human intellect, it nevertheless is the idea of the infinite being itself. Therefore, Malebranche says, "observe well that the proposition 'there is a God' is itself the clearest of

---

42. Nicolas Malebranche, *Dialogues on Metaphysics*, 2.5.

all propositions that affirm the existence of something else, and that is as true as this other one: 'I think, therefore I am.'"[43]

The question of the vision of ideas in God assumes *a priori* that one sees or knows that God exists. These two truths go together. "To fully explain what I mean, it would be necessary to show the soundness of the views of those who believe that God is the father of the light that enlightens all men, and that without this light, simpler truths would not be intelligible; and the sun, as bright as it is, would not even be visible. This conviction has led me to the discovery of this truth that seems like a paradox: that the ideas that represent creatures to us are perfections of God, which correspond to those same creatures and represent them."

In fact, this contrived theory is conditioned by the Cartesian legacy that Malebranche received. If the senses are unable to give certain, clear, and evident knowledge, the human soul would be enclosed within itself, without any communication with the outside world, at least with regard to the possibility of achieving true knowledge. But Malebranche is not disposed to deny the existence of the sensible world, so he had to resort to the theory of vision of things in God in order to preserve the human soul's access to the outside world.

e) Occasionalism

The topic of the vision of ideas in God is directly related to the present topic of occasionalism. Malebranche's position on the issue is again conditioned by his Cartesian inheritance. The dualism of the *res cogitans-res extensa* made explaining the interaction of creatures very difficult, especially with respect to the relationship between the human soul and the corporeal world. Once again, Malebranche will resort to a contrived theory as a way of solving a very ordinary existential question.

Earlier Malebranche had explained the origin of the ideas that the mind knows, but now he must explain the existence of corporeal bodies. Malebranche criticized Descartes' way of

43. Malebranche, *Dialogues on Metaphysics*, 2.5.

proving the existence of the world, because Descartes' thesis needed to first demonstrate the existence of a creator God, while Malebranche is of the opinion that reason can only prove the existence of a necessary God. The fact that God created the heavens and the earth is known only through revelation. Similarly, knowledge of bodies only comes through faith. The senses merely incline man to believe that corporeal bodies exist. Malebranche distinguished between supernatural and natural revelation. God uses the occasion of sensation to reveal the existence of other corporeal bodies. Though it may be a subjective fact, it is nevertheless evident that sensation reveals an act of God in man. Any sensation whatsoever, take pain for example, is a revelation. Feeling reveals an action of God through which man knows the existence of other corporeal bodies.

The senses make man believe that bodies exert a true causal activity. Some philosophers, Malebranche claimed, even talk of nature and the human faculties as causes of natural effects, but such affirmations are the result of original sin. Rather, there is no real cause except God: no natural cause is a real cause because it is merely an occasional cause. The true cause is one that has a necessary relationship with the effect; only the necessary Being has a necessary relation with his effects, thus only God is a true cause.

The divine causality is properly creative. Malebranche says that to cause is to create (displaying his Cartesian legacy of continuous creation), while creatures do not exert any real causation. Occasional causes particularly determine the general laws that God inscribed in the corporeal world. When a billiard ball collides with another, both spheres move, but it is God who produced the two separate movements. The collision is only the occasional cause of the distribution of their movements.

Malebranche explained this vision of the world by the principle of simplicity of the divine ways. Creatures and their movements are the work of the Wisdom and Power of God, and God does not do in a complicated way what he can do simply.

According to Malebranche, there are five types of general laws through which Divine Providence rules the world:

1) general laws of the communication of movement, in which an occasional cause is the collision between bodies;
2) laws of union of soul and body;
3) laws of union of soul with God;
4) laws that give the angels power over inferior substances;
5) laws through which Jesus Christ has received the sovereign power over all bodies and spirits, especially with respect to the distribution of goods and heavenly graces.

Although Malebranche intended to emphasize the transcendence of God and His infinite excellence over every creature, he compromised human freedom and divine freedom itself with his theory of occasionalism. In his *Dialogues on Metaphysics and Religion*, Malebranche summarized his unique occasionalist theory by the words of Theodore, a character in the dialogue:

"Therefore, Aristo, you cannot move your arm by yourself, change place, position, habits, do good or evil to other men, or bring about in the universe the slightest change. Here we are in the world with no power, rigid as a stone, stupid, like a log so to speak. Your soul can be united to the body as closely as you like, and therefore can stay in touch with all those who surround you, but what benefit can you draw from this imaginary union? How will you move even the tip of a finger or utter a monosyllable? What a pity! If God does not come to your aid you will exert but vain efforts, you will not conceive but impotent desires, because, just reflect a little, do you know what it takes to pronounce the name of your best friend, to bend or straighten the finger that you make more use of? (. . .) Despite the union of soul and body, as you like to imagine, lo and behold here you are dead and motionless, if God does not want to make his will agree with yours, his will is always effective while yours forever impotent. Behold, my dear Aristo, the solution to this mystery: creatures are immediately united to God, and they depend essentially and directly on Him alone. Since all creatures are equally impotent, they are not mutually dependent on each other at all. You can say, yes, they are linked together and depend on each other. I agree. But let it be clear that this is so only because of the immutable and always effective will of the Creator, and only as a consequence of the general laws that God has established and through which He directs the ordinary course of his providence. God wanted my arm to move at the same time that I want it myself."

f) Morality

Having understood Malebranche's metaphysical system, it is fair to ask what becomes of freedom. Malebranche distinguished two dimensions in human actions: the will and freedom. Will is prior to freedom, and has a necessary character—man cannot help but want the general good, which is God. The movement of the will is first and indeterminate, while freedom is defined as a determination of the will, the capacity to bestow or suspend the consent to the motions that lead the will to the good.

The will is nothing but the action of God in the soul. Freedom, on the other hand, has its proper activity, which can be determined to a particular good. But freedom is not a truly effective activity because freedom has a vincible character (it is not forced to choose this or that) and always requires the help of God.

Malebranche claimed that it is impossible to have a clear and distinct idea of freedom, though knowledge of it through consciousness or inner feeling is possible. The rationalist system of Malebranche will forever include the ultimate significance of free but ineffective activity—lacking any causality—as one of its unknowns.

Reminiscent of Augustinian thought, Malebranche thought that love of order was the most important virtue. He defines this virtue as submission to the divine laws. Original sin, thus, would be considered a disorder. One must ask for grace to restore the order that sin damaged.

* * *

Malebranche's philosophy is largely a continuation of that of Descartes. He took up once more the fundamental questions raised by Cartesian philosophy, though he never resolved them sufficiently, although he tried to give new explanations to these same issues without abandoning the rationalist perspective.

The question of method dominated much of Malebranche's reflection, just as it had for Descartes. From the beginning, Malebranche takes a metaphysical turn; he explains the problem of how the *res cogitans* connects to the *res extensa* through the action of God in the world. God himself coordinates all the activity of creatures.

Thus, in his theory of knowledge, Malebranche proposed the thesis of the vision of ideas in God. Just as in the Cartesian thesis, the soul somehow remains isolated from the world, without any way of establishing a relationship with it. The truth of an idea, according to Malebranche, is the truth of the idea in God. In a sense, the concept of truth is still the agreement between an idea and reality, but according to Malebranche, the idea is a reality in itself, not the result of a process of assimilation but an entity in itself to which reality must conform.

The problem of freedom and its paradoxes also come from a similar perspective. If man knows in and through God, and God knows all reality, and God is also the sole cause of his creatures' activity, there seems little room for free will in man. Even though Malebranche wants to distinguish between the will and freedom in order to protect autonomy of free human action, the paradoxes in his system remain.

2.5 BARUCH SPINOZA (1632–1677)

a) Life and Works

Spinoza was born in Amsterdam in 1632, in a Portuguese family of Jewish origin. He learned Hebrew and became familiar with the Scriptures. He studied mathematics, Latin, and Greek at the school of Van den Enden, a Dutch Christian doctor, where he also learned Cartesian philosophy. In 1654, on his own initiative, he left the synagogue, from which he was officially expelled in 1656. Although his primary interests were philosophical, to earn a living he also polished lenses. Between 1660 and 1663 he lived in Rijnsburg.

In 1663 he published *Renati Descartes Principia Philosophiae, More Geometrico Demonstrata* (*Principles of the Philosophy of René Descartes, Demonstrated Geometrically*). This is the only book published under Spinoza's name. Then he wrote *A Short Treatise on God, Man and His Well-Being,* and *Tractatus de Intellectus Emendatione* (*On the Improvement of the Understanding*), which he began but never completed. Once he moved to The Hague, he wrote *Tractatus theologico-politicus* (1670), and he began writing *Tractatus politicus* (1675), which he likewise will leave unfinished.

Spinoza rejected an invitation to be a professor of philosophy at the University of Heidelberg. Instead, he devoted the last years of his life to the magnum opus of his system: *Ethica more geometrico demonstrata.* This work was not published during his lifetime since it had been accused of being atheistic. Only after the philosopher's death would the book be made public in The Hague in February, 1677.

Spinoza's philosophy is based in part on Cartesian ideas, although there are profound differences between the two systems. The fundamental point of view of the philosophy of Spinoza is the unity of the world in a single substance. Spinoza fundamentally tried to answer the questions that Descartes had left open-ended. More indirectly, Spinoza was also influenced by the work of Giordano Bruno and other Jewish religious thinkers.

Spinoza's terminology is very similar to that of Descartes and of scholasticism. But the similarities are more terminological than conceptual, since Spinoza elaborated upon the fundamental concepts of the tradition he received in an original way.

Spinoza's rationalism differs from that of Descartes and Malebranche, mostly because Spinoza adopted a pantheistic worldview. Just the same, some characteristics remain common to all three rationalists, such as the special role given to reason as having the ultimate and autonomous application of human knowledge.

b) The Method and System of Spinoza

The goal of Spinoza's intellectual elaborations is "to eternally enjoy a supreme and constant philosophy." According to Spinoza, we arrive at this philosophy through the "knowledge of the union of the spirit with all of nature," which is to say, through the point of view of unity. To achieve this, we must purify the intellect so that it "will know things without error and in the best possible way."[44] Thus, "all science can be steered towards one direction and a single end: the achievement of the highest human perfection; and so everything in the sciences that does not serve to promote the attainment of our end will be rejected as useless: that is, in a word, all our activities and thoughts should be directed to this end."[45] The highest human perfection consists in knowing oneself to be part of the one substance.

Thus, Spinoza's philosophy is presented as philosophical soteriology: a knowledge of salvation through reason alone. This philosophical wisdom is rare, as most men must settle for a secondary path of wisdom: religion. Religious faith, according to Spinoza, is independent of philosophy. Philosophy "has truth for its end; while faith has obedience and piety as ends."[46] For this reason, the focus of *Tractatus theologico-politicus* is to explain the separation between faith and philosophy. Faith is a set of moral precepts that never reach God, who is the object of an intuitive act of reason. Faith is useful for peaceful co-existence among men and is a source of consolation for mere mortals.

---

44. Benedict de Spinoza, *On the Improvement of the Understanding*, 2.5.

45. Spinoza, *On the Improvement of the Understanding*, 2.16.

46. Benedict de Spinoza, *Tractatus theologico-politicus*, 13.

In Spinoza, the method is a result of the fundamental intuition of his system, that is, the unity of substance. The method is the way to arrive at the idea of the most perfect being. Since human thought is a part of divine thought, there is no room for a *transitus* of man to God. The method is also an attempt to unite the spirit with nature. To arrive at this idea, Spinoza started from the source and origin of nature: God. It is therefore a deductive method: the plurality of the world must spring forth from God in a necessary and intrinsically justified way. Despite the similarities, this is not a repetition of Neo-Platonism. Spinoza, in contrast, believes there is no separation between God and nature, or between God and multiplicity; rather, there only exists substantial unity and identity.

A thesis from the *Ethics* could be taken as the motto of Spinoza's philosophy: *ordo et connexio idearum idem est ac ordo et connexio rerum* (the order and connection of ideas is the same as the order and connection of things). His system proposes a clear parallelism between the real order and the order of ideas, harkening to the coming seventeenth-century rationalism.

Thus, the system of Spinoza starts with God, the metaphysically perfect being, who is the gnoseological first object of human knowledge. The connection between ideas and things will allow Spinoza to identify cause with reason, and metaphysical justification with logical deduction.

c) The Degrees of Knowledge

Spinoza distinguished different degrees of knowledge, according to their dependence on experience and according to the level of truth that each can achieve. In his treatise *On the Improvement of the Understanding*, Spinoza talked about four degrees of knowledge, while in the *Ethics* only three. The *Ethics* seems to be his definitive characterization of knowledge, in which he eliminated "knowledge by hearing" from the four types of knowledge listed in the treatise. Note that each degree serves as a starting point for the next degree, each level improving upon the previous one. The first two degrees are typically present in any man and are necessary for practical life.

First, knowledge gained through the senses constitutes what Spinoza calls 'ideas of the imagination.' Spinoza thought that other bodies in the human body interfere with this sense knowledge, thus producing inadequate and confused knowledge. Among the ideas of imagination are the universal ideas: "From similar causes, those notions called universal or general are born like man, dog, horse, etc."[47] Even though these ideas are false, confused, and misrepresenting of reality (given their origin in the senses,) they are useful for practical life.

The next degree of knowledge is reason. Rational knowledge is proper to common notions and adequate ideas of the properties of things. Rational knowledge is true knowledge, as defined by Spinoza, since the adequate idea is "the idea that is considered in itself, without relation to the object, has all the properties or intrinsic notes of the true idea."[48] Common ideas are clear, not confused, just like the universal ideas of the first degree of knowledge. They depend on the knowledge of thought and extension, which are the divine attributes that men can know.

The third and most perfect degree of knowledge is intuitive knowledge. Spinoza said that it proceeds "from the adequate idea of the formal essence of certain attributes of God to an adequate knowledge of the being of things."[49] In this level of knowledge, salvation is conferred through reason. Intuition is knowledge of the essences of things, not only of common notions: "because all things are in God and are conceived through God; it follows that from this knowledge we can deduce many things that can be known adequately, and thus

---

47. Benedict de Spinoza, *Ethica*, 2, prop. 40.

48. Spinoza, *Ethica*, 2, def. 4.

49. Spinoza, *Ethica*, 2, prop. 40.

form this third degree of knowledge."[50] The whole system of Spinoza aims to reach intuitive knowledge, which allows man to derive the God's essence.

Truth, idea, and objective essence are identical in Spinoza's thought. In his unitary vision of reality, the human mind is part of God's infinite intelligence. When the human mind reaches the third degree of knowledge, it is God who knows, not infinitely but still with some characteristics of the divine way of knowing.

d) God or Substance

The human mind is capable of acquiring an adequate knowledge of God. Man cannot imagine God, but he can understand him intellectually. According to Spinoza, knowledge of God does not start from some premise or from knowledge of something else. God is known and proven by himself through the human intellect that is united to him because it is a part of him. Knowledge of God, on the other hand, is the basis of knowledge of everything else, insofar as everything exists in God and nothing can be conceived without God.

The fundamental thesis of Spinoza's system is that God is known by himself and all of reality is known in Him. Here Spinoza breaks with Descartes, who thought that a proof of the existence of God was necessary to prove the world's existence. Spinoza's thesis clashes with Cartesian philosophy. While Descartes never solved the problem of duplicity in substances (*res cogitans* and *res extensa*), Spinoza professes original unity of the fundamental origin: God, the one and only substance.

With his new starting point, Spinoza does not need Cartesian methodical doubt. He sidesteps the problem of a deceiving God—the Dutch dismissed such an idea as a misconception of God. He is consistent with his fundamental pantheism, doing away with any need to prove the existence of God.

---

50. Spinoza, *Ethica*, 2, prop. 47.

1) *Substance, Attributes, Modes*

Spinoza defines substance as "that which is in itself and is conceived by itself, that is, that whose concept does not need the concept of something else for it to be formed."[51] In other words, God is the only substance. God is the absolutely infinite being, a substance consisting of an infinity of attributes, each of which expresses an eternal and infinite essence. The attributes have a substantive nature, so that they designate the divine essence: "God, or what is the same, all the attributes of God."[52] Man knows only two of these infinite attributes: thought and extension. Extension is infinite, one, and indivisible. "Extension is an attribute of God, or in other words, God is *res extensa*."[53] Together with the unity of substance, therefore, there is the myriad of attributes that constitute the divine substance.

This last thesis involves the unity of God Himself, since unity must extend to all that exists. Briefly stated, the oneness of the divine substance contains a certain tension between unity and multiplicity, which classical metaphysics conceptualized as specific moments of God and the world, respectively. The modes are "conditions of the substance, or what is in another thing and through which the thing is conceived."[54] The modes can be finite or infinite properties of attributes or actual things. Modes are effects in a formal deductive sense (*more geometrico*), not in the real sense of efficient causality. Since everything is in God, and the realm of ideas and the realm of things are connected, everything is deduced from God. Thus, the reality of the visible world is constituted by finite modes. Reality itself in its multiplicity is caused and simultaneously deduced by the single

51. Spinoza, *Ethica*, 2, prop. 1.
52. Spinoza, *Ethica*, 1, prop. 19.
53. Spinoza, *Ethica*, 2, prop. 2.
54. Spinoza, *Ethica*, 1, def. 5.

substance. Concluding his philosophical reasoning, Spinoza posited a triple identity: *Deus, sive Substantia, sive Natura.*

Spinoza distinguished between *Natura naturans* and *Natura naturata. Natura naturans* is in itself and is conceived by itself, corresponding to God as God. *Natura naturata,* however, is the whole of nature or the effects produced by the necessity of God's essence, and belongs to God as Nature or to Nature as deduced from God. "We must understand *natura naturans* as that which is in itself and is conceived by itself, that is, the attributes of the substance that express eternal and infinite essence, that is, God considered as a free cause. By *naturata,* however, I understand everything that follows from the necessity of the nature of God, that is, all the attributes of God, all the modes of the attributes of God, which without God can neither exist nor be conceived."[55]

Spinoza's distinction between *Natura naturans* and *Natura naturata* has proven insufficient to solve various problems of interpreting his fundamental theses, such as God's substantial unity and the diversity, infinity, and substantiality of his attributes and modes.

2) *Causa sui*

Spinoza and Descartes both thought that 'cause' can mean 'reason.' By *causa sui,* Spinoza understood those things whose essence implied their existence, whose nature cannot be thought about except as an existing thing. In this case, efficient causality is reduced to a logical sequence. But a parallelism between the logical order and the real order also makes the logical explanation an ontological cause: "all that follows formally from the infinite nature of God, follows also objectively from the idea of God in God, in the same order and with the same connection."[56]

---

55. Spinoza, *Ethica*, 1, prop. 29.
56. Spinoza, *Ethica*, 2, prop. 7.

Causa sui, in the logic of terms, is an inherently contradictory expression. However, Spinoza thought, as did Descartes in a certain sense, that this is the ultimate expression of the absolute independence and self-sufficiency of God. Cause and substance become identical.

Moreover, since any determination is, according to Spinoza, a negation, God is absolutely indeterminate. Among other characteristics of modern rationalist philosophy, there is a positive conception of infinity and indeterminacy. God's indeterminacy, for Spinoza, meant self-sufficiency and freedom. Something is free if it exists by the sole necessity of its nature and determines its own actions. Freedom is self-sufficiency, the absence of coercion, but not the capacity to make a free choice. God is a free cause, but he acts out of necessity because of his nature. Spinoza thus speaks about free necessity, not free will.

At this point, the system of Spinoza converted itself into a closed and absolute rationalism. Everything is God, God is *causa sui*, the reason of himself and therefore of everything. Freedom is the need to act according to one's nature, according to the proper cause. Between God, necessity, and freedom, man finds himself in a rationally closed circuit.

3) *The Issue of Pantheism and Atheism*

Spinoza's philosophy is pantheistic, or more technically, it is a panentheism: everything is in God; he is not transcendent because he is immanent to the world; the world is identified with God. In a strict sense, there is no world beyond the material world, insofar as everything is God.

If everything belongs to the same ontological level, then the 'pantheistic' system must either be atheist or truly pantheistic. In one possible interpretation of atheism, God is equated with nature and with absolute natural determinism. This atheism draws from an emphasis on the unity of substance and the identification of the world with the unique substance. A true pantheism would instead emphasize everything as God, including all nature and history. Regardless, in Spinoza's thought, the identification or non-distinction between finite and infinite, between the world and God, is very clear, and closes any possibility of transcendence. During Spinoza's own life, Verthysen made a clear statement summarizing the most common interpretation of his system: "He taught pure atheism."

One could say that Spinoza's religiosity was neither Christian nor Jewish. His religious doctrine was more of a deism that only called for the obedience of faith on the part of the ignorant. Spinoza's God is impersonal. God's intelligence is an infinite mode of the unique substance. Spinoza was far from any kind of anthropomorphism in his philosophical reflections on God, but he had to pay the price of depersonalizing God.

The identification of God with nature, aside from adding the problem of atheism as the ultimate consequence of pantheism, metaphysically constitutes the primacy of the identity over diversity in the created world. With this perspective, Spinoza's pantheism is a doctrine of metaphysical indifference.

e) Man

1) Soul and Body

As with almost all the authors of the seventeenth century, Spinoza inherited Cartesian dualism. Spinoza tried to solve the problem of the body-soul relationship by stating that they are two finite modes of the substance of God. In this sense, Spinoza did not accept the substantial dualism of Descartes. Neither the body nor the soul is a separate substance, because not even man is a substance: "To be substance does not belong to the essence of man;

substance does not constitute the form of man."[57] The reasoning behind this statement is consistent with the rest of his system. There is only one substance, and man is also identified with it. The essence of man, for Spinoza, "is constituted by certain modifications of the attributes of God."[58]

The soul is the idea of the body; the body is the object of the soul. Nothing can happen in the body without the soul necessarily knowing it. There is, therefore, a soul-body correspondence, but no real interaction or real unity, because there is identity: "a mode of extension and the idea of this mode are one and the same thing, but expressed in two different ways."[59]

Spinoza, following the footsteps of Descartes, explained the human body from a mechanistic, physical viewpoint, excluding any consideration of final causes. The soul, meanwhile, is more than just the idea of body—it also has consciousness, which is the idea of the idea, the idea that the soul has of itself.

The lack of unity between the soul and the body, and between the soul and consciousness, creates a problem that Spinoza resolves through the unity of God. Soul and body, and soul and the idea of the soul, do not have a true and proper justification from the point of view of unity, but only from the viewpoint of the unity of God, where all divisions are transformed into identity. Thus Spinoza believed that the only adequate knowledge the soul can have is not of the body or of itself, but only of the eternal and infinite essence of God.

---

57. Spinoza, *Ethica*, 2, prop. 10.
58. Spinoza, *Ethica*, 2, prop. 10.
59. Spinoza, *Ethica*, 2, prop. 7.

2) *Freedom and passions*

The human individual has a *conatus* or 'effort' to persevere in its being. More specifically, the determination or the way that the infinite power of God is expressed in each individual is called '*conatus*' when referring to the body, and 'will' when referring to the soul. It is called '*appetitus*' when referring simultaneously to both.

Spinoza denied that man has the faculties of intelligence or will, at least understood as the capacity to affirm, deny, or want. Consistent with his philosophy of metaphysical indeterminacy, Spinoza stated that "the will and the intelligence are the same thing."[60]

Man moves only by desires. Spinoza's Ethics translates into utilitarianism, in which the most important virtue is the pursuit of what is useful: "to act according to virtue is nothing else for us than to act, live, and preserve our being (these three things have the same meaning), under the guidance of reason, based on the search for our own profit."[61]

Freedom in Spinoza's system is not freedom of choice. Freedom is the perfect understanding of necessity, the perfect knowledge of the causes of action. Freedom consists in knowing that man works for causes and that these causes are necessary. Reason leads man to internalize and be conscious of necessity, which is the basis for living with freedom.

One must master any passion that might prevent him from knowing the causes of his actions and thus might result in a kind of slavery. The slavery of the passions is the denial of the knowledge of the causes for acting, opening the door to blind behavior: "I call slavery the impotence of man to moderate and control his passions. The

---

60. Spinoza, *Ethica*, 2, prop. 49.
61. Spinoza, *Ethica*, 4, prop. 24.

man under the dominion of his passions is not his own
master, but lies in the hands of fortune, and to such an
extent he sometimes is forced to do what is worse, though
he sees what is best."[62]

3) *Amor intellectualis Deo*

According to Spinoza, supreme happiness is *amor intellec-
tualis Deo*, the joy that follows the knowledge of God as
the eternal and unique cause, of which we form part. This
love, says Spinoza, is "the same love of God with which
God loves himself, not as infinite, but as can be expressed
by the essence of the human mind, considered under the
aspect of eternity,"[63] such that "the love of God for men
and the intellectual love of the mind for God are the same
thing."[64] This intellectual love must be interpreted within
the guidelines of Spinoza's system. It is not love for a
transcendent and personal God, but for a God in whom
we participate as modes. In short, supreme happiness
is an immanent activity of the spirit, fully attainable on
this earth.

f) Political Philosophy

Spinoza wrote his *Tractatus theologico-politicus*, in part, to bring
out the theological prejudices that impede the progress of philosophy. He also wanted to defend himself against charges of
atheism and to support a freedom of thought that opposes theology and faith.

His *Tractatus* elaborated a series of principles for scriptural
exegesis, which was a novelty for hermeneutics. His principles,
in fact, are considered the beginning of the historical method of
biblical exegesis.

62. Spinoza, *Ethica*, 4, preface.
63. Spinoza, *Ethica*, 5, prop. 36.
64. Spinoza, *Ethica*, 5, prop. 36.

The relationship between religion and politics is another prevalent theme of his *Tractatus*. Faith, says Spinoza, is a matter of obedience. Political power is entrusted with regulating sacred things. In the field of philosophy, by contrast, freedom prevails. In a free state, each individual can think what he wants and say what he thinks. This principle is not so much a consequence of the dignity of the human person, but a thesis corresponding to his moral utilitarianism. Freedom of thought must be defended by its utility to social living.

In the pages of the *Tractatus*, we catch a glimpse of a rupture between acting and thinking. The State can limit the freedom of the individual with respect to his external behavior, and the individual must obey even against his conscience. Manifesting an attitude very close to legal positivism, Spinoza believed that good and evil, right and wrong, are determinations established by political authority.

* * *

Spinoza's philosophy is deeply determined by the idea of God as the one and only substance. His rationalism revolves around this central thesis. From his metaphysical thesis about the uniqueness of substance comes his epistemological thesis about God as the first object of knowledge. The *Deus sive Natura* represents the starting and ending point of Spinoza's philosophy: between these extremes, all theoretical and practical physics of nature and human action can be derived.

His rationalism is undoubtedly Cartesian, as are the philosophical themes that he chose to discuss. However, the two thinkers differ radically in what concerns the overall view of the world. Despite many similarities on more basic topics, Descartes separates God and the world, the soul and the body, the order of knowledge and the will. In Spinoza, these distinctions remain very problematic, but only in a secondary or derived manner. Any distinction that Spinoza may have made between God and his manifestations, such as in his *Ethics*, belong merely to the plane of outward manifestation. There are no distinctions, however, from the viewpoint of unity, which is also the perspective of God. The world is *sub specie aeternitatis*, in which distinctions do not indicate an array of particular substances or of individual and free actions, but rather the one and only God as seen through his modes and attributes. Cartesian dualism is superseded in the philosophy of Spinoza, who annuls the ontological differences. Spinoza's ethics depend on this. One could say, though, that in reality Spinoza did not solve the Cartesian problem. Rather, his exaggerated assertion of the uniqueness of substance merely confronted the problem from a pantheist perspective.

Insofar as Spinoza introduced in philosophy an absolute point of view to consider all philosophical problems, his thinking will significantly influence succeeding rationalist thinkers, especially among the German idealists.

2.6 GOTTFRIED WILHELM LEIBNIZ (1646–1716)

a) Life and Works

Leibniz was born in Leipzig in 1646, the son of a professor of morals at the University of Leipzig. Leibniz was a kind of prodigy. As a child, he began reading his father's library, and at age fifteen he entered the university. In 1663 he wrote his bachelor's thesis, *On the Principle of Individuation*. After a period of dedication to law, in 1666 he wrote his first major work, *Dissertation on the Art of Combinations*.

In the same year, he obtained his doctorate at the University of Altdorf, a town near Nuremberg, having written his thesis *On the Enigmatic Cases of Law*. In Nuremberg he began his political and diplomatic career. He went to Paris, where he met certain personalities such as Arnauld, Malebranche, and Huygens, and further studied Descartes and Spinoza. Then he moved to London for a brief time, where he was admitted as a member of the Royal Society.

After studying some of Pascal's manuscripts, he discovered infinitesimal calculus, almost at the same time as did Newton. Leibniz also invented an algebraic machine. In 1676, he went to Hannover, passing through Amsterdam, where he met Spinoza. While working in the court of Hannover, he began writing a history of the house of Brunswick, a work in which he attempted to use new historical methods. He made two brief trips to Vienna and Rome during this period. Among the writings while in Hannover are *New System of Nature* (1695), *On the Ultimate Origination of Things* (1696), *New Essays on Human Understanding* (writing during a controversy with Locke and published posthumously in 1765), *Theodicy* (1710), *Principles of Nature and Grace* (1714), and *Monadology* (1714).

Leibniz died in November 1716 in Hannover. Anecdotally, it is noted that his funeral was attended only by his secretary.

b) Features of the Thought of Leibniz

1) The Outline of the System

Leibniz's work has many aspects. With an encyclopedic curiosity, he wrote about many topics with great depth. The vastness of his work is partially credited to Leibniz' capacity to think while writing. There are still some unpublished manuscripts among his enormous intellectual activity.

His ideas were developed gradually as his system matured. Along with this dynamic character of his thought, we also find a certain eclecticism. He knew the history of philosophy well, and he did not intend to found a new starting point for philosophizing, as had Descartes, taking, instead, any elements that he considered valid from the classical and modern tradition.

One main theme of his thought is the search for a universal science that could be a basic logic or a common language for all the sciences. This science, which Leibniz called *ars combinatoria*, would also have the nature of a universal method.

Another main theme of his philosophy was the idea of a universal harmony, a key element in his description of the cosmos. Such harmony belongs to the intrinsic principle of things, by which each element of the natural and human world has an ordered and harmonious relation with the totality of the universe. Leibniz believed that God predetermined universal harmony as a reflection of the divine perfection.

A third element of Leibniz's thought is the reappearance of the principle of finality, after it had been excluded from Descartes' philosophy. Leibniz recovered this principle from the classical tradition, correcting Descartes' mechanism.

A final element of Leibniz's system–not strictly philosophical, more derived from his philosophical theses—is his apologetic attempt to reunite all churches into one Universal Church. Aside from the construction of a theoretical ideal, this idea had a practical dimension in the political life of Leibniz. His ecumenism is founded on two philosophical theses that originate in the classical tradition: the claim that faith and reason do not contradict each other, and a need for a rational basis of human freedom as well as divine freedom and goodness.

2) Interpretations of his System

The importance of Leibniz's thought in the history of modern philosophy has resulted in various interpretations of his system. Wolff, through whom Kant eventually learned about Leibniz, considered him to be his immediate predecessor. Particularly in Germany, the metaphysics of the seventeenth and eighteenth centuries was dominated by Leibniz's work and that of others in his school. Kant, for one, had Leibniz's tradition in mind when he referred to metaphysical dogmatism. Hegel also gave considerable attention to critiquing Leibniz's system.

Interest in Leibniz's thought lasted into the twentieth century. Russell and Coutourat thought that Leibniz's system was a kind of logicism, from which logic metaphysics derived merely as a consequence. Cassirer, however, gave Leibniz the credit of being the first modern philosopher for making such a deep connection between philosophy and scientific thought. Other authors, like Baruzi and Friedman, highlighted the apologetic attempt of Leibniz, while Blondel, Guéroult, Belaval, Mathieu, and others interpreted his system from a metaphysical perspective, emphasizing the connection between Leibniz' philosophy and the *philosophia perennis*.

c) Logic and First Principles

1) The Project of a Universal Language

In his book, *Art of Combinations*, Leibniz proposed the existence of a universal language, which perhaps was his most original contribution to logic. Leibniz claimed that a profound unity exists between logic and mathematics, especially with regard to the universally intelligible character of both disciplines. He defined logic as the art of using the intellect, which means that logic is, or at least should be, a universal science. But a universal science requires a universal language based upon a certain alphabet of human thoughts. By this alphabet and language, Leibniz was trying to convert reasoning and logical processes into a kind of calculus. With this transformation, logic could proceed arithmetically; the universal language would perform the function of a general algebra. Thus in a conversation, Leibniz suggested, instead of getting into an argument, the interlocutors could resolve things by saying: let's count.

The vast potential of the *Ars combinatoria* can be found in its universality, since, by the unity of method and of criteria, it can be applied to the various fields of knowledge.

While others have interpreted Leibniz's work to be a panlogism, a certain absolutizing of logic, we think that his logic in the *Ars combinatoria* is rather a *modus dicendi*, which expresses a reality that simultaneously transcends logic itself, and gives it a foundation. An analysis of his epistemology and logic will cast more light on this universal language.

2) *Truth and first principles*

Leibniz' epistemology is found mainly in the *New Essays on Human Understanding*. He took on many and varied interests and opinions in epistemology, unprecedented by earlier thinkers. He critiqued British empiricism, the Aristotelianism in vogue at the time, and he gave a new twist to the Cartesian innate ideas.

The soul, according to Leibniz, is not a *tabula rasa*, as the empiricists claim. Instead, he used a different physical image, a veined block of marble: "ideas and truths are innate and manifest as inclinations, dispositions, habits, and natural potentialities."[65] Sense experience is the occasion to awaken in the subject these notions that it virtually possesses. The senses only give particular or individual truths, but sense knowledge activates the higher faculties and innate notions that are present in an obscure manner in the depths of the faculties themselves.

Leibniz defines truth as a statement whose subject contains the predicate. In all true affirmative propositions, whether necessary or contingent, universal or particular, the notion of the subject in some way contains the notion of the predicate. Leibniz claimed that the analysis of true

65. Gottfried Wilhelm Leibniz, *New Essays*, 5.45.

propositions demonstrates this fact. We must analyze the truths to reach simple elements, which are the ideas: "the analysis is this. We resolve a given term into its formal parts, that is, we define it. Then we resolve these parts in their parts or give the definition of the terms of the first definition, until we reach the simple parts or the indefinable terms."[66]

A definition is the analysis of ideas; the analysis of ideas allows us to reach the simplest ideas that cannot be defined. At this point the idea, if it is a simple element that cannot be further analyzed, is the innate idea. Although he could have proven the thesis of innatism, Leibniz considered the innate idea to be evident, a first principle that needs no demonstration. Thus, the truth is based on the immediate evidence of the innate ideas. These simple ideas are the basic elements of the universal language of *Ars combinatoria.*

Taking into account these considerations on truth and innatism, Leibniz distinguished between truths of reason and truths of fact. The former are necessary, while the latter are contingent. In other words, it is impossible for any proposition that opposes the truths of reason to be true. The truths of fact, however, may have opposite propositions: "that God exists, that all right angles are equal to each other, are necessary truths. But that I exist or that in nature there are bodies effectively having right angles are contingent truths."[67] Truths of reason are known *a priori*, that is, independent of experience: they are known in themselves and by themselves. Truths of fact, on the other hand, depend on experience, that is, they are known *a posteriori.* According to Leibniz, the former are based on the principle of non-contradiction, while the latter are

---

66. Gottfried Wilhelm Leibniz, *Ars combinatoria*, 4.64.

67. Gottfried Wilhelm Leibniz, *Necessity and Contingency*, 3.400.

based on the principle of sufficient reason. This does not mean that the truths of fact can be contradictory; more accurately we say that they are not necessary, although they have a sufficient reason for which the predicate can be included in the subject.[68] Truths of reason are analytical in a limited respect, since they can be resolved into primitive ideas. Truths of reason are also eternal, true in this world and in any other. By contrast, truths of fact are infinitely analytical, never adequately proven. It is impossible to boil them down to their primary evidence or first foundational principle. Only God sees clearly how the predicate is included in the subject in the truths of fact. He also understands *a priori* the perfect reason of contingency, while men know the truths of fact only through experience. The truths of fact are contingent, existential (non-essential), and are based on the principle of sufficient reason (*nihil esse sine ratione*).

Leibniz, aside from addressing the issue of the first principles in relation to truth, also considered them in relation to God. In God, the principle of non-contradiction corresponds to his intelligence, the realm of the eternal truths. The principle of sufficient reason, however, is related to the will, that is, with the choice God makes among the infinite possible essences. God indeed could create infinite possible worlds, but he has created a single one, which implies a divine choice among endless possibilities. God created the possibilities that can co-exist in this concrete world that God has chosen.

There is a third principle related to God in the system of Leibniz. This is the principle of fittingness, which can be formulated as, "God always chooses the best." From this principle it follows that God gave existence not only to the best of the possibilities for this world, but that this world is

---

68. See Gottfried Wilhelm Leibniz, Letter, 7.200 in *Die philosophischen Schriften* (Berlin: C.I. Gerhardt, 1875).

the best possible world. Leibniz, however, rejected divine voluntarism. The divine will is related to the divine intelligence, because the goodness of the world comes from both. God had objective reasons for creating good things; those objective reasons reside in the possibilities that God chose and in some way demand their creation.

At this point in Leibniz's thought, divine freedom becomes a problematic subject: if God must necessarily choose the best possible world, he would not be free in his choice or in the act of creating. Moreover, the concept of "the best possible world" is not very convincing. Every finite reality, by the very fact of being limited, cannot be an absolute "best." Finite reality can always be made more perfect, otherwise, it would cease to be finite. Leibniz's ultimate goal, however, was to show how all the complex realities of the world depend on God and divine freedom.

d) Metaphysics

1) Possibility and Essence

In this section we will review some of the elements we have discussed in the logical theory of Leibniz. There we studied them from the standpoint of the first principles. Now we look at them from the metaphysical perspective. The foundation of Leibniz's metaphysics is the theory of possibility. In this aspect of his doctrine, Leibniz inherited a tradition spanning the ancient and medieval, Arabic and scholastic schools. Suarez's influence is also very noticeable.

The German thinker established certain equivalence between essence, reality, and possibility. Possibility is the same as intrinsic non-contradiction, the non-impossibility of the terms, or the compatibility of the notes proper of the essence. In other words, the possible is what is not-impossible.

But the non-contradiction of an essence is also presented as a demand or a claim of existence. Existence depends on the amount of essence, the degree of perfection of each essence. The greater the perfection, the nearer the essence is to full existence. An essence, before it exists, is a possible essence in a sense, already somewhat perfect since it only lacks existence for it to be completely real.

The question of the best possible world, referred to above, fits into this perspective. In what Leibniz called the 'battle of the possibilities to obtain existence,' there comes into play the principle of compatibility among the possibilities. God, in compatibility or co-possibility, finds the ultimate objective reason to create this world, which is the best among the possible worlds, and in which the best possible and compatible essences are called into being. The co-possibility of this world is the best of the harmonies possible.

From this point of view, it seems that the supreme principle of existence is that of sufficient reason, which depends on the will of God. God never chooses capriciously; he follows the principle of fittingness, that is, the law of the best.

2) The Monads

The more mature metaphysical system of Leibniz, which contains many of the elements we have previously analyzed, is that found in his famous work: *Monadology*. *Monad* comes from the Greek *monos*, which means unit. The monad is a simple substance, unextended, indivisible and immaterial, which is the basic unit of the composite substance.[69] With the monadic theory, Leibniz opposed ancient and modern materialistic atomism. Moreover, by positing a plurality of individual substances, he rejected Cartesian dualism and Spinoza's concept of one substance.

---

69. Gottfried Wilhelm Leibniz, *Monadology*, 1.

The monad is mainly characterized by unity. With a graphic phrase, Leibniz indicated that monads cannot suffer changes at the hands of other creatures: "the monads have no windows." They have no beginning nor end; they are eternal and incorruptible. God created them, and only he can annihilate them. All monads differ from each other. They have an internal principle, which Leibniz calls the force, which confers on the monads an active character.

The qualities and internal actions of the monads are called perceptions and appetitions. Perception is the representation of the compound in the simple. It has a passive nature and indicates the perfect conformity of each monad with the entire universe, since each perception represents the universe, in its own particular way, according to a certain point of view.[70] Each monad has its own perceptions, no matter whether they compose an animal, vegetable, or mineral body. But only some monads enjoy conscious perception. Strictly speaking, the soul is a monad that possesses conscious perceptions. Appetition is active in character, and consists of the principle that produces a change from one perception to another.[71] Monads are essentially active, with an infinite number of degrees of perfection, culminating in rational souls or spirits that are truly "images of the divinity."[72]

3) Pre-established Harmony

Leibniz claimed that monads share no mutual influences, but he refused to accept Malebranche's occasionalism. In order to explain causality in the universe, then, he posited a pre-established harmony: "God first created the soul or any other actual unity, so that all will be born of it

70. See *New System of Nature*, 4.484.

71. Leibniz, *Monadology*, 15.

72. Leibniz, *Monadology*, 83.

from its own depths through a perfect spontaneity with respect to itself, and yet with perfect conformity with external things."[73]

An ordering intelligence causes each monad to comply with the rest of the universe according to a preexisting established harmony between the perceptions of monads and bodily movements. The mutual influence between monads is not real, just apparent. The interaction always and necessarily happens through God. It is God, indeed, who has established harmony "in the beginning of things, after which every thing moves on in the phenomena of nature, according to the laws of soul and body."[74]

As an example of pre-established harmony, Leibniz talked of two synchronized clocks. God is the watchmaker, the two watches do not influence each other, and, by contrast with Malebranche's occasionalism, the constant vigilance of the watch maker is unnecessary. Leibniz' true rejection of occasionalism is still doubtful after this explanation, especially since human freedom finds itself in a problematic position with this perspective.

e) Dynamics and the Notion of Force

One of the key elements of the Leibnizian system, clearly stated in his monadological theory, is the notion of individual substance. According to Leibniz, "the nature of an individual substance or of a complete being consists in having a notion that is so complete that it is sufficient to understand it and to allow the deduction of all the predicates that are attributed to the subject."[75]

---

73. Gottfried Wilhelm Leibniz, *New System of Nature*, 4.484.

74. Leibniz, Letter, 3.143.

75. Gottfried Wilhelm Leibniz, *Discourse on Metaphysics*, 8.

The notion of force is linked to that of substance. Force is an intrinsic principle of the things themselves, existing prior to extension and introduced by God into the substances. It is, in other words, the intimate nature of bodies, the formal principle and energy that comes from the actions of the corporeal substance. The idea of force is closely related to the presence of an intelligent designer, God, the foundation of finality in the created world.

With the notion of force, final causality reappears. The dynamics and the metaphysics of Leibniz rejects Cartesian mechanics, which Leibniz dismisses as a product of the imagination. Physics is subordinated to arithmetic through geometry, and it is subordinated to metaphysics through dynamics. But while he was critical of Cartesian mechanics, Leibniz did not want to return to the classical notions of potency in Aristotelian and scholastic traditions. Force is active, not passive. Once force is admitted to the system, we can explain all the bodily motion in a mechanistic way.

Leibniz's physics has other important principles, such as the law of continuity, which claims that nature has no jumps, only a gradual scale of perfections, and the consideration of space as a set of relationships and not as an absolute reality, an idea that, as we shall see, would be taken up by Kant a few years later.

f) Theodicy

In 1710, Leibniz published his *Essays of Theodicy*, which attempted a justification of God's existence, defending divine goodness against the objections of Pierre Bayle, who said that an omniscient and powerful God is rationally incompatible with the presence of evil in the world. In this section we analyze Leibniz's proofs of God's existence, his notion of the divine essence, and the problem of evil in relation to divine freedom.

1) *The Existence of God*

Leibniz followed the classical arguments for the existence of God, but he added his personal touch. The German philosopher thought that all classical arguments can be valid if properly developed. Some of these arguments are explained below.

a) *Cosmological Argument.* Since things are contingent, we must find the cause of the world's existence. This cause is the *ens a se*, that is, the being that possesses in itself the reason of its existence, an existence that consequently is necessary and eternal. Although he shares a certain similarity with the Thomistic argument, Leibniz believed that the principle of sufficient reason applies to God, and, in rationalist fashion, he identifies cause with reason.

b) *The Argument from pre-established harmony.* Leibniz gives a new spin to the classic proof based on final causality. Substances cannot interact, yet still we observe some coordination between them. Thus we must postulate the existence of a God who is the source of order. For Leibniz, this argument *per se patet.* But the problem with this proof is that it relies on an *a priori* of his system — the theory of monads and pre-established harmony — which in turn would have to be justified.

c) *Argument from the eternal truths.* Leibniz made an explicit reference to St. Augustine in this proof. The eternal and necessary truths, being prior to the existence of contingent beings, should find its foundation in the existence of a necessary substance, namely God. Since the eternal truths are not fictitious, they must have a metaphysical principle, that is, "they should have their existence in an absolute and metaphysically necessary subject, that is, God."[76]

---

76. Leibniz, *Monadology*, 44.

d) *The Ontological Argument.* He elaborates upon a Cartesian proof: "Only God, or the necessary being, has the privilege to exist necessarily if it is possible. And since nothing prevents the possibility of what has no limit or negation, or contradiction, this is enough to prove *a priori* the existence of God."[77]

The Kantian critique to the ontological argument, as we study in a later chapter, appears to be valid also for this case: the ontological argument only proves that the concept of God is possible. In other words, it only demonstrates the absence of contradiction within this concept (negative possibility), but it does not demonstrate the positive possibility that arises from the essence of the thing itself.

2) *The Essence of God*

Leibniz said that God is an *ens a se*, the necessary, eternal, ultimate reason for the universal harmony in things. He is the prime unity, from which all other unities or monads have been created. There is identity between essence and existence in God, but the essence precedes the existence and thus contains it. The formal content of God is *aseity*: "God has existence in himself, that is, by essence."[78] Put another way, God is the sufficient reason of himself. Leibniz's concept of aseity is analogous to Descartes' and Spinoza's concepts of *causa sui*.

Leibniz also reasons that there is a formal difference between the divine intelligence and will, even though the divine will acts together with the divine intelligence: "to affirm that a will does not presuppose knowledge of what one wants, is a game of words." In his concept of God, Leibniz slipped into a kind of anthropomorphism in two ways. First, he claimed that man obtains knowledge about

---

77. Leibniz, *Monadology*, 45.
78. Leibniz, Letter, 1.212.

God more through the *via positiva* than the *via negativa*. Second, he thought that human and divine attributes differ by degree and not by essential differences. Leibniz pointed out the infinity of God and human finitude as the main difference between God and man, but in this he risked neglecting the analogical meaning of the comparison, instead tending toward univocity.

3) Creation, Freedom, and the Problem of Evil

Leibniz admitted the existence of a creator God, outside and superior to the world. For him, creation meant passing from the possibility of being to the actuality of being, that is, to bring possible essences to existence through the law of sufficient reason and the principle of fittingness or the law of the best. Leibniz's view of creation does not consider coming into existence to be an absolute novelty in being, as does the classical conception of *creatio ex nihilo*. Leibniz's theory of creation from possible essences conceptually endangered divine freedom. His system, in a sense, required God to create the most perfect possible essences.

Leibniz defended himself against his critics using a different semantic distinction. He said that God acts with moral—not metaphysical—necessity and determinism. As far as human freedom is also conceptually threatened by his theory of pre-established harmony, Leibniz does not offer a completely satisfactory answer.

Leibniz believed in a metaphysical evil, which he explained as the limitation inherent in all creatures. He also proposed a moral evil—sin—a result of human freedom and its metaphysical evil, since sin is a result of deficient knowledge. As a result of this reasoning, Leibniz reduced moral evil to ignorance. He explained himself in the *Theodicy*: "We, who have derived all things from God, where do we find the principle of evil? The answer is to be sought in the ideal nature of the creature, insofar as this nature is contained in the eternal truths that are in the intellect of

God independent of his will. We must, indeed, consider that there is an original imperfection in the creature before sin, because the creature is limited in his very essence, and therefore he cannot know everything. He can be deceived and can make further mistakes."[79]

The origin of evil, then, in Leibniz's opinion, is ultimately metaphysical. This assertion introduces sharp discord when considering philosophical questions such as how God can create and will evil, or the question of pre-established harmony. Leibniz preferred to solve the contention, attempting to justify a certain necessity of evil, by resorting to the latter question: to create the best possible world, God also had to create imperfection.

g) The Republic of Spirits or the City of God

Leibniz's system culminates in a Republic or City of Spirits, which is a realization of his ecumenism. Superior to the rest of the universe, the spirits can come to know each other and God by the act of reason. They therefore have a moral quality. Because of this moral quality, God is regarded as the head of all intelligent people and as absolute monarch of the most perfect republic. All the spirits gathered under the rule of God form a moral world within the natural world. Just as God is the best architect of the physical world, so is the best Republic that of which God is King.

This republic of spirits is also called the kingdom of grace. Sometimes it seems that Leibniz conceived supernatural grace as a continuation of nature. It would seem that his most authentic attitude would be to admit only two realms in the universe: the natural world and the moral world, in mutual continuity and harmony. Many have interpreted Leibniz's system as tending toward a naturalization of the supernatural.

---

79. Gottfried Wilhelm Leibniz, *Theodicy*, 4.115.

Leibniz also developed a theory of natural religion, in which reason is the natural voice of God. Reason must justify divine revelation, giving legitimacy to faith. Leibniz said that supernatural revelation was necessary because of the wrong use men have made of their reason. Christ converted natural religion into a law, giving it the authority of a public dogma. This natural religion is a sufficient light for guiding men in their behavior and leading them to the knowledge of God and the practice of virtue. The two fundamental truths of this religion are the existence of God as the ultimate reason of things and the immortality of the soul.

* * *

The multiple interests of Leibniz are reflected in his philosophy. His system clearly forms part of the rationalist tradition, which, in a certain sense, acquired its cultural dominance because of Leibniz's work. From a historical standpoint, rationalist philosophy never again had such a prominent representative.

Christian Wolff, although an important figure as the link between rationalism and the Enlightenment, would not commandeer the depth of thought that the great rationalists had. With Leibniz, we arrive at the threshold between rationalism and the Enlightenment. The German philosopher concludes the first moment of modern philosophy.

Leibniz was a careful thinker, steeped in the most debated metaphysical and epistemological issues of his time, as well as in the modern scientific issues, especially concerning mathematics and physics. He displayed an impressive scholarship, which may explain why his relations with the history of philosophy are so diversified. The force of his thought is especially felt in his metaphysics and in the intermediate field between science and philosophy. His speculation on the latter is defined principally by his theses on the individual substance, where we can easily find elements of the classical, medieval, and modern traditions. Leibniz's thoughts on divine and human freedom and on the much debated problem of evil have also had lasting importance.

Leibniz's metaphysics, faithful to the rationalist model of his time, is an optimistic metaphysics. Kant would eventually subject Leibniz's model of rationality to a careful criticism, after it had been exaggerated during the philosophical enlightenment, arising just after Leibniz's death.

2.7 GIAMBATTISTA VICO (1668–1744)

a) Life and Works

Giambattista Vico was born in Naples in June 1668. He belonged to a financially modest family, but with intellectual interests. Not surprisingly, his father was a librarian. Giambattista first began his humanistic studies under the guidance of the nominalist Antonio del Balzo and later, he followed the teachings of Giuseppe Ricci, a disciple of Scotus. He also learned from the courses of Felice Acquadies, professor of civil law at the University of Naples. Forced by illness to leave college, he became a tutor to the nephews of Monsignor Geronimo Rocca in Vatolla. In that place he deepened his humanistic studies by reading the Greek and Latin classics.

In 1695 he returned to Naples, where he obtained the chair of Latin Eloquence and Rhetoric from the University of Naples. Between 1699 and 1708 he prepared inaugural lectures for the academic year. The seventh "inaugural oration" is of particular importance. It is entitled *De nostri temporis studiorum ratione*.

In 1710 the first of the three volumes of the *De antiquissima Italorum sapientia ex linguae latinae originibus emenda* appeared.

1713 marked the start of Vico's most productive period. He carried out historical and philosophical research, and studied the legal thought of Grotius. In 1716 he published *Quattro libri intorno alle imprese di Antonio Carafa*. In 1720, the work *De universis iuris uno principio et fine uno*, was written to obtain the first chair of laws; it was a failed venture because of the insurmountable opposition he faced.

Vico's most important work, written amid financial difficulties and family problems, is the *Scienza Nuova*, whose full title reads: *Principi di una scienza nuova d'intorno alla natura delle nazioni, per la quale si ritrovano i principi di altro sistema del diritto naturale delle genti*. The first edition was published in 1725. It was then edited anew with some modifications in 1730 and 1744. Vico's masterpiece went unnoticed in Europe, and was not received well in Italy. Vico died after the third edition of the *Scienza nuova*, when he was 76 years old.

He was a counter-cultural thinker; he has nearly been ignored by academic historians for centuries. His thought aroused some interest in Goethe, Coleridge and Michelet, but we must wait until the twentieth century to find a Vico that is appreciated, especially through the work of Benedetto Croce.

b) The Critique of Cartesian Rationalism

In the inaugural lecture of the academic year 1708, Vico formulated one of the ideas that would become the definitive element of his thought: the critique of the Cartesian claim to universalize the geometric-mathematical method.

The Cartesian method is not universally valid, Vico argued, because the structure of the universe is not mathematical, as Galileo thought. If geometry can pride itself because of its clarity and distinction, these features are not designed to make possible the true knowledge of the very structure of reality. Clarity and distinction are due to the fact that it is man that created the propositions of geometry: *verum est factum*, the rule, the criterion of the truth of something, arises from its having been done or produced. If geometry is so clear, it is simply because men have been its inventors.

Later we will see how Vico applied this truth to the moral world. In his early works, when he criticized Cartesian rationalism, Vico emphasized the radical difference between geometric-mathematical knowledge and physical knowledge. Men built the first, while physical propositions were not created by us: they are not human creations like mathematical entities, and they must be proven by experiments.

According to Vico, the Cartesian criterion of truth, clarity and distinction cannot be applied to one of the widest areas of our knowledge: the world of probability, which is something that is between the true and the false. Law, politics, art, in short everything that contains the concept of Vico's *mondo civile*, should be studied through a speculative perspective radically different from the Cartesian method, because different situations require different methods.

Vico not only criticized the universalization of the Cartesian method: he also disagreed with the French philosopher regarding his starting point of philosophizing, namely the *cogito ergo sum*. The Cartesian principle, regarded by many as the dike to contain the skepticism of the libertines, can only affirm the consciousness of existence, but not its knowledge.

Consciousness accepts the existence of a fact; knowledge finds out the causes of that fact. The Skeptics also admitted facts, but they did not admit the knowledge of their causes.

Let's read this radical critique by Vico of the Cartesian cogito: "The skeptic does not doubt that he thinks. Even more, he is so sure of this that he seems to see it. Neither does he doubt that he exists. But he maintains that the certainty he has that he thinks is consciousness and not knowledge, that is, a vulgar knowledge that any idiot can attain, and not a rare and sought truth, which is required for meditation of a philosophy."[80]

c) Verum est factum

The clarity and distinction that Vico attributed to geometry, as we have just seen, was due to the fact that men created those

80. Giovanni Battista Vico, *De antiquissima Italorum sapientia*, 1.3.

mathematical entities. In this sense, the criterion of the truth of a thing is the fact of its having been produced. Vico, on the other hand, also realized that men do not create all things. From here arose the criticism of Vico regarding the application of the geometrical method to the natural world.

However, the *verum est factum* criterion does apply to the moral world: man is an actor and producer in history. Laws, literature, language, institutions are human products. Man can more easily know the world that he makes and transforms. The self-knowledge of the human sciences, different from that of geometry, is deeper than the knowledge given by the physical sciences. The reversal of the Cartesian epistemological position is clear: the human sciences now occupy a privileged position regarding the possibilities of attaining the truth.

In the *De antiquissima Italorum sapientia*, Vico explained the principle *verum est factum* using linguistic analysis: "In Latin *verum* and *factum* have a reciprocal relationship, or to use a traditional word in the schools, 'they are convertible to each other' (*convertuntur*). From this it is lawful to conjecture that the ancient Italic scholars agreed on these thoughts: that truth is the same thing as fact, and that God is the first truth because he is the first maker and creator."[81]

d) The mondo civile. The Discovery of History

For Vico, the *Scienza nuova* is history, the science that seeks to know the civil world as a product of the human soul. The ultimate goal of the *Scienza nuova* is the determination of the universal and eternal law of history and the ways in which that eternal law is manifest in the history of every people.

But historical science, as something new, needs to be given its bases. Vico based his arguments on the epistemological

---

81. Vico, *De antiquissima Italorum sapientia*, I, 1.

principle of *verum est factum*, and he had recourse to the authority of those who in his *Autobiography* he considered its four
authors:

> Plato, the philosopher who contemplates man as he should be;
>
> Tacitus, the historian who presents man as he is;
>
> Francis Bacon, who inspired Vico to undertake this proj-
> ect of the new science, where analysis should not be at the
> expense of synthesis (perhaps the same title *Scienza nuova*
> has something to do with the *Novum Organum* of Bacon).
>
> Hugo Grotius, the philosopher of law.

Vico's historical science is a vital synthesis between the universal and the particular, between philosophy and philology.
According to Vico, philosophy cannot be abstract, *a priori*, in
relation to factual truth. At the same time philology is in need of
a theoretical framework. Under the name of philologists, Vico
grouped all those concerned with establishing the origins of
languages and customs, or those who study the succession of
the specific facts of a people.

Philosophy should provide the truth, while philology must
give certainty: what is certain, the concrete historical fact, is the
benchmark of truth: the theoretical system that explains universal history. Therefore, philosophy without philology is empty:
it would be an abstract philosophy, like Cartesian philosophy.
And philology without philosophy, the isolated historical fact,
without a system of references, is blind.

The level of philosophy, the science of truth, is found in the
study of the ideal eternal history, that is, in finding the ideal
necessity—the ought to be—of man. But the being of man is
socio-historical in nature. The study of the facts reveals the fundamental aspects of man: his ideal aspirations and his weak-
nesses, the influence of man in the social environment, and the
influence of the environment on human nature.

Philosophy and philology are mutually interwoven, so
that they can provide a scientific understanding of history,

presenting the particular developments of different societies, but integrated into a theoretical framework, that is, in the ideal eternal history.

Vico presented an overview of world history divided into three stages or ages:

The age of the gods, or first stage of civilization, based on three principles: religion, marriage and burial of the dead;

The age of heroes, which developed the first forms of socio-political organization;

The age of men, characterized by democratic republics and awareness of the dignity of the rational being.

When he dealt with the stages of civilization, Vico offered an anthropological view opposed to Cartesian rationalism: the essence of man is not reduced to reflective reason. In the first two stages of civilization, sensitivity and poetic imagination guided the lives of men. Studying a primitive historical period from the point of view of the age of men, the stage of reason, is a wrong scientific attitude and it prevents the knowledge of a historical period in its specificity.

Vico's vision of universal history is completed with the theory of *corsi* and *ricorsi*. The Three Ages of civilization reappear in the course of the centuries, and they follow one another based on their own frame of mind. The poetic imagination leaves the way clear for reflective reasoning, which will be criticized later by skeptical reason, and which in turn will restart the cycle with the primitive mentality.

Nevertheless, the successive phases do not occur according to a deterministic law. Copleston wrote: "Vico does not say that historical events are determined or that in each cycle, groups of events that are similar have to occur. Neither does he state, for example, that Christianity is a religious phenomenon that has value only with respect to a specific cycle, so that it has to give way in the future to another religion. What recurs is not the fact or the particular historical event, but the general framework in which the facts occur. Or rather, what recurs is the cycle of mentalities."[82.]

World history is the work of man, and at the same time, the work of Divine Providence. Vico spoke of the hetero-genesis of purposes: men act freely with their will; they propose particular ends, but it is always divine design that is accomplished in world history. History is the scope of the civil world, the world made freely by men, while men are guided *suaviter et fortiter* by the Wise and Eternal Providence.

Vico was a counter-cultural thinker, and as such he presents a difficult historiographical problem: his insertion into a particular philosophical tradition. We decided to treat his thought briefly at just about the end of our discussion of rationalism. The philosopher from Naples, endowed with a great freedom of spirit, opposed the universalization of the Cartesian method, and opened modern philosophy to the world of history. The human sciences can now enjoy a dignity that had been denied them by seventeenth-century mathematicism. With his anthropological insights, Vico is a precursor of Romanticism. His new epistemological premises make him a precursor of the renaissance of historical and social science in the nineteenth and twentieth centuries.

Sources

René Descartes, *Oeuvres complètes*, Adam-Tannery ed. (Paris: Vrin, 1897–1909).

Galileo Galilei, *Opere* (Torino: UTET, 1965).

Gottfried Wilhelm Leibniz *Die philosophischen Schriften* (Berlin: C.I. Gerhardt, 1875).

N. Malebranche, *Oeuvres complètes*, Andre Robinet, ed. (Paris: Librarie J. Vrin, 1958).

---

82. Frederick Copleston, *History of Philosophy, Vol. VI: Wolff to Kant.* (New York: Image Books, 1963).

Blaise Pascal, *Oeuvres complètes*, Leon. Brunschvicg, Pierre Boutroux, and Felix Gazier, eds. (Paris, 1904–1914).

Benedict de Spinoza, *Werke*, C. I. Gerhardt, ed. (Heidelberg, 1925).

Giovanni Battista Vico, *Opere*, (Bari: Laterza, 1914–1941).

PART THREE
EMPIRICISM

After studying the most important representatives of continental rationalist philosophy, we now turn our attention to the major British empiricist authors. We are facing an authentic philosophical tradition whereby a continuity between these philosophers is evident. Thus, the first stones of empiricism laid by Bacon would coherently end in the skepticism of Hume. Clearly there are major differences between Bacon's epistemological confidence and Hume's theory of knowledge. But between one and the other, almost two centuries of empiricist thought pass by, within which the starting theses, at first moderate, potentially contained the extreme forms that would lead empiricism into a serious skeptical crisis. Kant would later have to confront this crisis in the eighteenth century.

3.1 FRANCIS BACON (1561-1626)

a) Life and Works

Francis Bacon was born in London in 1561. He was only twelve years old when he entered the University of Cambridge, where he stayed until 1575. In this period, he got to know and reject Aristotelian philosophy. He stayed for a time in Paris, and then returned to London. In 1579 he began his early political career.

In 1603 he wrote an autobiographical preface for a work he had thought of writing: *Cogitationes de natura rerum* (*Thoughts on the Nature of Things*). Starting from 1604 he wrote his major scientific and philosophical works: *The Advancement of Learning*

(1604), *The Advancement and Proficience of Learning Divine and Human* (1605); *Cogitata et visa de interpetatione naturae* (*Thoughts and Conclusions on the Interpretation of Nature*, 1607–1609); *Redarguitio philosophiarum* (*The Refutation of Philosophies*, 1608).

Between the years 1613 and 1618 he was the Lord Chancellor of England and was appointed Baron of Verulam. In 1621 he ended his political career when he was accused of corruption. The previous year he had published *Instauratio magna* (*Great Instauration*), a vast project divided into six parts. The second, completely dedicated to the scientific method, is his most famous work: the *Novum organum*. The last parts of the *Great Instauration* were never completed. The last five years of his life were devoted to historical studies. He began an unfinished utopian work called *The New Atlantis* published, like many of his works, after his death which occurred in London in 1626.

b) The Knowledge and Mastery of Nature

Just like Descartes, Bacon wanted to found all human knowledge again, but from a new point of view: the English philosopher had the aim of reaching a knowledge that was total, complete and comprehensive. At the same time, according to Bacon, knowledge has a social and pragmatic purpose, which is subject to the truth of utility: "what is more useful in practice is more true in science."[83]

In the *Novum organum* he explained very clearly the new purpose that knowledge must pursue, "the true and legitimate goal of the sciences is to provide human life with new inventions and resources."[84]

Elaborating on the practical purpose of learning, Bacon affirmed: "The power of man lies only in science: man can do only as much as man can know." It is a matter of knowledge for the sake of power. Therefore, "the path to power and to science

---

83. Francis Bacon, *Novum Organum*, 2.4.

84. Bacon, *Novum Organum*, 1.81.

are very near each other and are almost the same."[85] Knowledge is at the service of man and is meant to take over nature, to dominate it.

To achieve this dominion, a necessary prerequisite is a good knowledge of nature. The role that observation plays regarding empirical data is essential. Hence the need to introduce a method that can guide experience. In *Novum organum*, Bacon made a bet that technology would triumph over nature: the value of science then becomes its application at the service of technology, enabling man to transform nature.

c) Method and Division of the Sciences

A new method is needed in order to found a new science. The method proposed by Bacon consists in: "obtaining axioms starting from the senses and from particular facts, then rising continuously and progressively until arriving, in the end, at the most general principles."[86]

Bacon rejected syllogistic deduction, considering it as an illegitimate procedure. In the *Novum organum* he presented his method in two parts: the *pars destruens*, which consists of a correction of the intellect (*emendatio vel expurgatio intellecti*), and the *pars construens*, which is the art of interpreting nature.

1) Expurgatio intellecti

Bacon holds that is necessary for the human intellect to have a heavy load to carry, to keep it firmly on the ground. Reason must remain true to the data given by experience, resisting the temptation of anthropomorphism, which is to consider nature as analogous to man. In the investigation of nature, man finds certain mental habits and prejudices that must be criticized and abandoned. Prejudices that, according to Bacon, threaten the intellect and that impede it from

---

85. Bacon, *Novum Organum*, 2.4.

86. Bacon, *Novum Organum*, 1.19.

getting down to things and approaching them. He calls these prejudices "Idols."

There are four types of idols: Firstly, *tribal idols*, which are founded on human nature itself, and are due to the weakness of the senses and of the intellect. These idols lead men to approve of generally accepted opinions.

The second type of prejudices are the *idols of the cave*, that belong only to the individual man. Each individual man has his own cave where the light of nature is corrupted. These idols are the product of one's own education, customs and readings. Bacon includes respect and admiration for the ancients among these idols.

The *idols of the Forum* arise from language, and lead us to imagine that reason is founded on words. Vulgar language frequently uses manners of speech that lead to mistaken concepts. Common language—that of the market, or *forum*—is a source of errors, and human disputes are often linguistic.

Finally, there are the *theater idols*, made up of the different philosophical theories, which are nothing but comedies. Bacon was referring to: sophist philosophy, identifying it with Aristotelianism; empirical philosophy, one that focuses on a few experiments; and to superstitious philosophy that mixes philosophy with theology, as the Pythagoreans and the Platonists did.

For Bacon, therefore, the human intellect is an *enchanted mirror, full of superstitions and ghosts*, that must be cleaned for it to reflect things and actions, and not just probable arguments and reasons.

2) *The interpretation of nature*

Once the intellect is free from prejudices, from idols, we must proceed to the interpretation of nature through induction. Bacon's induction consists in, above all, the collection of empirical data that will serve as the basis of science. Bacon called this first stage *natural history*. The new induction must be complete, and it must take into account exceptions, variations, refutations, etc., that occur in nature. Therefore, it is not just simple enumeration, as Bacon saw Aristotelian induction. With Bacon's induction we obtain the *true method of experience*, that is, the final alliance between the intellect and the senses.

The final aim of the method and of human knowledge is to "discover the form, or the real specific difference, or the *natura naturante*, or the source of emanation" of all things.[87] But what did "form" mean for Bacon? It is hard to tell. It seems as though there were two main meanings: a) form as essence: "the form of the thing is the same as the thing itself: *ipsissima res*";[88] and b) form as law: "when we talk about forms we mean those laws and determinations of pure act that determine and constitute any simple nature, such as heat, light and weight."[89]

Bacon uses Aristotelian language, but changes the meaning of the terms. In the spirit of his system, the form could be identified with a natural law that constitutes the very essence of a thing. In Bacon, therefore, the aim of induction is to discover the forms or the natural laws of things.

3) The Division of Science

Bacon divided the sciences according to the faculties that they cultivate: the memory is the faculty proper to history; the imagination to poetry; while reason is the faculty of philosophy.

For Bacon there is a first philosophy, which is a kind of universal science prior to any division of knowledge, and that deals with the most fundamental and general axioms. Among these, Bacon cites the familiar adage: *quae in*

---

87. Bacon, *Novum Organum*, 2.1.

88. Bacon, *Novum Organum*, 2.13.

89. Bacon, *Novum Organum*, 2.17.

eodem tertio conveniunt, inter se conveniunt and fundamental notions like that of being and non-being.

After first describing this philosophy, Bacon goes on to divide human knowledge into its various parts, taking as criterion their material object. Thus, Bacon speaks of divine philosophy or natural theology, which deals with the knowledge of God obtained through the light of human reason.

Then comes the philosophy of nature, which is divided into speculative and operative philosophy. To the first division—speculative—belong metaphysics, which studies the formal and final causes of things, and physics, which deals with natural or efficient causes. To understand what Bacon meant by metaphysics it is necessary to keep in mind the change he made to the Aristotelian meaning of the term. For Bacon, formal causes are natural laws, the fixed principles of material nature. Final causes, which were theoretically admitted in Bacon's metaphysics, are in reality left aside. Bacon's famous and disrespectful phrase leaves no room for doubt: "the search for final causes is sterile, and just like a virgin consecrated to God does not produce anything."[90] Based on these distinctions, it is reasonable to say that both physics and metaphysics are concerned with the material world. Francis Bacon's metaphysics is not a contemplative knowledge, but a practical one, and its object is reduced to the corporeal world.

To the second division—operative—belongs the application of physics and metaphysics. More specifically, mechanics is applied to physics, and magic is applied to metaphysics. In his system, magic is the practical application of the science of occult forms. There are many aspects of material nature that are unknown to us; once discovered, they can be put at the service of human life.

---

90. Francis Bacon, *The Advancement of Learning*, 5.

The third part of knowledge, after divine philosophy and the philosophy of nature, is the philosophy of man, which leads to the philosophy of the body, the soul, and society or civil philosophy. Bacon considered the arguments concerning the immortality of the soul as more suitable for divine philosophy or natural theology. However, he says that in man there are powers that go beyond the limitations of matter. Thus, in the Baconian division of knowledge there is a place for logic (*doctrina circa intellectum*) and ethics (*doctrina circa voluntatem*).

d) A Precursor of the Technological World

Bacon presented a very large project, but he did not contribute anything significant for the development of empirical science. He had some eminently modern views. He created an intellectual environment favorable to experimental science, and put the problem of method at the center of philosophical speculation.

Bacon also clearly separated the scope of reason and of faith. In his view, scholastic philosophy, based on Aristotle, claimed to found a rational theology capable of knowing and defining the divine essence. But Bacon's fundamental task was to study nature, where God has manifested himself.

Bacon proposed the *credo quia absurdum* as a fundamental religious attitude, and he promoted an image of man dedicated to the transformation of nature as the only possible task after original sin. There is no room, therefore, for contemplation, but only for the philosophy of doing, of producing, although certainly not completely deprived of a moral and religious context. Still, the absence of a scientific basis for faith will lead to an attitude typical of Puritan fideism on the one hand, and a concern for temporal business on the other.

Bacon is presented in the history of philosophy as a precursor to the technological man. Knowledge as a means for gaining power, the need to find a scientific method to make man's dominion over nature more effective, and the consideration of metaphysical problems as alien to philosophical knowledge would be lines of force that would develop the English empiricist tradition to come.

In this sense, Benedict XVI considers Francis Bacon to be a milestone of modern culture. There is an epochal change in the sixteenth century, based on "the new correlation of experiment and method that enables man to arrive at an interpretation of nature in conformity with its laws and thus finally to achieve "the triumph of art over nature" (*Novum Organum I, 17*). The novelty—according to Bacon's vision—lies in a new correlation between science and praxis. This is also given a theological application: the new correlation between science and praxis would mean that the dominion over creation—given to man by God and lost through original sin—would be reestablished (cfr. ibid. I, 129)."[91]

Pope Benedict XVI argues that in Bacon, there had been a substitution of faith in the redemption wrought by Christ by faith in technological progress. The hope for a better world is rooted in "the newly discovered link between science and praxis. It is not that faith is simply denied; rather it is displaced onto another level—that of purely private and other-worldly affairs—and at the same time it becomes somehow irrelevant for the world. This programmatic vision has determined the trajectory of modern times."[92]

91. Benedict XVI, Encyclical on Christian Hope *Spe Salvi*, (November 30, 2007) 16. Vatican website: www.vatican.va.

92. Benedict XVI, *Spe Salvi*, 17.

3.2 Thomas Hobbes (1588–1679)

a) Life and Works

Born in Malmesbury, England in 1588, Thomas Hobbes was the son of an Anglican pastor. He studied at Oxford, and worked as a tutor to the son of Lord Cavendish. After a trip to the continent, he focused on the study of history and the classics. He had contacts with personalities from the British intellectual circles, among whom was Francis Bacon.

On a second trip to the continent he did mathematical research, and on a third trip (1634–1637) he met Galileo, Mersenne, Gassendi and Descartes. When he returned to England, the political situation was deteriorating: strife, Charles I sentenced to death, civil war, the Puritan dictatorship were some of the difficult circumstances of seventeenth-century England that Hobbes lived through.

In 1640 he wrote *Elements of Law, Natural and Politic*, which he showed only to his circle of friends. Due to the political chaos and a concern for his life, Hobbes decided to move to Paris, where he remained until 1651. He wrote the *Objectiones ad Cartesii meditationes de prima philosophia*. In 1642, while still in Paris, he published *De cive*.

In 1651, during the government of Cromwell, he returned to England, where he published his most famous work *Leviathan*. During this period, he also wrote *De corpore* and *De homine*, which together with *De cive* form a trilogy under the name *Elements of Philosophy*.

He devoted the last years of his life to the translation of Greek classics. He died in 1679 at the age of 91.

b) The Formation of Hobbes' Thought

1) Unity and system in the project of Hobbes

In his autobiography, Hobbes claims to have been brought into the world prematurely: the world then was dominated by the terror aroused by the arrival of the Invincible

Spanish Armada, off the coast of England. Partly joking and partly seriously, the philosopher of Malmesbury wrote that fear was his twin brother. Indeed, the ultimate aim of the thought of Hobbes was the establishment of peace and order among men, so as to stay as far away as possible from the possibility of a violent death. To understand more deeply this purpose, it is necessary to consider the socio-political circumstances of seventeenth-century England, where internal disagreements and civil war conditioned the ordinary life of the British people. Hobbes's project was mainly political and would be based on a set of philosophical principles, which were contained essentially in his *Elements of Philosophy*.

Hobbes's philosophy is unitary; he thought of the universe as a set of bodies: natural bodies and political bodies. This doctrine, which we might call *corporealist*, is evident from the titles of his work. If for Hobbes philosophy is the science of bodies, then there are natural or physical bodies: *De corpore*; human bodies: *De homine*; and an artificial body, the political body: *De cive*.

Taking this *corporealism* as a basis, Hobbes constructed a materialist system with a pragmatic purpose. Assuming some elements of the thought of Francis Bacon he said that "the end of knowledge is power (*scientiam propter potentiam*)."[93] Hobbes excluded any metaphysical and theological concept from philosophy, following the tradition begun by Bacon.

According to Hobbes, "the subject of Philosophy, or the matter it treats of, is every body of which we can conceive any generation, and which we may, by any consideration thereof, compare with other bodies, or which is capable of composition and resolution; that is to say, every body of whose generation or properties we can have any

---

93. Thomas Hobbes, *De corpore*, 1.16.

knowledge. . . . Therefore it (philosophy) excludes theology, I mean the doctrine of God, eternal, ingenerable, incomprehensible, and in whom there is nothing neither to divide nor compound, nor any generation to be conceived."[94]

2) Elements and Characteristics of the System

Hobbes's philosophical system can be characterized by the following elements:

a) *Materialism:* reality for Hobbes is just material, to the point that he saw a contradiction in the concept of an incorporeal substance. The spirit would be a corporeal body, but one that is so subtle that it cannot be perceived by the senses. The spirit, then, is "a colorless figure, a body without dimensions."[95] From this radical materialism, it is logical to exclude from the purview of philosophy any reality that cannot receive an explanation from the point of view of its generation.

b) *Mechanicism:* any change that occurs in reality was explained by Hobbes in a quantitative way. Movement is the universal cause. Matter and motion, understood as change of quantity, can explain any sensible phenomenon, all human knowledge and voluntary acts.

c) *Concern for methodology:* Like Descartes, Hobbes considered error as the result of a lack of method for reasoning well. Hobbes's method was inspired by the physics of Galileo. The English philosopher thought that human reason simply performs calculations. Analysis and synthesis, addition and subtraction, allow us to go from the known to the unknown, following the order of generation.

---

94. Hobbes, *De corpore*, 1.1.8.
95. Thomas Hobbes, *The Elements of Law, Natural and Politic*, 1.11.4.

d) *Sensism and nominalism:* Hobbes said that our thoughts are just images or representations of bodies expressed by names. Thoughts are produced in us by sensations, the source of all thoughts is what we call sense, because there is no conception of the human mind that has not been before, in whole or in part, generated in the sense organs.[96]

In Hobbes's perspective there is no room for universal concepts: there are only common names. The name is a word used arbitrarily by man. Universal is just the name of a name, since there are only individuals and individual names. Common names do not refer to reality, but only to what we think of it: the representation that the senses have of reality.

Since sensitive knowledge is individual and contingent, the foundation of science lies in a rationalization of experience through language, which replaces things by their names. Language is the guarantee and foundation of science. Consequently, science is reduced to names, and thus Hobbes establishes a discontinuity between real truth and scientific truth. For Hobbes, the theory of science thus becomes a mere convention.

3) First Philosophy and Philosophy of Nature

According to Hobbes, the first philosophy consists in the "correct definition of the most universal names."[97] These names are basically: body, time, place, cause, potency, act, quantity and movement. The proper object of philosophy is the body, that is, "that which does not depend on our thinking and coincides with some part of space."[98]

In his philosophy of nature, corporealism together with mechanicism, provide the explanations for all reality. The

---

96. See Thomas Hobbes, *Leviathan,* 1.1.

97. Hobbes, *Leviathan,* 4.46.

98. Thomas Hobbes, *De corpore,* 2.8.1.

main cause of all that happens in the world of bodies is motion. For Hobbes, motion is "the first door that opens to the knowledge of all things physical."[99] Any change or action between bodies can be explained by motion. There are two types of motion: vital, which begins with generation and is never interrupted during life (for example, the circulation of blood, respiration, etc.); and animal and voluntary motion (walking, talking and moving one's limbs at will).

c) Anthropology and Morals

Consistent with his basic materialism, the Hobbesian conception of human nature differs profoundly from the previous philosophical tradition. Man, for Hobbes, is a set of material elements. The fundamental value of man is his life, understood as mere conservation.

The two key building blocks of human nature are the passions and reason. Passions are an effect of the action of external bodies on the brain, which is transmitted to the heart, as the center of the human body. They originate vital movement.

The two main passions are desire and aversion: they are two movements that make man approach the desired object or turn away from the rejected. The most radical natural human desire is the desire for power that ends only with death.

The higher powers of man also depend on the body. Mental discourse is determined by the sensations. For Hobbes, intelligence and imagination are identical. The only difference between animal and human imagination lies in curiosity, which Hobbes relates to sagacity, and which has its origin in the memory.

---

99. Hobbes, *De corpore*, introduction.

Reason is presented as merely instrumental with respect to the passions: it serves as a means for the passions to attain the objects that they tend to. The will, in turn, is considered as a combination of appetite, fear and hope. It is, for Hobbes: "the ultimate appetite or the ultimate aversion that is in immediate contact with action or omission."[100]

In a materialistic and mechanistic system like that of Hobbes, there is no room for freedom. The English philosopher reduced freedom to the absence of external obstacles; to do what one pleases. More specifically, freedom is identified with the freedom of movement.

In the moral sphere, Hobbes defined the good as the object of an appetite or desire. Evil, however, is the object of hatred or aversion. There are no absolute goods or evils: good and evil are concepts ultimately dependent upon individual interest.

"Continual success in obtaining those things which a man from time to time desireth, that is to say, continual prospering, is what men call Felicity; I mean the Felicity of this life. For there is no such thing as perpetual Tranquillity of mind, while we live here; because Life itself is but Motion, and can never be without Desire, nor without Feare, no more than without Sense. What kind of Felicity God hath ordained to them that devoutly honour him, a man shall no sooner know, than enjoy; being joys, that now are as incomprehensible, as the word of School-men, Beatifical Vision, is unintelligible."[101]

"Felicity of this life, consisteth not in the repose of a mind satisfied. For there is no such Finis Ultimus, (utmost ayme,) nor Summum Bonum, (greatest good,) as is spoken of in the Books of the old Morall Philosophers."[102]

---

100. Thomas Hobbes, *Elements of Law*, 1.6.

101. Hobbes, *Leviathan*, 1.6.

102. Hobbes, *Leviathan*, 1.11.

d) Political Philosophy

1) The State of Nature

Starting from a nominalist concept of human nature, Hobbes believed that man is an asocial individual. Before entering into any society, man lived in a *state of nature*.

Hobbes was not the first to speak of this pre-social state: it is a *locus communis* of Roman and medieval legal tradition. We have also seen this concept when dealing with libertinism. In the English philosopher, this state of nature is described quite strongly, demonstrating his materialist anthropology.

In this *status naturae*, natural law does not have a moral nature, but merely a factual one. In the system of Hobbes there is no room for a concept of a natural law of moral nature, because the system lacks an understanding of human nature that is imbued with finality or teleology.

For Hobbes, every man in the state of nature has a right to everything: *Natura dedit omnia omnibus*, nature has given everything to everyone. This fact is the cause of a state of generalized war among men who, driven by their instincts, demand for themselves the full blessings of nature.

This is the war of all against all—*bellum omnium contra omnes*. This creates a state of contradiction of man with himself and with others, in the sense that, the universal right of an individual goes against the right of another. Thus, *homini homo lupus*, man is a wolf to man; the individual becomes the declared enemy of the others.

From the above we can conclude that Hobbes identified right with power. Man is characterized essentially by the desire for an ever-greater power. Hobbes wrote in the *Leviathan*: "So that in the first place, I put for a general inclination of all mankind, a perpetual and restless desire of Power after power, that ceaseth only in Death. And the cause of this, is not always that a man hopes for a more intensive delight, than he has already attained to; or that he cannot be content with a moderate power: but because he cannot assure the power and means to live well, which he hath present, without the acquisition of more."[103]

Hobbes distinguished between natural right and natural law. Law means obligation; right, in contrast, is freedom understood as power.

"A law of nature, (Lex Naturalis,) is a Precept, or general Rule, found out by Reason, by which a man is forbidden to do, that which is destructive of his life, or taketh away the means of preserving the same; and to omit, that by which he thinketh it may be best preserved."[104]

Concretely, according to Hobbes, natural law obliges us to seek peace. From this fundamental law, Hobbes deduced twenty other natural laws. The collection of all these precepts is the only principle of order in the state of nature, and is a rule of selfish individual behavior. If peace is sought it is not for the sake of the good of the others but for one's own preservation. This natural law is the means to achieve the civil state.

According to Hobbes, the state of nature is not necessarily a historical state of humanity. Rather, it is a theoretical attempt to express the natural condition of men considered as such, regardless of specific historical circumstances. But we must also take into account the historical context in which Hobbes elaborated his doctrine.

---

103. Hobbes, *Leviathan*, 1.14.
104. Hobbes, *Leviathan*, 1.14.

2) *The Social Pact*

The most effective way to preserve peace is for each one to renounce his own rights and freedom—his own power—to the extent that this waiver could lead to establishing peace among men. It may entail a pact between individuals, which will cause the state of war to cease. The pact is not just a waiver, but a mutual cession of the right of every man over all things.

The social contract is necessary but not sufficient for establishing peace. We must institute a power that rules over the parties. The original pact of Hobbes had a peculiar nature:

"This is more than Consent, or Concord; it is a real Unity of them all, in one and the same Person, made by Covenant of every man with every man, in such manner, as if every man should say to every man, 'I Authorise and give up my Right of Governing my self, to this Man, or to this Assembly of men, on this condition, that thou give up thy Right to him, and Authorise all his Actions in like manner.'"[105]

The transfer of individual rights converts the crowd into a unity, resulting in the state, called the *Leviathan* or mortal god. This state is a unique person called the sovereign. The people are subjects or citizens. The power of the sovereign is absolute, and irrevocably retains the rights of the citizens. Hobbes wanted the state to be a real guarantee for safeguarding peace. "The state is the force that constrains the wolfish nature of man and makes him become social, by means of the fear that such a force infuses in men, so as to maintain peace and guarantee security. This is the reason why the state is conceived by Hobbes as a mortal god, to which men owe, after the immortal God, their earthly life."[106]

---

105. Hobbes, *Leviathan*, 2.17.

106. Mario D'Addio, *Storia delle dottrine politiche*, vol. 1 (Genova: ECIG, 1992), 443.

The absolute nature of the sovereign power is derived from the sum of the individual powers that men have ceded through the pact. This cession is irrevocable, for otherwise it will be impossible to keep the peace. Consequently, any right of resistance to political authority is nonexistent. Civil laws are the will of the sovereign, the unique and supreme legislator.

To the sovereign power also belong the following: the administration of justice, the appointment of all civil servants, the right to reward or punish subjects and the possibility of conferring dignities and honors.

According to Hobbes' particular anthropological conception, in the state of nature there was no criterion for determining what was just and unjust. In that state, man had every right to use all means he deemed suitable for defending his life. After the pact, however, which gives rise to the state, the criterion of justice is established by positive law. The strength of the sovereign power determines what is just and unjust through rules provided with sanctions.

Hobbes's doctrine of property is inserted in this context: the sovereign power conditionally recognizes private property, since he retains absolute power over all things.

For Hobbes, in the civil state "right is the freedom that the law allows us."[107] It is the sovereign power that determines the amplitude of individual freedom. The individual has full freedom only in those actions about which the laws say nothing.

The absolute nature of the State extends to the religious sphere. If in the state of nature man can worship God according to the way he thinks most appropriate, once the social compact is established, the individual gives this right to the State as well. In the society of the Leviathan there can

---

107. Hobbes, *The Elements of Law, Natural and Politic,* 2.10.5.

only be one religious cult: the diversity of religions is a continual cause of discomfort and controversy.

According to Hobbes, the identification of political power and religious power is grounded in the Holy Scriptures. For Hobbes, obedience to God is made manifest in obedience to human law. Political authority is presented as a religious mediator. The civil sovereign is the head of the Church, and he will decide on doctrinal disputes and the canonicity of Scripture. Obviously, in this last aspect of his doctrine many historical-religious circumstances of seventeenth-century England had their influence.

* * *

A feature of much of modern philosophy is to take the physical and mathematical sciences as a model to imitate in philosophy. Mechanicism and corporealism—the application of physical and mathematical principles to all of reality—led Hobbes to political absolutism and to the consequent reduction of freedom. "In the elements of Hobbes's first philosophy there can be found *in nuce* all that would constitute his political system. (. . .) The best method to prove the truth or falsity of principles is to bring them to their ultimate consequences. This is what Hobbes did. Hence the usefulness of the study of his work."[108]

---

108. Alfredo Cruz Prados, *La sociedad como artificio* (Pamplona: EUNSA, 1986), 380–381.

3.3 JOHN LOCKE (1632–1704)

a) Life and Works

John Locke was born in 1632 in Wrington, near Bristol. He studied at Westminster. In 1652 he joined Christ Church College, Oxford University, intending to follow an ecclesiastical career. He obtained the title of Bachelor and Master of Arts and in 1659 became part of the school's faculty, teaching Greek, rhetoric and moral philosophy. After a few years he decided to abandon the ecclesiastical career, and became interested in medicine, natural sciences and chemistry.

In 1664 he wrote his first book, *Essays on the Natural Law*. In 1665 he moved to London where he worked at the service of Lord Ashley-Cooper, future first Earl of Shaftesbury. In the British capital, he made contacts with several scientists including the chemist Boyle, and he also joined the Royal Society. After the political demise of his protector, he returned to Oxford in 1674, where he graduated in Medicine. In 1675 he went to France and remained there until 1678.

He then returned to London to work for the Earl of Shaftesbury. But in 1682, the Earl was accused of treason, and was forced to flee to Holland. Locke also left England and went to the Netherlands. From there, he was actively involved in political intrigues, preparing William of Orange to ascend to the throne of England.

In 1689 he returned to England after the revolution of 1688, now that the political situation had changed. In this period, he published his most important works: *Essay Concerning Human Understanding*, *A Letter Concerning Tolerance*, and *Two Treatises of Civil Government*. In 1693 he published *Some Thoughts Concerning Education*, and in 1695, *The Reasonableness of Christianity, as Delivered in the Scriptures*. From 1700 onwards he retired to Oates (Essex), where he died in 1704.

b) General Outline of Locke's Thought

Locke's works deal primarily with two major areas of philosophy: the theory of knowledge and political philosophy.

Although these fields seem unrelated, they are connected in such a way as to give Locke's thought a certain coherence and consistency.

In the *Essay Concerning Human Understanding*, which is one of the first modern attempts to present the critical issue in all its radicalism, Locke asked about the scope of our knowledge: that is, what things can we know, and with what degree of certainty.

This study is not the result of curiosity, but responds to an eminently practical purpose: if one knows the limits of knowledge, one can employ the mind for useful things. Good use of the intellect can be a remedy to laziness and skepticism. According to Locke, what we need to know are "things necessary for living a life suited to human nature."[109]

The critique of knowledge in Locke's thought has a predominantly methodological character, but it isn't only about method, since it is pursued at the service of the true end of philosophy: to live a decent life with peace and happiness.

Locke is, strictly speaking, the first proponent of British empiricism. Despite obvious differences in perspective, he was influenced by Descartes. He was also influenced by Bacon and Hobbes. We can also find elements of the medieval nominalist tradition in his thought. Moderation is one of the salient features of the empiricism of Locke; it is also manifest in his political theory.

c) Theory of Knowledge

All of Locke's epistemology is found in the *Essay Concerning Human Understanding*. In his introduction, Locke explained that he wanted to examine the capacity of the intellect to carry out an investigation on the origins of knowledge, the power of the intellect and the certainties it can attain. To carry out this study, the British philosopher used the historical method, that

---

109. John Locke, *Second Treatise of Government*, 2.15.

is, showing the way through which reason arrives at the ideas of things.

The *Essay* is divided into four books:

the first is a debate with innatism;

the second studies the origin of ideas, sets the empiricist principle and explains simple and compound ideas;

the third is about the relationship between words and ideas;

the fourth examines the degrees of knowledge.

1) Controversy with Innatism

Locke criticized the theory of innate ideas, which had been defended, as we have seen, by Descartes and Leibniz. The privileged opponent of Locke is the latter philosopher. Recall that Leibniz wrote his *New Essays on Human Understanding* precisely to get into controversy with Locke.

Locke rejected the foundation of innatism: universal assent. For Locke, it is not true that there is universal agreement on the content of the alleged innate ideas. Different peoples have ideas that are profoundly different on countless aspects of reality; also, children and the mentally handicapped have no idea about the principle of identity, nor of non-contradiction and of fundamental moral principles.

Moreover, according to Locke, to fail to apply methodical doubt to the innate principles would be incompatible with the Cartesian claim of reaching an absolute principle without any presuppositions. Against Leibniz, Locke claimed that sense knowledge is the origin of ideas and first principles. For Leibniz, however, sense knowledge served as an occasion for awakening the understanding of the innate ideas.

Nevertheless, Locke's empiricism is not at odds with all kinds of rationalism. There is a rational desire to control the contents that reason receives, and yet these do not depend on reason but rather, come from experience.

154 A History of Modern Philosophy

2) The Origin of Simple Ideas

For Locke, idea means any content of the mind, any object of the act of thinking, taken in a broad sense. Sometimes he called the same act of perception "idea," thus making his epistemological exposition unclear.

Locke says that all knowledge comes from experience. He gives two aspects of experience: first, the external experiences or sensations, which are the source of most of our ideas. Second, the internal experiences or reflections, consisting of the various activities of the mind.

Thus, sensations and thoughts are the only sources of our ideas. In turn, Leibniz defined sensation as "an impression or motion made in some part of the body, that produces some perception in the understanding."[110]

The intellect can only reflect on the sensations after perceiving them.

Simple ideas are the materials of knowledge. All knowledge and each bit of knowledge are constructed starting from simple ideas, which are the subject of perceptions.

For Locke, simple ideas are clear and distinct. They correspond to the real properties of the bodies. They come to the mind through a sense or through various senses. Regarding them, the intellect is passive.

With respect to the origin of ideas, from an analytical point of view, there are also simple ideas that come from the combination of sensations with reflection, and finally, others that come solely from reflection; for instance, the very idea of perception.

The theory of simple ideas is largely due to the Cartesian principle of clarity and distinction. However, there is a clear difference in that the sensory origin of ideas in Locke is rejected by Descartes's system.

---

110. John Locke, *Essay Concerning Human Understanding*, 2.1.23.

Locke also distinguished between ideas and qualities. Ideas are perceptions within the mind, while qualities are modifications of matter in the bodies. Qualities are the cause of perceptions that occur in the mind. In other words, qualities are, "the power to produce any idea in our mind."[111]

Ideas are in the mind, and qualities are in the bodies. Primary qualities—which Locke also called original—are inseparable from a body, and the senses find them in any particle of matter. These primary qualities are the cause of the simple ideas of solidity, extension, shape, motion, rest and number.

Secondary qualities (colors, sounds, flavors), however, do not belong to bodies themselves, but have the "power to produce various sensations in us by their primary qualities."[112] In this point, Locke defended a position very close to that of Descartes: he denied the complete objectivity of the secondary qualities. However, he did not think of them as innate ideas of the mind, but only as modes of the primary qualities.

3) The Compound Ideas: Substances, Modes, Relations

Up to this point in our discussion of the *Essay Concerning Human Understanding*, Locke has treated the mind as something passive. Now, Locke adds that there are compound ideas, formed from simple ideas on which the mind acts by varying and multiplying them, beyond the limit allowed by sensations and reflections.

Compound ideas are of three main types:

a) *Substance:* It is an idea born from the observation of the fact that a certain number of simple ideas go together, so that they are thought to belong to the same thing.

---

111. Locke, *Essay Concerning Human Understanding,* 2.8.8
112. Locke, *Essay Concerning Human Understanding,* 2.8.10.

At this point it may be that we come to think of there being a substrate on which these ideas exist. For Locke, substance is simply an assumption produced by our ignorance about the inner nature of things: "we have no idea of what it is, but only a confused and obscure one of what it does." For Locke, substance is an operating principle that we need as a hypothesis to explain reality, but it lacks an experiential basis.

According to Locke there are two types of substances: bodily and spiritual. But we cannot know them because we can only have clear and distinct ideas of primary qualities of body and spirit. Despite this limitation of human knowledge, "The infinite wise Contriver of us, and all things about us, hath fitted our senses, faculties, and organs, to the conveniences of life, and the business we have to do here. We are able, by our senses, to know and distinguish things: and to examine them so far as to apply them to our uses, and several ways to accommodate the exigencies of this life."[113] Therefore, man can attain sufficient knowledge to take care of his vital needs.

b) *Modes:* These are "complex ideas which, however compounded, do not have the supposition of subsisting by themselves, but are rather considered as dependences on, or affections of substances." There are simple and mixed modes. Simple modes are combinations of the same simple idea (for example, the number twenty is a combination of the idea of unity, i.e. many ones). Mixed modes arise from the combination of different simple ideas, for example, the idea of beauty.

c) *Relations:* They are the ideas that the mind gets by comparing simple ideas. Relations do not exist in reality but only in the mind, because every relation is concerned

---

113. Locke, *Essay Concerning Human Understanding*, 2.23.12.

about and ends with the ideas we receive from sensation or reflection.

Locke concluded the second book of the *Essay* by establishing a division between the ideas. Firstly, every simple idea is adequate, and is an effect of the primary qualities of things. The complex idea of substance, however, is inadequate. The only real ideas, that is, those that correspond to something real, are those that come from the primary qualities.

Reality, therefore, in Locke's thought appears as somewhat fragmented, as it is reduced to phenomena connected together eidetically, which cannot give a plausible explanation of the intrinsic unity of things.

4) The Universal Language and Ideas

We will now consider the third book of the *Essay*. For Locke, words are sensitive external signs by which we convey to others invisible ideas. They are arbitrary and conventional vehicles of thought, unlike ideas which are natural signs of things.

Language is needed to provide the foundation for science. Things are particular, but most of our words are general. General words are signs of general ideas; Locke also called them abstract ideas.

What is an abstract idea? It is an idea that has been separated from all circumstantial connotations of time and space. The general character of a word is an invention of the intellect, and does not belong to things or ideas, which are always particular.

In Locke, abstraction does not allow for the knowledge of real essences. Lockean abstraction is rather a subtraction of some properties that are not considered common to a particular genus or species. The deep problem of Locke's epistemology is this impossibility of knowing the real essences of things. The generalization of words fits only the nominal essences, but does not apply to the real constitution of things. In Locke's epistemology, the real essences remain unknown.

5) The Degrees of Knowledge

Human knowledge, according to Locke, has as its immediate object our own ideas. Consequently, we can say that Locke's epistemological theory is a representational theory, which he shares in common with rationalist and empiricist philosophy. The idea is a representation of the thing, and has a certain consistency in itself. The intellect knows only ideas or representations; although they refer to the primary qualities of things, they do not present the things in themselves to the intellect, but only their representation.

The fundamental types of knowledge are:

Intuitive knowledge: this is the knowledge that the mind has of its own ideas.

Demonstrative knowledge: this is the knowledge obtained when the mind perceives the agreement or disagreement among ideas. This knowledge is less certain than intuitive knowledge.

Sensitive knowledge: this knowledge falls more in the realm of faith or opinion. If we assume as did Locke, as well as Descartes, that knowledge is characterized by certainty, then sensitive knowledge would not be knowledge, strictly speaking.

Intuitive knowledge, however, requires sense knowledge, because the ideas are effects of sensations, but this does not imply that mere sensations constitute knowledge as such.

If sensitive knowledge lacks certainty, how can we know the existence of different realities? Locke said that we have the knowledge of our own existence by intuition; of the existence of God by demonstration; and of other things by sensation.[114] In this point, Locke followed an argumentative scheme inspired by Descartes. He considered that man knows his own existence intuitively from his own mental operations.

Starting from the existence of the self, Locke demonstrated the existence of God as eternal being required by the temporal contingency of the self. The existence of things, however, is only probable, since we can only be sure of the things that impress directly on us. But since the probability of the existence of things we have not experienced directly is very high, such probability guarantees the normal development of human life.

Faith that comes from human testimony or experience is a probable knowledge. However, if the witness is not human but divine, his testimony gives us certainty with no room for doubt. We must therefore ensure that we have genuine divine revelation. This is a task for reason, which thus becomes the judge of the veracity of the testimony of faith.

d) Moral Philosophy

Although Locke did not write any specific moral treatise, his interest in morals is present in all his works.

According to him, "All desire happiness. If it be further asked, what it is that moves desire? I answer, happiness, and that alone. . . . Happiness, then, in its full extent, is the utmost pleasure we are capable of, and misery the utmost pain; and the lowest degree of what can be called happiness is so much ease from all pain, and so much present pleasure, as without which any one cannot be content."[115]

Locke further specified the concept of happiness: in its maximum degree, it is the greatest pleasure we are capable of. Thus

---

114. Locke, *Essay Concerning Human Understanding*, 4.3.21.
115. Locke, *Essay Concerning Human Understanding*, 2.21.42–43.

the classical *eudaimonia* is transformed into a doctrine of pleasure. Good and evil, accordingly, are just names we give to
things that cause us pleasure or pain. From the gnoseological
point of view, the moral good and evil do not have any reality
in themselves, since they are relations, that is, they are one of
the types of complex ideas studied earlier, and are found in
the mind.

According to Locke, moral ideas are a collection of simple
ideas, but from the time that they are valued as good or bad,
they become relative because they are now put in relation to
some rules: the divine law, the civil law and the law of opinion.

> The divine law, which is identified with natural law, deter-
> mines what a sin is and what a duty is.
>
> Civil law determines what constitutes a right.
>
> The law of opinion classifies actions into virtues or vices.
> These laws can contradict each other. A duel, for example,
> may be a sin, yet not constitute a crime and even be consid-
> ered a virtuous or vicious action, depending on the customs
> of different peoples.

All of these manifest the relative nature of Locke's morality:
Locke opened the way for the idea that the decisive criterion of
morality is the desirability or usefulness of an action.

Locke used some key concepts with regard to the analysis
of moral action:

> Freedom, which for him is the power of any agent to do or not
> do a particular action;
>
> The will, which is the ordering power that prefers and
> chooses, directs and determines the exercise of freedom.
> The reason that moves the will is always restlessness, which
> causes a desire that determines the will. It is clear that this
> determination is not necessary or mechanical because the
> judgment of the intellect examines whether the good that it
> is considering forms or does not form part of true happiness.

In Lockean morality there is no absolute good. God is only a guarantor, enabling men to give multiple solutions to the problem of the objectivity of morality.

e) Political Philosophy

In Hobbes, we may recall that there was a close relationship between anthropology and political philosophy. That relation will not be as close in Locke, but no great contradictions will arise between these two philosophical fields, except for some reflections about the theory of natural law in his political philosophy, that is closer to the classical tradition.

Locke's political philosophy, as was the case of Hobbes's, is closely linked to the historical circumstances of the latter part of seventeenth-century England: the dictatorship of Cromwell, the Glorious Revolution of 1688, the accession of William of Orange to the throne of England and the substantially successful attempt to establish stable and harmonious relationships between Parliament and the Crown.

The two most important works of political philosophy written by Locke are the *Two Treatises of Government*.

The first treatise, written in controversy with Robert Filmer, author of *The Patriarch*, stated that family power was of the same nature as political power. Locke tried to show that the formation and maintenance of political power and the political organization of society is based not on the traditional power of the *paterfamilias*, but on the consensus among men.

In the *Second Treatise of Government*, Locke presented his proposal for the political organization of society. Like Hobbes, Locke referred to a state of nature and to a state of political or civil society. But as we shall see, Locke's ideas are placed in a different perspective from that of Hobbes. Whereas the latter wanted to ensure order and peace, and for this reason wanted to reinforce the absolute nature of authority, Locke aimed to safeguard the individual rights of citizens and therefore limit political power.

1) State of Nature and Social Contract

A first important concept in his political philosophy is that of natural law. This law is not innate: we get to know it, like everything else, from sensory experience. It is mandatory; it is the rule of moral conduct and God is its author. In the second treatise Locke would identify natural law with reason, without excluding reference to God. The rationality of the natural law causes it to be present to us as a law of convenience, through which men can form a community.

In Locke, the state of nature is a state of freedom, governed by the natural law, where equality reigns: "being all equal and independent, no one ought to harm another in his life, health, liberty, or possessions."[116] In this state, the only valid law is the natural law.

"The natural liberty of man is to be free from any superior power on earth, and not to be under the will or legislative authority of man, but to have only the law of nature for his rule."[117]

However, as there are men with disordered passions, the absence of an authority would allow for some in the state of nature to fail to obey the natural law. This creates a state of war, which is not the same as Hobbes' state of war, because it is a state of limited war: temporary, and not generalized. This state of war is the source of the social pact, which is "this one of agreeing together mutually to enter into one community, and make one body politic"[118] and so ends the fighting.

For Locke, man is not asocial. Man is social by nature, but the society of the state of nature is a pre-political society and lacks some essential elements that shape society as a political body.

---

116. Locke, *Second Treatise of Government*, 2.6.
117. Locke, *Second Treatise of Government*, 4.22.
118. Locke, *Second Treatise of Government*, 2.14.

Consensus is the fundamental concept for understanding the pact proposed by Locke. Men give rise to civil society through a consensus or a convention with other individuals, so that the society thus created allows for a comfortable, safe and peaceful life and the quiet enjoyment of their own goods. Civil society aims to safeguard natural rights: the right to life, health, liberty, and property. The right to property is fundamental in Locke's social theory, and will open the way for Adam Smith's economic theory.

2) The Political and Civil Society

Once constituted by the social compact, the political community would organize the defense of the rights of citizens by establishing, through general consensus, a political law that is recognized, impartial judges to resolve disputes and a power sufficient enough to ensure obedience to the laws and to make the decisions of the judge efficacious.

The political community moves by the force of the majority. The soul that gives form, life and unity to the political community is the legislature. The executive and the judiciary powers must reside in people who are not the same legislators. There is also a federal power, which deals with international relations.

Natural liberty is transformed, in the political community into civil liberty. Such liberty consists in not being subordinated to any power other than the law. Locke stresses that freedom is not a concept contrary to law. The laws formulated in parliament are a defense against the oppression of an absolute and arbitrary power. Therefore, the branches of government should be limited and should monitor each other. Locke, in controversy with Hobbes, presented the first systematic analysis of the liberal principle of the separation of powers. In order to avoid the arbitrariness of power, Locke also spoke of the obligation of the legislature to obey natural law.

3) Religion and Tolerance

In 1689, Locke wrote *Letters Concerning Toleration*. The church and the state, he said, are two distinct societies. The first is a free society of men who come together because of a mutual agreement to serve God publicly according to the way they deem most appropriate, for the salvation of their souls.

The State, however, deals with civil goods, and the power of rulers must not extend to things that touch on the salvation of souls. The Church, for its part, ought to encourage and advise, but not coerce.

Rather than a distinction, Locke's theory proposed a separation between church and state. The state can be intolerant of doctrines that threaten the things necessary for the preservation of civil power. Among these doctrines, Locke quotes atheism and Catholicism, considered by Locke as a bigoted creed, which decreases the independence of political power.

He presented his vision of the Christian religion in his essay *The Reasonableness of Christianity*. The minimum creed is to believe that Jesus is the Messiah. Revelation is necessary and serves to reinforce the law of reason or natural law. Jesus, by the gospel revelation, has transmitted to us a universal moral law.

Christianity is the only true religion, because it contains the essential beliefs that man can assent to with his reason. Despite this assertion that savors of rationalism, there is room in Locke's thought for supernatural truths. In the postscript to a letter to Edward Stillingfleet, written in 1697, he wrote: "Sacred Scripture is, and will always be the constant guide of my assent and I will listen to it always because it has the ineffable truth about things of utmost importance. I wish we could say that there are no mysteries in it, but I must admit that for me there are and I fear that there will always be. Where I lack the evidence of things, I find a sufficient basis for me to believe: God has said this.

Therefore, I will immediately condemn and reject any doctrine of mine, as soon as it is shown to me that it is contrary to any doctrine revealed in Scripture."

* * *

Locke's work is a major stage in modern philosophical thought. He was the first to present the critical problem in all its radicalness, although his theoretical vacillations will be clarified later by the more coherent empiricism of Berkeley and Hume. His epistemology elicited deep thought in England and Europe. At the same time, his moderate political philosophy sealed the fate of modern constitutionalism, giving rise to political and institutional concepts that after three centuries still enjoy wide acceptance.

3.4 GEORGE BERKELEY (1685–1753)

a) Life and Works

He was born in Kilkenny (Ireland), in a family of English origins. He studied at Trinity College in Dublin. Having completed his ecclesiastical studies, he became an Anglican minister and professor at the same College. In 1709 he published his first major work: *An Essay towards a New Theory of Vision*. The following year he finished writing *A Treatise Concerning the Principles of Human Knowledge*. In 1713 he published *Three Dialogues between Hylas and Philonous*. In that same year he moved to London.

In 1721 he wrote in Latin *De motu*, and he decided to go to Bermuda, for evangelical purposes. In 1729 he went to Rhode Island where he preached and founded a literary and scientific society, while awaiting transfer to Bermuda. But this trip could not be made, and so he returned to London where he published the *Alciphron*, a philosophical defense of Christianity.

He was appointed Anglican Bishop of Cloyne, Ireland, in 1734 and remained there until 1752. In the last years of his life he was dedicated to pastoral activity and philosophy. In this period, he published an essay on political economy: *Siris, a chain of philosophical reflections and inquiries, concerning the virtues of tar-water* (1744), which became his most famous work. Berkeley died in Oxford in 1753.

In his philosophy he received influences from Locke and Malebranche. From his early writings we can clearly see the central thesis of his thought: immaterialism.

b) General Outline of Berkeley's Thought

Berkeley's work has a deep religious inspiration and an apologetic purpose. In his *Treatise concerning the Principles of Human Knowledge* he wanted to refute skepticism and to prove the existence and immateriality of God, and the immortality of the soul.

For Berkeley, the right use of reason is the best ally of true religion. Therefore, it is necessary to develop a theory of knowledge which, for Berkeley, is at the basis of all philosophical knowledge. The Irish philosopher's epistemology is presented as a radical empiricism. To understand Berkeley's philosophical project, we must not forget its primary goal, which is religious in nature. Its extreme epistemological position was meant to serve his religious theses.

A quotation from the *Treatise concerning the Principles of Human Knowledge* is sufficient to demonstrate this purpose: "For, after all, what deserves the first place in our studies is the consideration of God and our Duty; which to promote, as it was the main drift and design of my labours."[119]

c) The Problem of Knowledge

In the preface to the *Treatise concerning the Principles of Human Knowledge*, Berkeley said that Locke had moved away from empiricism. For Berkeley, there are no general or abstract ideas. To speak of an abstract or universal idea is a contradiction, because every idea is particular: we know only our ideas, which

119. George Berkeley, *A Treatise concerning the Principles of Human Knowledge*, 1.156.

are the same as the impressions of the senses. These impressions are always particular, and from them we cannot obtain a general idea.

Men, said Berkeley, think they have universal ideas, but this is so only through language. Men also think that abstract ideas are attached to words, and so they use words instead of ideas. It is necessary to set ourselves free from the misleading use of words, by trying to limit our thoughts to the ideas, without words.

The critique of abstract ideas is the *pars destruens* of his theory. The positive part revolves around the question of the relationship between ideas and perceptions. Berkeley's gnoseological attempt is summarized in the following passage from the *Dialogues*:

"I do not pretend to frame any hypothesis at all. I am of a vulgar cast, simple enough to believe my senses, and leave things as I find them. To be plain, it is my opinion that the real things are those very things I see, and feel, and perceive by my senses. These I know; and, finding they answer all the necessities and purposes of life, have no reason to be solicitous about any other unknown beings. A piece of sensible bread, for instance, would stay my stomach better than ten thousand times as much of that insensible, unintelligible, real bread you speak of. It is likewise my opinion that colours and other sensible qualities are on the objects. I cannot for my life help thinking that snow is white, and fire hot. You indeed, who by snow and fire mean certain external, unperceived, unperceiving substances, are in the right to deny whiteness or heat to be affections inherent in them. But I, who understand by those words the things I see and feel, am obliged to think like other folks. And, as I am no sceptic with regard to the nature of things, so neither am I as to their existence. That a thing should be really perceived by my senses, and at the same time not really exist, is to me a plain contradiction; since I cannot prescind or abstract, even in thought, the existence of a sensible thing from its being perceived. Wood, stones, fire, water, flesh, iron, and the like things, which I name and discourse of, are things that I know. And I should not have known them but that I perceived them by my senses; and things perceived by the senses are immediately perceived; and things immediately perceived are ideas; and ideas cannot exist without the mind; their existence therefore consists in being perceived; when, therefore, they are actually perceived there can be no doubt of their existence. Away then with all that skepticism, all those ridiculous philosophical doubts."[120]

It is not about transforming things into ideas, but rather ideas into things. Berkeley wanted to abolish the distinction between real being and a being of reason, and between the idea and the thing known. Berkeley's idea is not: *that through which* (representationist thesis) or *that in which* (realist thesis) you know something, but precisely the idea itself is the very thing that is perceived:

"It is evident to anyone who takes a survey of the objects of human knowledge, that they are either IDEAS actually imprinted on the senses; or else such as are perceived by attending to the passions and operations of the mind; or lastly, ideas formed by help of memory and imagination—either compounding, dividing, or barely representing those originally perceived in the aforesaid ways."[121]

According to Berkeley, knowledge is limited to the world of experience of consciousness itself. The being of things is to be perceived. The so-called new beginning of philosophy is the famous *esse est percipi*. In the *Treatise*, Berkeley explained the meaning of all propositions of existence according to this new principle of knowing and being:

"The table I write on I say exists, that is, I see and feel it; and if I were out of my study I should say it existed—meaning thereby that if I was in my study I might perceive it, or that some other spirit actually does perceive it. There was an odour,

120. George Berkeley, *Three Dialogues Between Hylas and Philonous*, 3.
121. Berkeley, *Treatise*, 3.1.

that is, it was smelt; there was a sound, that is, it was heard; a colour or figure, and it was perceived by sight or touch. This is all that I can understand by these and the like expressions. For as to what is said of the absolute existence of unthinking things without any relation to their being perceived, that seems perfectly unintelligible. Their ESSE is PERCIPI, nor is it possible they should have any existence out of the minds or thinking things which perceive them."[122]

The Irishman supported two types of beings: the spirit, that is, the agent who perceives, and the perceived ideas. Therefore, the principle of Berkeley par excellence is: *esse est percipi aut percipere.*

The last step of this delusional idealism, as Kant calls it, is the cancellation of the distinction between primary and secondary qualities. According to the rationalist and empiricist traditions, secondary qualities are only modifications of the knower: they are not real. For Berkeley, every quality is secondary and exists only in the mind.

The notion of matter or material substance outside the perceiver is intrinsically contradictory and tends, according to Berkeley's particular conception of creation and the conservation of beings, to the affirmation of atheism and materialism, since it would be an absolute existence in a sense, and would thus be placed on the ontological level of the existence of God.

"The great danger is that extension were made to exist outside the mind. If it existed outside the mind, it must be recognized as infinite, immutable, eternal, etc. This is the same as making God extended (which I consider dangerous), or to make an eternal, unchanging, infinite, uncreated, being exist next to God."[123] The explicit rejection of the notion of material substance puts immaterialism at the core of the thought of George Berkeley.

---

122. Berkeley, *Treatise*, 3.3.
123. George Berkeley, *Philosophical Commentaries, Notebook B,* note 290.

d) Immaterialism

Berkeley's epistemological theory is extremely radical, since the only realities that are the immediate object of our knowledge are ideas. Berkeley suppressed real things as the object of our act of knowing, and their position is occupied by ideas. The only difference left between beings is that of subject and object. This difference belongs to the epistemological order, permitting us to classify Berkeley's system as idealism. However, this is an empirical idealism, since the origin of ideas is sensory experience.

For Berkeley to transform ideas into things, he first had to transform things into ideas. He did this in three steps:

1. Reduce things to sensations or affections or passions of the intellect, regarding which the soul remains passive.
2. Affirm that the sensible qualities are subjective.
3. Make sensitive qualities relative to the state of the subject that perceives them.

Thus, for Berkeley, ideas, feelings and things that we perceive have the same meaning. When people talk about things, they often imagine that they are external material substances, but in reality they are just a set of sensations.

"And as several of these are observed to accompany each other, they come to be marked by one name, and so to be reputed as one thing. For example, a certain colour, taste, smell, figure and consistence, having been observed to go together, are considered as one distinct thing signified by the name APPLE. Other collections of ideas constitute a stone, a tree, a book, and the like sensible things—which as they are pleasing or disagreeable excite the passions of love, hatred, joy, grief, and so forth."[124]

Berkeley looked for the cause that produces the continuous succession of ideas. He thought this to be the spirit, which

124. Berkeley, *Treatise*, 3.1.

is not itself an idea, but rather a simple, undivided and active being. When the mind perceives, it is called the intellect; and when it acts on the ideas in any other way, it is called the will. The collection of ideas, or complex ideas, is the work of the will.

Although Berkeley identified ideas with things, when he referred to the objects of knowledge he preferred to use the term *ideas* and not *things*. The term *thing* is broader, since it includes both ideas and spirits. Berkeley did not deny the reality of things: he only denied their material nature, and the fact that they exist outside the mind. Thus, for Berkeley, all reality is spiritual.

If the concept of matter outside the intellect that perceives is inherently contradictory, the cause of things—that is, of our ideas—must be a spiritual substance. To arrive at this cause, Berkeley distinguished between images and ideas.

Images depend on the will and manifest the active nature of the human spirit. Thus we can arrive, say, at the image of a unicorn.

Ideas, however, depend on the senses, and show the passive nature of the human spirit.

"But, whatever power I may have over *my own* thoughts, I find the ideas actually perceived by Sense have not a like dependence on my will. When in broad daylight I open my eyes, it is not in my power to choose whether I shall see or no, or to determine what particular objects shall present themselves to my view; and so likewise as to the hearing and other senses; the ideas imprinted on them are not creatures of my will. There is *therefore some other will or spirit* that *produces them*."[125]

The senses impress upon the intellect, thus producing ideas. But since there are no external material substances, something else must provoke the ideas. Berkeley concludes that the ideas that depend upon sensations must be placed there by the Author of nature, and are therefore considered as real things. But immediately afterwards, Berkeley insists that ideas and images exist only in the mind and not outside of it.

---

125. Berkeley, *Treatise*, 29.

e) The Existence of God

Following the above arguments, we can say that for Berkeley, nature reveals its Author. The proof of his existence is immediate:

"Sensible things do really exist; and, if they really exist, they are necessarily perceived by an infinite mind: therefore there is an infinite mind or God."[126]

Although the limited mind of man cannot actually perceive all things, things still do exist. But if *esse* is identified with perceptibility, something will exist only when a mind perceives it. Therefore, things unperceived exist since God always perceives all things actually, and is not only their cause, but also the mind that contains and holds them.

This thesis, which for Berkeley is persuasive, nevertheless seems to go beyond the *esse est percipi*: how can we perceive the existence of something that cannot be perceived? We must admit a metaphysical principle that goes beyond the strict limits of perception. In his last works, Berkeley employed a broader sense of perception that allowed him to prove the existence of God from causality.

According to Berkeley, causality makes direct reference to the action of God in the world. Causal relations belong exclusively to God, an assertion that reflects some elements of the system of Malebranche. When we find a certain connection between two ideas, we do not verify a relationship of cause and effect: there is only a connection between the sign and the thing signified.

This statement leads to Berkeley's theory of divine visual language: "God speaks to men using arbitrary signs, external and sensible, which bear no resemblance or necessary connection to the things that they mean and suggest; and that, through countless combinations of these signs, we discover

---

126. Berkeley, *Dialogues*, 2.2.

and we know an infinite variety of things."[127] This divine language is the medium by means of which God speaks to us and governs us.

The visual language theory reveals voluntarist and occasionalist elements that, similarly to what happened with the system of Malebranche, tend to reduce the divine transcendence. As regards morality, the human good—happiness—is eternal life. Therefore, faith in God, in the future life and in moral duties are the only wise principles. Moreover, one can observe a certain legalism in his moral theory: the goodness of an action lies in obedience to the laws, which have their origin in a decree of the divine will. This decree does not take into account personal judgment on the factual circumstances of moral action. Therefore, in his moral theory, the voluntarism of the divine visual language reappears.

Berkeley's epistemological theory demonstrates the logical consequence of empiricism: without a theory of abstraction, empiricism must remain within the limits of pure subjective sensation. The religious context in which Berkeley's thought moves led him to maintain two fundamental metaphysical principles: the existence of God and the spirituality and immortality of the soul. But what endured of his philosophy was his radical empiricism, which led to the skepticism of Hume.

3.5 DAVID HUME (1711–1776)

a) Life and Works

He was born in Edinburgh in 1711. He began studies in law, but then abandoned them to engage in philosophy and literature. In 1724 he moved to France, where he remained for some years. While there, he wrote *A Treatise on Human Nature*, published in London in 1738. It is his major work, although it did not obtain the effect desired by its author. In 1742 he wrote *Essays Moral*

---

127. George Berkeley, *Alciphron*, 4.7.

and Political. After a failed attempt to obtain a professorship at the University of Edinburgh, he accepted the post of secretary to General St. Clair, with whom Hume traveled through different European countries.

During this period, he reworked the *Treatise.* In 1751 he would see the first fruits of that reworking: he published *Philosophical Essays concerning Human Understanding,* whose second edition will be named *An Enquiry concerning Human Understanding.* In 1751 he also published *An Enquiry concerning the Principles of Morals.* Other works of philosophical interest are: *Dissertation on the Passions* and *Four Dissertations,* both published in 1757.

Hume also wrote a history of England, and discourses about political issues. He was appointed secretary of the British Embassy in Paris, where he lived between 1763 and 1766. From 1769 until his death in 1776 he lived in Edinburgh. After his death, his *Dialogues concerning Natural Religion* and a brief autobiography were published.

b) The General Outline of Hume's Thought

In *A Treatise on Human Nature,* Hume affirmed that in a certain sense, all knowledge depends on the science about man. Anthropology is the basis of all knowledge. We must reestablish the science of human nature to end philosophical disputes, which are simply consequences of an erroneous method. Hume's new method, following the line of British philosophers who preceded him, will be based on experience and observation.

The idea that philosophy has a very practical purpose, which we have seen in many modern philosophers, is present in Hume; philosophy serves to find the best way through which men can become happy. To this end, Hume developed his theory of knowledge. He thought that for men to be happy, they must keep to the data of experience and reject the illusory pretensions of metaphysical reasoning.

The theory of knowledge should help man to verify his capabilities and powers. With a radical empiricism as the basis of his epistemology, Hume would be led towards extreme skepticism. The timid assertions of Lockean empiricism, deepened and radicalized by Berkeley, come to their ultimate conclusion with Hume's epistemological theory.

c) Theory of Knowledge

1) The Notion of Experience

Hume said that if we want to build a philosophy that has the same accuracy as physics, it is essential not to exceed the limits of experience. Man cannot go beyond the experimental area, if he does not want to run the risk of entering a chimerical world. The affirmation of experience as the only area of scientific knowledge is the basic principle of the philosophy of Hume.

Throughout his work, Hume argued on various interpretations about the ultimate meaning of experience.

One of them is to identify experience with a bundle of sensations, vivid and immediate sense impressions, that man receives.

But another meaning of experience would be given by the set of common perceptions that are rooted in custom. In the first case we have an actual experience of feeling; in the second, experience refers to the past, where memory plays a determining role.

We can say therefore that taken in the first sense, experience is the contact we have with sensible phenomenon, with the immediate reality that impresses upon the senses. Sensation is characterized by its vividness and immediacy.

Custom however, is the guide of human life since it makes experience become useful. Without the influence of custom, man would always be in the dark about any matter of fact, except for those things that are presented immediately in sensation.

2) *Impressions and Ideas*

Later, we will discuss the important role that Hume gave to custom. For now, we will briefly look at the various types of perceptions he presents. Hume claimed that the contents of consciousness are of two kinds: *impressions* and *ideas*. The difference between an impression and an idea lies in their different degrees of intensity. Impressions have a greater degree of force and vivacity; they include all forms of sensation, passion and emotion. Ideas, however, are weak images that impressions leave in the mind and in reasoning.

These distinctions are important when establishing the truth of a philosophical notion. If we want to discern the meaning of a philosophical term, it is necessary to clarify from which impression the notion was derived. If we cannot determine any original impression, that philosophical term is meaningless.

Every idea is necessarily derived from an impression. The impression is sensed, whereas the idea is thought. Intellectual knowledge, for Hume, is none other than weak sensible knowledge. Impressions can be sensations or reflections. Sensation is the ultimate foundation of our knowledge, and it comes from unknown causes. Reflections are derived from our ideas, but the original source is always a sensation.

Humean agnosticism concerning the causes that produce sensations ends up making impressions become the ultimate content of consciousness. Consciousness has no opening to external reality: it is enclosed in itself and merely knows it's own impressions. Sensations do not give us any indication of anything that is beyond the sensation itself; and the senses cannot distinguish between the subject and the external objects.[128]

---

128. See David Hume, *A Treatise of Human Nature*, 1.4.2.

3) The Association of Ideas and their Effects

Although sensations are independent of each other, the imagination and the memory unify the impressions and ideas that flow from them. Imagination and memory perform this operation following three principles: resemblance, contiguity in space and time, and the cause-effect relationship.

These three principles are qualities of the imagination. Hume needed this explanation to clarify the natural tendency man has to consider the agreement between knowledge and reality as normal. Hume spoke of a kind of pre-established harmony between the course of nature and the succession of our ideas,[129] but without abandoning his radical agnosticism.

The most significant effect of this association of ideas is that of the complex idea. Like Locke, Hume classified complex ideas into substances, modes and relations. Among the relations, first there are natural relationships, which are defined by the three types of association and second, there are philosophical relations, which originate from the comparison of ideas without any connecting principle. Substances and modes are reduced to the natural associations or relations of ideas. They are, according to Hume's definition: "nothing but a collection of simple ideas that are united by the imagination, and have a particular name assigned them, by which we are able to recall, either to ourselves or others, that collection."[130]

4) Abstract Ideas

Following the criticism of Berkeley regarding the abstract ideas of Locke, Hume said that every idea is particular. If I think, for example, about the general idea of a line, I will always have an idea of a line with a certain degree of

---

129. See David Hume, *An Enquiry concerning Human Understanding*, 5.2.

130. Hume, *A Treatise of Human Nature*, 1.1.6.

quantity and quality. Hume welcomed abstraction, but only as the individuation of the original impression of the idea. I can compare two ideas under the principle of similarity, but I will never manage to conceive of a common nature between the two ideas. The universal, for Hume, is only nominal, never essential.

The constitution of general ideas is a product of custom, which tends to always put a particular idea under a general name. The general idea is usually nothing more than a signifying function of names, which goes beyond the nature of the idea.

5) Relations of Ideas and Matters of Fact

We just saw that Hume distinguished between two types of relations: natural and philosophical. Among the philosophical ones, there are two broad classes: those that depend only on the ideas, and those that depend on experience. The first are the ones that can be an object of demonstrative knowledge and are called relations of ideas. Geometry, Algebra and Mathematics are based on these types of relations.

The second—philosophical relations dependent on experience—are called matters of fact. Unlike the relationship of ideas, they can change without changing the related ideas. Hume gave a very clear example: the fact that in any triangle the sum of its angles is equal to two right angles is a relation of ideas, and therefore invariable. In contrast, the relation of contiguity and distance between two objects can change without necessitating any change in the objects themselves or in their ideas. The greater or lesser distance depends on a matter of fact, not of reason. Men do not have demonstrative knowledge about such matters: we can only have moral or probable knowledge about them.

Consequently, demonstrative science regarding questions on quantity and number is possible. However, for the majority of other matters that form part of knowledge—that is, matters of fact rooted in experience—the only knowledge possible is moral knowledge. In a strict sense, knowledge is only demonstrative; whereas moral knowing is closer to a belief.

d) The Critique of Causality

Knowledge of cause and effect is not *a priori*, as rationalists claimed. Consistent with his basic empiricism, Hume argued that in the event that this knowledge is possible, it should come from the senses, that is, from experience.

Every inference that man performs starting from experience is the effect of custom, not reasoning. The inference or causal connection of any matter of fact or real existence always derives from some object present in the memory or the senses, and from a habitual union of two objects. On the other hand, when the mind assents to this inference, in reality it makes an act of belief. Causal inference is the result of belief and habitual union between two objects.

In the cause-effect relation, according to Hume, there are different types of relations.

The first is the relation of contiguity: whenever the two objects considered as cause and effect are contiguous.

Then we have the relation of temporal priority of the cause with respect to the effect.

Third, there is another relation called a *constant conjunction*. Nevertheless, according to Hume, these three types of relations do not give a full explanation of the cause-effect phenomenon. In the idea of this relation, there is an essential element called the *necessary connection*.

The problem lies in the fact that man does not have sense knowledge of the necessary connection. Experience can only observe the conjunction, but not the hidden force that moves from cause to effect. Consequently, Hume claimed that the necessary connection between cause and effect is the work of the imagination:

"The first time a man saw the communication of motion by impulse, as by the shock of two billiard balls, he could not pronounce that the one event was *connected*; but only that it was *conjoined* with the other. After he has observed several instances of this nature, he then pronounces them to be *connected*. What alteration has happened to give rise to this new idea of *connexion*? Nothing but that he now *feels* these events to be connected in his imagination, and can readily foretell the existence of one from the appearance of the other. When we say, therefore, that one object is connected with another, we mean only that they have acquired a connexion in our thought, and give rise to this inference, by which they become proofs of each other's existence: A conclusion which is somewhat extraordinary, but which seems founded on sufficient evidence."[131]

Hume does not claim to solve the mystery of causality. On the contrary, based on his radical empiricism, which makes him think that perceptions are the only beings present in the mind, he only wants to give a reason for the way the common man connects diverse facts, the reason being *custom*. Custom, for Hume, is a true principle of human nature that makes things easier for ordinary life. However, this principle does not overcome his deep skepticism, which leads him to present the solution to the problem of causality as merely pragmatic.

e) The Outside World and the Subject's Identity

1) Belief in the External World

Man naturally tends to think that an external world exists. This same inclination makes man consider that the images presented by the senses are external objects themselves. However, against this peaceful and universal opinion, philosophy teaches us that we only know an image or perception, and we

---

131. Hume, *An Enquiry concerning Human Understanding,* 7.2.59.

are unable to explain what relationship there is between a supposed external object and sense image.

The connection between the outside world and sensible knowledge is a problem that has to be solved without leaving the realm of experience, since it is a matter of fact. We cannot have recourse to the veracity of God as Descartes had done, because this would not account for the errors of the senses: if God is the guarantor of our senses, they would be infallible, which is not the case.

Moreover, faithful to the modern tradition, Hume believed that the secondary qualities of objects are subjective, together with some primary qualities, such as extension and solidity.

Hume recognized that the problem of the existence of the external world is unsolvable from a gnoseological viewpoint. In the thinking of Hume, there is room only to affirm that there is a tendency of human nature, which produces the opinion of the continuous and distinct existence of bodies. This opinion originates in the imagination that acts on two qualities of impressions: consistency and coherence, which present the world as something real and lasting.

2) The Identity of the Self

Hume, in perfect continuity with his professed radical empiricism, gave this definition of the mind:

"That what we call a mind, is nothing but a heap or collection of different perceptions, united together by certain relations, and supposed, though falsely, to be endowed with a perfect simplicity and identity."[132]

The only source of self-consciousness is a sensation that does not correspond to any perception, but only to a figment of the imagination. This sensation occurs when we reflect on our perceptions. The identity of the self depends on the laws of association of ideas already alluded to: resemblance, contiguity and causation.

---

132. Hume, *A Treatise of Human Nature*, 1.4.2.

The skeptical conclusion (founded on epistemological grounds) about the possibility of establishing one's identity, did not convince even Hume. There is a kind of drama between Hume the philosopher and Hume the ordinary man. The ordinary Hume says: "Here then I find myself absolutely and necessarily determined to live, and talk, and act like other people in the common affairs of life." But he effectively decreed the defeat of philosophy, which is now unable to solve the ordinary problems of human existence.

f) Morality

Hume tried to save the dichotomy between philosophy and natural tendencies with his moral theory. Although we cannot establish the identity of the self from an epistemological point of view, it can be done from a moral standpoint, through a practical study of the passions and personal interest.

Morality cannot be based on reason. After Hume's critique of causality, the principle that the "ought to be" should depend on being or on human nature cannot be valid. The foundation of morality, for Hume, is in the feelings, more specifically, in the passions.

Hume's morality focuses on the concepts of pleasure and pain. Virtue produces a pleasant impression and vice, an unpleasant one. The ultimate reason for human action is the avoidance of pain and the desire for pleasure. Morality, therefore, is reduced to a mere sentiment imbued with necessity, while the scope of reason is subordinated to the passions.

Reason can never constitute sufficient grounds for action. It can only show the passions the most appropriate means for attaining happiness. We quote this famous passage from the *Treatise*:

"Reason is, and ought only to be the slave of the passions, and can never aim for any other office than to serve and obey them."[133]

___

133. Hume, *A Treatise of Human Nature*, 1.4.7.

The passions are closely related to perceptions. As we may recall, Hume thought that perceptions can be impressions or ideas. Impressions can be original (impressions of sensations) or secondary (impressions of reflections). Passions belong to this second type and are divided into direct and indirect ones.

The direct passions are those that arise immediately from pain or pleasure, such as desire, aversion, grief, joy, expectancy, fear, despair and security.

The indirect passions also come from pain or pleasure but, in their constitution, other qualities come into play. These are the passions of pride, humility, ambition, vanity, love and hatred.

Among the factors involved in the formation of the passions, Hume attached particular importance to sympathy, which is the tendency of the subject to enter into relationships and communication with other subjects. The cause of sympathy is the similarity between men, and it is an element that introduces a kind of altruism in human relations.

In *A Treatise of Human Nature*, once he addressed the issue of the passions, Hume began a study of the will and of freedom. For Hume, the will is not a faculty. It is just a mode of the passion of "desire":

"Of all the immediate effects of pain and pleasure, there is none more remarkable than the WILL."[134]

Hume defined the will more specifically:

"By the will I mean nothing but the internal impression we feel and are conscious of, when we knowingly give rise to any new motion of our body, or new perception of our mind."[135]

In this regard, the will is regarded as an internal impression, and thus it is not voluntary. This consideration presents a major obstacle in the affirmation of freedom. Hume argued that the necessity that reigns in the material world also reigns in the world of human actions.

---

134. Hume, *A Treatise of Human Nature*, 2.3.1.

135. Hume, *A Treatise of Human Nature*, 2.3.1.

Freedom is just a false sense of indifference that we have in the face of our actions, which leads us to imagine that our will is not subject to anything else. But in reality, we can never be free from necessity, even though we *experience* the feeling of freedom.

"A spectator can commonly infer our actions from our motives and character; and even where he cannot, he concludes in general, that he might, were he perfectly acquainted with every circumstance of our situation and temper, and the most secret springs of our complexion and disposition. Now this is the very essence of necessity."

In the thought of Hume there is room only for a certain kind of freedom: the freedom of spontaneity that does not preclude necessity as such. It is in contrast with force or violence that ordinary people consider the idea of necessity. Freedom of spontaneity means absence of coercion or violence. If necessity means uniformity in the causal relationships, the connection between the cause and action in human actions would be as constant as in natural operations. Hume's conclusion is obvious: both the natural world and the human world are part of the realm of necessity.

g) Politics and Religion

According to Hume, man has a great desire for sociability. All human desires refer to society: pleasure is less if it does not rejoice in the company of others. For Hume, the greatest punishment that a man can suffer is absolute loneliness.

When analyzing the origin of society, Hume moved away from the individualistic positions of Hobbes and Locke. Necessity, instinct, the congenital weakness, cause man to be in the midst of society from the beginning of his existence. Man naturally tends to seek his own interests, but at the same time this selfish tendency is tempered by a tendency to disinterested benevolence. The bond that strengthens and unites society is not an alleged original contract, but the common interest that men have in preserving society. For this common interest to prevail over private interests, governments are established, whose main task is to enforce laws for co-existence. "Common interest and utility beget infallibly a standard of right and wrong among the parties concerned."[136]

Hume dedicated two specific works to the philosophy of religion, the *Dialogues Concerning Natural Religion*, and *The Natural History of Religion*. Hume thought that the study of religion should be done from the perspective of anthropology. What must be studied is not so much the essence and the attributes of God, but the religious sentiment that man possesses. The method of the philosophy of religion will be the same as that of Hume's entire philosophical project: experience and observation.

For Hume, religion is a kind of philosophy. As with any other kind of knowledge, religion cannot go beyond the realm of experience, if it claims to be true: "All the philosophy, therefore, in the world, and all the religion, which is nothing but a species of philosophy, will never be able to carry us beyond the usual course of experience, or give us measures of conduct and behaviour different from those which are furnished by reflections on common life."[137]

In his *Natural History of Religion*, Hume tried to establish the origin of religious feeling. The philosopher believed that this source is the fear of death, the fear of unhappiness reserved for the bad and the desire of happiness promised to the good. These feelings are actually passions. The passions are at the basis of religious sentiments and they are the cause of "the universal propensity to believe in an invisible, intelligent power."[138] According to Hume, this tendency is the mark that the divine creator left imprinted on his work. The historical religions have distorted the image of the divine, mixing true religion with superstition, bigotry and intolerance.

For Hume what is the true religion? Skepticism reappeared with renewed vigor: "The only point of theology in which we shall find a consent of mankind almost universal, is that there

136. David Hume, *An Enquiry concerning the Principles of Morals*, 4.

137. Hume, *An Enquiry concerning Human Understanding*, 11.

138. David Hume, *The Natural History of Religion*, 15.

186 A HISTORY OF MODERN PHILOSOPHY

is an invisible, intelligent power in the world; but whether this power be supreme or subordinate; whether confined to one being or distributed among several; what attributes, qualities, connexions, or principles of action ought to be ascribed to those beings—concerning all these points there is the widest difference in the popular systems of theology."[139]

God is considered an object of worship in the temple rather than an object of discussion among schools of thought. Religion is a psychological fact that cannot be eliminated from human nature, and is reduced to a simple feeling that is instinctive in nature, without any rational or supernatural basis.

* * *

David Hume's philosophy brought empiricism to its ultimate consequences. This current of thought, which began with the technological confidence of Francis Bacon, ended with the defeat of a philosophy that is not even able to assert the identity of the self. Skepticism reappeared on the scene. Kant would have to deal with the crisis caused by the extreme empiricism of the Scottish philosopher.

Sources

Francis Bacon, *The Works of Francis Bacon*, James Spedding, Robert Leslie Ellis, and Douglas Denon Heath, eds. (London: Longmans & Co. 1858).

George Berkeley, *The Works of George Berkeley, Bishop of Cloyne*, Arthur Aston Luce & Thomas Edmund Jessop, eds. (London: Nelson, 1948).

Thomas Hobbes, *The English Works of Thomas Hobbes of Malmesbury*, William Molesworth ed. (London: Longman, Brown, Green, and Longmans, 1839–1845).

David Hume, *The Philosophical Works* (London: T.H. Green & T.H. Grose, 1974–1875.)

John Locke, *The Works of John Locke*, Thomas Tegg et al., eds., (London 1853).

---

139. Hume, *The Natural History of Religion*, 14.

PART FOUR
THE ENLIGHTENMENT

4.1 THE ENLIGHTENMENT: AN INTRODUCTION

A*ufklärung*, Enlightenment, *Illuminismo, Les lumières, Ilustración*, are words used in different languages to identify a cultural movement, a way of seeing the world, a *Weltanschauung* that while containing obvious philosophical elements exceeds the strictly philosophical realm.

Chronologically, the Enlightenment belongs to the eighteenth century, and is a predominantly European cultural phenomenon, whose most important developments occurred in England, France and Germany. The historical period marked by the Enlightenment was full of intellectual and philosophical stimuli but at the same time lacked a figure that can be considered an obligatory reference point. In this sense, it is analogous to the Renaissance period. There was a philosophical environment that encompassed everything: in this lies its specificity: the enlightenment was an atmosphere, a way of thinking.

Immanuel Kant tried to define this new state of culture. In a pamphlet entitled *What is the Enlightenment?* Kant answered the question as follows:

"Enlightenment is man's emergence from his self-imposed immaturity. Immaturity is the inability to make use of one's understanding without direction from another. This immaturity is self-imposed, when its cause lies not in the lack of understanding, but the lack of resolution and courage to use one's own understanding without direction from another.

Sapere aude! Have courage to use your own understanding! So this is the motto of the Enlightenment."[140]

As we can see from the definition of Kant, the theoretical key to understand the Enlightenment is the role given to reason. But what is reason? It is not the rationalist reason of seventeenth-century metaphysics, even if the Enlightenment inherited its optimism in the powers of reason. It is rather the idea of reason proper to the British empiricists: an adherence to the data of the senses and the results of experiments.

Reason in the Enlightenment is no longer the place of spirits, the reservoir of innate ideas, but is rather a faculty, understood as the capacity to know. It is an inexhaustible capacity or force, which will lead us to the knowledge of the unfathomable mysteries of nature. The attachment of eighteenth-century reason to sensory experience will promote the development of the natural sciences: botany, chemistry, zoology, natural history and medicine.

On the other hand, faith in the ability of reason is manifested in another key concept for understanding the Enlightenment: the notion of progress. The intellectuals of this period thought that the Enlightenment would lead to a more humane, prudent and comfortable life.

The Enlightenment would be the first time in history in which a new discipline emerged: the *Philosophy of History*. With it men undertook an analysis of the history of man from a universal and progressive standpoint. History is seen as the development of reason, which takes man out of medieval darkness and into the light of rationality.

This optimistic and progressive vision of history is closely related to another feature of Enlightenment reason: the rejection of tradition. For the Enlightenment, all social or spiritual phenomena that cannot be explained by human reason are a myth or superstition.

---

140. Immanuel Kant, *Was ist Aufklärung?* Ak 8.35.

Thus, the anti-traditionalism of the Enlightenment is embodied in the rejection of revealed religion, especially Catholicism, and in the theoretical construction of deism, that is, a religion without mysteries, cut to the measure of reason; it finds it sufficient to affirm the existence of God, the immortality of the soul and the afterlife.

The enlightened attitude towards religion will become manifest in Germany with the process of the rationalization of dogmas; and in England and France with the defense of tolerance, which in this period will often have religious indifferentism as a basis.

Along with the rejection of revealed religion came the desire for social change. The hereditary transmission of power, social inequality dependent on the circumstances of one's birth, the colonial pact of different lands, appear to the Enlightened as inexplicable from a rational standpoint. Thus, the Enlightenment, inspired by Locke's political theory, would present a liberal and democratic political program which, in France, would be identified with the revolutionary program.

Unfortunately, the alliance between Throne and Altar, characteristic of the *Ancien Régime*, did not help people to understand the difference between the historical circumstances and the divine aspects of the Catholic Church. Attacks against the established social order—which were largely necessary and just, in defense of the dignity of the human person—were directed against the Church. Thus, because of the misunderstanding of one party with the other, the political and social philosophy of the eighteenth century bears the stamp of anti-Catholicism, though there are important exceptions.

Law and morals, two basic areas of human knowledge, suffered major changes in this period. Enlightened morality is secular, that is, it does not have any relation with transcendence, and it rather manifests important utilitarian features. At the same time, natural law, which the second scholasticism presented as united to the transcendent destiny of man, would also be secularized. The new natural law would tend toward the affirmation of the absolute autonomy of temporal affairs.

Rationalist systems of law would arise, based on a strongly voluntarist vision of positive law.

The Enlightenment was an elite cultural movement. The bourgeoisie was the social group where the new principles most vigorously developed. After some time, the categories of Enlightened thought would spread throughout Europe and America, setting up a form of popular thought.

The belief in progress puts the Enlightenment in relation with positivism; the concepts of morality and politics link up with liberalism and utilitarianism; the universal vision of history and the affirmation of rationality in its development relate the enlightenment's attitude to Hegel and in a sense, to Marx.

However, the increased awareness of some aspects of the dignity of the human person made manifest the Christian *humus* that served as the basis for modernity, although such a *humus* is often hidden under strong forces of secularization, understood as total and absolute autonomy of the temporal with respect to the transcendental.

4.2 THE ENGLISH ENLIGHTENMENT

In England, the Enlightenment basically focused on the areas of religion and morality. This does not mean that the Enlightenment did not have other interests, especially in the realm of empirical science. Moreover, a most important intellectual figure in the British Isles during this period, who would have a decisive influence on the development of European philosophy, particularly in Kant's system, was not a philosopher but a scientist: Sir Isaac Newton (1642–1727).

a) The Physics of Newton

Newton completed the worldview offered by Galileo, Copernicus and Kepler; he is considered to be the father of modern physics. Among his most famous works must be mentioned *Philosophia naturalis principia mathematica* (1687, 1713 and 1726) and *Optics* (1704).

Newton rejected and proved false the Aristotelian doctrine of the distinction between the laws of terrestrial and celestial bodies. Then he successfully applied his scientific method in various fields of research, which assumed that all phenomena of motion in nature can be deduced mathematically from the principles of mechanics.

However, Newton did not agree with Galileo regarding the mathematical structure of reality. Mathematics is a methodological tool, but the scientific method is based on experience: we must first discover the laws of mechanical nature inductively, starting from experience, so that we can proceed by deduction.

Newtonian science is a science of phenomena: "All that does not proceed from phenomena should be defined as a hypothesis; and hypotheses, both the metaphysical and the physical, either occult or mechanical qualities, have no place in experimental philosophy. In this, propositions are inferred from the phenomena and they are generalized by induction. Thus was discovered impenetrability, mobility, the momentum of bodies and consequently, the laws of motion and gravity."[141]

Although Newton rejected the use of assumptions, there are two concepts in his physical system that were in themselves assumptions. These were *absolute time* and *space*, of which he gave a theological interpretation. These authentic "speculative hypotheses" form the field in which things move. In the universe there is no empty space. The world of Newton is still a mechanistic world. At the same time, it is a world where God is involved not only with its creation and preservation, but also actively, by correcting any imperfections in the movements.

b) English Deism

The topic of religion was a privileged field of speculation of the enlightened English court. By Deism we mean a movement of religious thought which, in spite of a certain uniformity, presented various theoretical attitudes.

---

141. Isaac Newton, *Philosophiae naturalis principia mathematica*, 2.

The predecessor of the eighteenth century deists is Lord Herbert of Cherbury (1583–1648). Among his works may be mentioned *Tractatus de veritate* (1624), *De causis errorum* (1645) and *De religione gentilium* (1645, 1663). Cherbury believed that all men have common notions, which are *a priori*, universal and certain. They are impressed by God in man, and man knows them through a natural instinct. Sensitive knowledge would not be possible without resorting to these concepts.

Some of these common notions are the basis of so-called natural religion. For Cherbury, the five truths, which are or should be supported by all religions are: the existence of a supreme being; the obligation on the part of men to worship this being; the moral life is the most important religious cult; vices and sins must be expiated by repentance; and the existence of another life where reward or punishment will be given according to one's behavior.

Lord Herbert of Cherbury wanted to achieve a *pax religiosa*. Bearing in mind the historical circumstances of the wars of religion in Europe, Cherbury did not reject the possibility and usefulness of revelation. Rather, he considered reason as the ultimate judge of revealed truth.

John Locke, as we have seen, wrote in 1695 *The Reasonableness of Christianity*, which evidenced a strong tendency toward the rationalization of dogma. Many British intellectuals followed in Locke's footsteps. However, deism strictly speaking radicalizes this trend.

Concerning this trend of rationalizing religion, Copleston wrote: "The Deists were rationalists who believed in God. . . . Eighteenth-century Deism meant de-supernaturalizing of religion and the refusal to accept any religious propositions on authority. For the Deists, reason, and reason alone, was the judge of truth in religion as elsewhere."[142]

---

142. Frederick Copleston, *A History of Philosophy, vol. 5: Hobbes to Hume* (London-New York: Continuum, 2003), p. 163.

The most important authors of this movement are John Toland (1670–1722), with his work *Christianity not Mysterious* (1696), and Matthew Tindal (ca. 1656–1733), who wrote *Christianity as old as the Creation, or, the Gospel a Republication of the Religion of Nature*. Another author worth mentioning is Henry St. John, Viscount of Bolingbroke (1678–1751), who presented Christ as God's instrument to confirm natural religion.

The intellectual attitude of Samuel Clarke (1675–1729) was different. He was an Anglican priest who sought to demonstrate the rational nature of the faith in open controversy with Hobbes and Spinoza. By means of twelve propositions, Clarke showed the existence of God and of some of the divine attributes. An admirer of Newton, he related Newtonian absolute space and time with the divine existence, an issue that would provoke a controversy with Leibniz. But he moved away from the deists as he affirmed the moral necessity of revelation, given the current state of humanity. Within revelation there are truths that are beyond the capacity of reason, yet do not contradict reason.

Anglican Bishop Joseph Butler (1692–1752) strongly opposed the deists. Author of the book *The Analogy of Religion, Natural and Revealed, to the Constitution and Course of Nature*, he wanted to show that the belief stating that Christianity is true is not unreasonable and, if it were, then the belief systems about nature would also be unreasonable. In the acceptance of revelation or of some natural truths, like the immortality of the soul, there are always difficulties. However, also in the field of knowledge of nature's system there are also analogous difficulties, and this is not a valid reason to reject knowledge of the natural world.

c) Moral Philosophy

The other field of study typical of the English Enlightenment is moral philosophy. The two great exponents of English ethical thought of this period are Anthony Ashley-Cooper, Earl of Shaftesbury (1671–1713) and Francis Hutcheson (1694–1746).

Ashley-Cooper is known for his *Inquiry concerning Virtue and Merit*. He believed that man has innate moral ideas that incline him to seek his own good, which must be harmonized with the good of society.

In controversy with Hobbes, he did not think that men are evil by nature. Benevolence is an essential part of morality and it has its roots in human nature. Every man also enjoys a moral sense, which makes it possible to distinguish between right and wrong behavior.

Morality, based on virtue, is autonomous with respect to religion. Virtue must be sought for its own sake. This, however, does not mean that Shaftesbury rejected transcendence. True virtue includes piety towards God. Therefore, "the perfection and elevation of virtue is due to faith in God."

Meanwhile, Hutcheson followed in the footsteps of Shaftesbury. He proposed ideas with a utilitarian bent, which would be taken up in the nineteenth century by Bentham and by John Stuart Mill:

"Comparing the moral quality of actions in order to provide a criterion for our choices among the various actions proposed, or to find which of them has the highest moral excellence, we are led by our moral sense of virtue to judge in this way: to equal degrees of happiness which we hope will follow the actions, virtue is in proportion to the number of people to whom the happiness will be extended . . . so that action is best which procures the greatest happiness for the greatest number of people, and the worst action is that which causes unhappiness to the greatest number."[143]

In Hutcheson we find a sense of happiness that is rather hedonistic, and a tendency to identify morality with the aesthetic: together with the moral sense men have the aesthetic sense. Influenced by Butler, Hutcheson tried to unite morality with metaphysics and theology, but he will be remembered in

---

143. Francis Hutcheson, *Inquiry into the Origin of Our Ideas of Beauty and Virtue*, 2.3.

history as a forerunner of the utilitarianism of Bentham and John Stuart Mill.

4.3 THE FRENCH ENLIGHTENMENT

While we tend to think that the Enlightenment was a typically French phenomenon, we cannot forget that its first followers were English. To this chronological fact must be added the profound influence of the English Enlightenment on the French. The popular image of the French Enlightenment—*les Lumières*—is due to the radicalization of some theoretical enlightened attitudes which in the British Isles appeared under the cloak of moderation. Excesses have always had a greater resonance in the collective memory, and materialism, atheism, the attacks on the Catholic Church and the horrors of the revolutionary Terror are characteristic elements of the popular image of the French Enlightenment.

Although these elements are true, not all manifestations of eighteenth-century French thought can be forced into this scheme. There is a common family air within which we must make distinctions. In the following pages we will try to provide an overall picture of these *philosophes*, who are important not so much for the depth of their ideas, but for the influence they had on popular categories of thought.

a) Pierre Bayle, the Precursor

Pierre Bayle (1647–1706), whom we have seen when we studied libertarianism, is considered by most historians as the main precursor of the *philosophes*. Bayle presented a set of theoretical principles which would be extensively developed during the eighteenth century.

The author of the *Historical and Critical Dictionary* believed that the theological disputes between Catholicism and Protestantism and between Catholic schools of thought, are all confusing and useless. The cause of these disputes is the lack of clarity in judgments and the presence of prejudices. Basically, all agree on the fundamental things. If theological controversies are so frequent, metaphysical disputes are even more so. Whatever one may say concerning the rational demonstration of the existence of God or the immortality of the soul, there will always be demonstrations to prove the opposite.

In addition, there remains the problem of evil in the world, incompatible with the existence of a powerful, infinite and omniscient God.

Faced with metaphysical and theological disputes we are left with no option but the practice of tolerance. Tolerance is the only rational response to the various points of view on things beyond the power of reason. Furthermore, it is necessary to separate religion and morality. According to Bayle, the life lived by men of all time shows that there is no inextricable link between religious belief and moral practice. So he did not see any problem in asserting the possibility of a society of atheists who act in a morally upright manner.

The critique to the intellectual attitude of Bayle, considered by some as akin to atheism, arose from everywhere. In controversy with Bayle, Leibniz attempted to give a response to the problem of the relationship between divine omnipotence and the existence of evil. However, tolerance as the basis for civil coexistence—which in Bayle has strong connotations of indifference—and the separation between religion and morality are the inheritance Bayle left for future generations.

b) The Encyclopedia

If unanimity among historians to consider Bayle as the great forerunner of the Enlightenment is almost complete, then likewise is the affirmation of the importance of the *Encyclopédie* as a symbol of the new current of thought. The *Encyclopédie ou Dictionnaire raisonné des arts et des métiers* was the work of many authors, under the guidance of Diderot and D'Alembert. The latter retired from writing in 1758. The Encyclopedia consisted of thirty-five volumes, published between 1751 and 1780. The editing of the work was not easy, since the French government considered some items as detrimental to both political power and to the authority of religion.

As with any work in which many minds intervened, the entire Encyclopedia is uneven from the philosophical and scientific standpoint. Authors such as Montesquieu, Turgot, Rousseau, D'Holbach appeared alongside others who are rather unknown.

However, what interests us most when dealing with the Encyclopedia are not matters of detail, but rather the basic spirit and purpose of this work. The purpose was to provide the reader of its time with a body of information on the elements of the past and present, and to lay the foundations of a future society that would be more humane and rational. It was not a purely scientific or instructive aim: in the end, the encyclopedic project sustained an ideology of a rationalist nature that questioned the certainties received by tradition, and judged, although moderately for reasons of political prudence, the very foundations of political power and of the Catholic Church.

As a child of its time, the Encyclopedia must not be seen only as an anticlerical manifesto. This would not be fair since there are articles concerning faith written with sufficient orthodox standards. Moreover, the Encyclopedia served as a positive revaluation of the popular arts and crafts. Indeed, for the first time the curious reader was offered an almost complete picture of manual trades, agricultural techniques, and the various complicated processes of craftsmanship. Empiricism, which is at the origin of the Enlightenment, along with many elements of rationalism and mechanicism (the consideration of the material universe as a vast machine), served as an adequate theoretical framework for the rehabilitation of the technical trades.

The two main promoters of the Encyclopedia, as we have already mentioned, were Denis Diderot (1713–1784) and Jean Le Rond D'Alembert (1717–1783).

Diderot received influences from Shaftesbury. He wrote *Essai sur le mérite et la vertu*, which is a translation of Shaftesbury's work with personal additions. He was in Russia, where he engaged in philosophical conversations with his protector, the Empress Catherine II. As regards his religious attitudes, he went through different stages, which included elements of deism, pantheism and atheism. Diderot did not present a stable philosophical system, and in order to obtain an overall picture of his thought we ought to combine the materialism of his *Le rêve de D'Alembert* (*The Dream of D'Alembert*) with the moral idealism of some of his articles in the Encyclopedia.

The thought of D'Alembert seems to be more consistent. Besides being a philosopher, he was a great mathematician and physicist. From the point of view of his philosophy, the Preliminary Discourse of the Encyclopedia has special importance. D'Alembert considered Locke as the father of scientific philosophy and welcomed the progress of philosophy in the Age of the Enlightenment. At the core of his philosophy there is a firm phenomenalism, which is an authentic positivism *avant la lettre*: both the philosopher and the scientist ought to describe and relate the phenomena observed empirically. To go beyond the phenomenon is to go beyond the capabilities of knowledge.

As regards morality, D'Alembert thought that it is based on a sense of duty towards others: an awareness that will support the establishment of a civil society founded on the agreement between one's own interest and the ends of society: happiness and the common welfare.

c) Materialism

If the symbol of the French Enlightenment is the Encyclopedia, the two most interesting theoretical developments—one because of its radicalism and the other because of its vast historical consequences—are materialism and its socio-political theory.

Regarding materialism, its most classic representative is Julien Offray de La Mettrie (1709–1751). In his famous book *L'homme machine* (*Machine Man*), and also in his *Histoire Naturelle de l'Âme* (*Natural History of the Soul*) and *L'Homme Plante* (*Plant Man*), he developed a base materialism that made everything, including ideas, depend on sensitivity. The key to understanding what man is resides in the physiological processes. The difference between man, animal and plant is just one of degree. An agnostic in the religious field and a hedonist in morals, this physician-philosopher proposed one of the possible radical developments of enlightened empiricism. One of his works is entitled: *L'Art de Jouir* (*The Art of Enjoying*).

Along the same materialist lines, we find Baron Paul d'Holbach (1723–1789). He was born in Germany but was French in education. D'Holbach wrote the most important text about materialism in the eighteenth century: *Système de la nature ou des loix du monde physique & du monde moral* (*The System of Nature, or Laws of the Moral and Physical World*, 1770).

This author professed a certain atomism: all things are the result of a conjunction of atoms structured in different ways. The principles of motion are not external, but rather internal to things: attraction and repulsion between atoms. In the case of man, these two principles are called love and hate.

Man, like all other things, tends to preserve his own existence. Self-love, therefore, is the main driving force of human life. This tendency is not incompatible with the search for general welfare. As an enemy of all forms of religiosity, D'Holbach believed that ignorance and fear are the origin of the notion of divinity, and that religion increases anxiety and fear. Once religion is eliminated, we can change the political system of the *Ancien Régime*, and replace it with something more rational. It is clear that d'Holbach did not advocate for a violent revolution.

Etienne Bonnot de Condillac (1715–1780) was not a materialist strictly speaking, but his radical sensism relates him to this school of thought, though he gave room in his system to the spirit and transcendence.

Condillac published in 1746 *Essai sur l'origine des connaissances humaines* (*Essay on the Origin of Human Knowledge*), which showed him to be a faithful disciple of Locke. For him, all knowledge has an empirical origin, whether as a simple or complex idea. Condillac, however, developed his own thought and arrived at personal epistemological positions. In the *Traité des systèmes* (*Treatise of Systems*, 1749) he strongly criticized the metaphysical systems of the seventeenth century: Descartes, Malebranche, Spinoza and Leibniz started with definitions, and then using a geometric method, arrived at conclusions that are arbitrary. We certainly have to systematize knowledge, but we must start from phenomenal data provided by the senses.

In the *Traité des sensations* (*Treatise on Sensations*, 1754) Condillac veered away from Locke to assert that even mental operations like judgment, wanting and comparing are only transformed sensations.

To convince the reader that our only source of knowledge is sensation, Condillac proposes an analogy: imagine a statue that is deprived of all knowledge. Based on one of the crudest senses, the sense of smell, Condillac reconstructs the whole process of knowledge to arrive at intelligence itself.

In a later work, *Essay Concerning Human Understanding*, he explained that the will is determined by an illness of the spirit; it feels the need for a good that is absent. This discomfort or concern is the first principle of all the habits of our soul. This same argument is developed in the *extrait raisonné* (Summary), subsequently added to the *Treatise on Sensations*, and the *Treatise on Animals*. For this reason, there are voluntarist interpretations of Condillac's system, since all passions and ideas depend on the determination of the will.

Despite appearing as a thorough materialist, this French philosopher categorically affirmed the existence of God as supreme cause, and the existence of the immaterial and spiritual soul.

The soul is not a set of sensations, but a single center that unites them. Moreover, regarding the existence of bodies and their qualities, Condillac maintained a cautious position: "Everything that could and should be reasonably inferred is that bodies are beings that cause sensations in us, and have properties of which we know nothing for sure."[144] In short, as noted, Condillac's materialism is *sui generis*, open in a sense to the spirit and transcendence.

The materialism of Claude Adrien Helvetius (1715–1771), however, seems to be less open to transcendence. In his book *De l'esprit* (*On Mind*) he reduced all human capacities to sensory perception. This reductionism applies also to the ethical life, where the fundamental principle of behavior is the pursuit of pleasure. Education should teach men to harmonize their personal interests—the pursuit of pleasure—with the general interest of society, which would ultimately lead to greater pleasure. For this process of education to be effective in society, political freedom must prevail and natural religion should be generalized.

d) Social and Political Theory

The other speculative line that has attracted the attention of historians is the social and political philosophy of the French Enlightenment, where three philosophers, with their ideas, have succeeded in changing the way ordinary people think. We are referring to Montesquieu, Voltaire and Rousseau.

Charles-Louis de Secondat, Baron de La Brède et de Montesquieu (1689–1755), went down in history as the great defender of political freedom and the division of powers. A historian, public servant and a man with a curious spirit, his first book came out in 1721 under the name of *Lettres persanes* (*Persian Letters*). There, Montesquieu criticized the religious and political institutions of France, through a satirical view that the author attributed to a Persian traveler.

But the most important work of the philosopher of Bordeaux is *De l'esprit des lois* (*The Spirit of the Laws*) published in 1748 after seventeen years of preparation. Montesquieu made a comparison between different societies in this voluminous work. Following an empirical-inductive method, he intended

---

144. Étienne Bonnot de Condillac, *Treatise on Sensations*, 4.5.

not only to present a vast collection of data, but he also wanted to understand the cause of the diversity of institutions and ways of life.

Thus, our author came to establish general laws of society. The systems of positive law are different, and the reasons for these differences are many. Among these, Montesquieu pointed out the character of a people, the climate, geography, commerce, and the forms of government. All these circumstances form the spirit of the law.

From the analysis of specific data provided by the study of each society, Montesquieu could establish a theory of law that, in a certain sense, approached the classical doctrine of natural law: for the French philosopher there exist laws of nature, "so called because they derive from our being."[145] Montesquieu admitted the existence of a natural moral law that precedes the system of positive law. He also affirmed the existence of a God, Creator and Preserver of the world, who established fixed rules of justice.

The best known part of his work, which will actually influence subsequent political philosophy to a great degree, concerns the forms of government. For Montesquieu, the forms of government are three: Republican, which can be democratic or aristocratic depending on the number of people involved in the direction of the supreme power, the monarchical and the despotic. The difference between the last two is the fact that, in the case of a monarchy, the king reigns taking into account some fundamental rules, while in the despotic state, the despot governs by caprice.

Any form of government is ruled according to a principle. In the republic, the guiding principle is civic virtue; in the monarchy, honor; and in despotism, fear.

"There is this difference between the nature of government and its principle; its nature is what makes it be such, and its principle, which makes it act. One is its particular structure,

---

145. Charles-Louis de Secondat, Baron de La Brède et de Montesquieu, *De l'esprit des lois*, 1.2.

while the other is human passions that set it in motion. However, the laws must be relative to the principle of each government and to its nature."[146]

In addition to the classification of the forms of government, which shows the relationship between the thought of Montesquieu and classical political thought, there is another concept that will endure: the separation of powers.

"Freedom can consist only in being able to do what we want, and not being forced to do what we do not want."[147] This freedom entails the separation of political powers. The legislative, executive and judiciary powers should be independent of each other, in order to avoid despotism and the tyrannical abuse of power. Montesquieu admitted that he got this idea from the English constitution, whose main purpose was to safeguard political freedom.

If these ideas of Montesquieu had a vast influence in Europe and America, the critical attitude of François Marie Arouet, better known as Voltaire (1694–1778), also enjoyed great popularity.

Voltaire wrote a lot and very effectively, with an elegant French satirical style. He did not have a system, but in his writings there is a common spirit: the critique of tradition, which runs throughout his work.

Voltaire argued that the seventeenth-century metaphysical systems are artificial, and that Cartesianism leads to Spinozism. However, he thought that Newton leads to true theism, where we recognize a supreme God who created all things. Moreover, he thought that Newton rediscovered final causes, which are the most valid proof for the existence of God.

Very close to Locke in his epistemological empiricism, Voltaire doubted the spirituality of the soul, and he identified freedom as a term that men have invented to designate the known effect of any unknown cause.

---

146. Montesquieu, *De l'esprit des lois*, 3.1.
147. Montesquieu, *De l'esprit des lois*, 11.3.

While rejecting freedom in a psychological sense, he was an avid advocate of political freedom, not in the democratic sense (Voltaire always despised the masses) but in the sense of freedom for philosophers. Voltaire intended to replace the dogmas of the Church with the principles of Enlightenment philosophy. He went to extremes to defend religious tolerance, and ended his writings with the phrase *Écrasez l'infâme* (Crush the loathsome), where the loathsome was the Catholic Church.

Voltaire was not a profound philosopher, but he achieved something few philosophers achieve: to mold the thought categories of broad intellectual sectors. Confidence in the progress of the enlightenment and a consideration that faith is an obstacle to this progress would be the leitmotif of subsequent thought.

Regarding Jean-Jacques Rousseau (1712–1778), the last of the exponents of the triad mentioned above, we are presented with a historical classification problem. This citizen of Geneva was not exactly a man of the enlightenment. He declared himself against the attitude of the *philosophes*, whom he described as "zealous missionaries of atheism, and even more, dogmatic tyrants."

His revaluation of the inner feelings, the consciousness that man is not only reason, but mainly heart, represent a theoretical exit from the Enlightenment and a bridge to Romanticism. But at the same time, his rationalist construction of the Social Contract, the revolutionary political thesis he proposed, and the milieu in which he developed his doctrines allow us to classify him within the field of the Enlightenment.

He was born in Geneva in 1712, the son of a watchmaker. Rousseau received a poor education because of the absence of his mother, who died shortly after birth. He spent his early childhood in Geneva, and then afterwards he went to Piedmont and France, where he stayed most of his life. From Calvinism he converted to Catholicism; but he later on decided to embrace a natural religiosity.

Rousseau was sentimental, passionate, and contradictory. The author of *Émile* or *On Education*, he had several children whom he abandoned to an orphanage. He presented elements that provide for interesting psychological study. In the last years of his life he seemed to have suffered from a mental illness, manifested in a persecution complex. He died in Erménonville in 1778.

Among his most important works from the point of view of the history of philosophy, we must mention the *Discours sur les sciences et les arts* (*Discourse on the Arts and Sciences*, 1750), the *Discours sur l'origine et les fondements de l'inégalité parmi les hommes* (*Discourse on the Origin and Basis of Inequality among Men*, 1758), and three books published in 1762: *Julie, ou la nouvelle Héloïse* (*Julia or the New Heloise*), *Du contrat social* (*The Social Contract*) and *Émile*. Works of an autobiographical type, which showed his pre-romanticism, are: *Rousseau Judge of Jean-Jacques*, the *Confessions*, and *Rêveries du promeneur solitaire* (*Reveries of a Solitary Walker*).

Rousseau did not present a system, although he defined his work as a *système du coeur* (system of the heart) However, it is possible to single out a basic principle of his philosophy: nature has made man good and happy, but society has degraded him and has made him miserable. In his *Discourse on the Arts and Science*, Rousseau tried to give an answer to the question about the positive influence of culture in the ways of men. The Genevan considered the eighteenth-century man as denatured and alienated, since he no longer responds to himself, but depends on the opinion of others. The society of the *Ancien Régime* denatured European man: it is necessary to return to the origin, "listen to nature," Rousseau wrote.

The *Discourse on the Origin and Basis of Inequality among Men* was an attempt to rediscover authentic human nature. Rousseau, in its pages, presented the *homme naturel* that is, original human nature. In the thinking of the Swiss philosopher, nature and culture are contrary concepts: culture is artificial, the unnatural; nature is identified with the original and the spontaneous.

Rousseau artistically described man in the state of nature: "This being thus constituted, stripped of all supernatural gifts that he may have received, and all artificial faculties, that he has acquired through long progress; in a word, considering him as he had come out of the hands of nature, I see an animal weaker than the others, less agile, but overall, more advantageously organized than all others; I see him satisfy himself under an oak, quench his thirst in the first stream, finding his rest at the foot of the same tree that has provided his food, behold all his needs are met."

The natural man is still a pre-rational being, happy and kind; we understand this natural goodness to mean everything that can contribute to the preservation of his life. Being asocial, enjoying the chance to satisfy all his material needs, all men were equal and free: freedom is based on a pre-rational internal sentiment. Freedom, therefore, and equality are natural rights of men.

The circumstances outside of the state of nature changed; man developed his rational faculties that were in potency; in order to meet his needs, now unsatisfied because of the changes from the original state, man slowly moved away from the state of nature.

The origin of eighteenth-century society is a social contract, based on economic inequality, which tramples on basic human rights. We must re-establish society, though a return to the state of nature is impossible; we must lay entirely new foundations, which are in line with the original rights of men.

The social contract is Rousseau's political proposal. After analyzing original human nature and finding out the changes undergone by the influence of culture and unjust social institutions, Rousseau arrived at the constructive moment: "The problem is to find a form of association which will defend and protect, with the whole common force, the person and goods of each associate, and in which each—while uniting himself with all—may still obey himself alone and remain as free as before."[148]

---

148. Jean-Jacques Rousseau, *The Social Contract*, 1.6.

The theoretical purpose of the political formulation of Rousseau is to safeguard man's original freedom and equality. For this to be achieved, it is essential to observe a clause in this contract: "the total alienation of each associate, together with all his rights, to the whole community."[149]

In the society of the contract, natural freedom is transformed into civil freedom. The power that arises from the contract—the sovereignty or general will of the people—is made up by the rights of all the citizens. In this sense, the popular will that legislates is the citizen's will, because all of them form part of the power that is of the community, which safeguards the individual's rights and is erected as sovereign. This correlation is freedom, which is defined as the "obedience to a law which we prescribe to ourselves."[150]

For Rousseau, freedom is autonomy and self-legislation. This idea will be taken up by Kant, who will put it at the basis of his moral system. Equality becomes legal equality. The law is the declaration of the general will and is the same for all.

While it is clear that Rousseau's ultimate intention was to defend the rights which he considered an integral part of human nature, some of the institutions he proposed tended toward totalitarianism. Rousseau explained that as men come together in society for the common good—the defense of freedom and equality—the general will that arises from the alienation of the rights of individuals would necessarily tend toward the same common good.

Moreover, Rousseau added that nobody wants to harm himself. However, the lack of a concrete content of this common good which is oriented towards the general will makes Rousseau's system end up in formalism, capable of receiving different institutional configurations. The only real content of this common good is freedom as self-legislation and legal equality, which are formal rights.

149. Rousseau, *The Social Contract*, 1.6.
150. Rousseau, *The Social Contract*, 1.8.

In *The Social Contract*, on behalf of an absolute, indivisible and infallible general will, the right of association and freedom of education are denied, and religious freedom is reduced. It was the price to pay for the rediscovery of some natural rights, not sufficiently founded on a notion of human nature and incapable of justifying not only its origin, but also its transcendent purpose.

4.4 THE GERMAN ENLIGHTENMENT

In Germany, the Enlightenment went through several stages. The amplitude of the interests of the German Enlightenment, the prestige obtained by the main universities and influence of some theses, made the *Aufklärung* the precedent of the golden age of German philosophy and literature, which has among its leading men Kant, Goethe and Hegel.

The first phase of the German Enlightenment is represented by two legal philosophers: Samuel Pufendorf (1632–1694) and Christian Tomasius (1655–1728). They developed a doctrine of natural law with a rationalist bent, where the precepts of justice are deduced from general and rational laws and principles. Both philosophers, but more specifically Tomasius, separated natural law from metaphysics and theology. The metaphysical analysis of man, carried out by the second scholasticism to give foundations for natural law, was replaced by a psychological analysis of human tendencies and passions.

With Christian Wolff (1679–1754) the second phase of the German Enlightenment began. He was a university professor at Halle and was an archetypal representative of the philosophy that a few years later Kant would call dogmatic. Wolff had the aim of creating a complete philosophical system.

Being a disciple of Leibniz, and taking metaphysical elements from the second scholasticism, particularly Suarezian essentialism, his system was a gigantic, logical-formal, complete and consistent construction, although removed from sensitive reality. In this system, logic played a basic methodological role. The principle of non-contradiction and sufficient reason formally constitute the bedrock of all knowledge. Science can be rational or empirical and each has a theoretical aspect and practical applications. Not having great originality, we can say that Wolff is an eclectic. He left philosophical posterity with a terminology that would enjoy great success. After Wolff the term ontology would be used to refer to metaphysics; critical theory would refer to the theory of knowledge: and theodicy would replace natural theology.

Wolff was at the same time a sincere believer and a rationalist. So he did not hesitate to consider reason as a judge of the faith. This theoretical position earned him the opposition of the Pietists, who carried Wolff into exile, although he returned to his homeland under the protection of the king. This fact of Wolff's life allows us move on to the more specific area of the *Aufklärung*: philosophy of religion and in particular, the relation faith-reason.

In eighteenth-century Germany, there was a religious group called the Pietists. Originally Lutheran, Pietism stressed the importance of the inner aspect of religion: faith is manifested primarily in sentiment and in personal religiosity rather than in dogmatic truths. Although this attitude may seem contrary, or at least not very favorable, to the *Aufklärung*, pietistic mistrust against all types of metaphysics and scholastic theology managed to unite two seemingly antithetical movements.

The third period of German Enlightenment takes place in the latter part of the government of Frederick the Great (1712–1786), King of Prussia, a friend of English and French philosophers, and protector of Voltaire. The king himself wrote some philosophical works, such as the *Essay on Love of Self considered as the Principle of Morals* (1770).

The introduction and translation of some books of the English deists Toland and Tindal favored the development of a current of German deism. In this intellectual environment we must mention Hermann Samuel Reimarus (1694–1768), Jewish, and a strong advocate of natural religion. In a work published posthumously by Lessing, and had as title *Apology and Defense of the Rational Worshipers of God*, Reimarus maintained that the only divine revelation was the natural world itself. The super-natural revelations were only human inventions, and the very same miracles were an offense to God, who wanted to create a world organized and governed by a rational system.

Another Jewish philosopher with deist convictions was Moses Mendelssohn (1729–1786), who did not share the hostility of Reimarus against supernatural revelation. Mendelssohn was interested above all in the relationship between religion and political power, advocating for tolerance and the non-intervention of the State in religious matters.

Gotthold Ephraim Lessing (1729–1781) is the philosopher of greatest importance in the field of the philosophy of religion during the German Enlightenment. This author will also be important as the link between the aesthetic ideas of Baumgarten (a disciple of Leibniz), and Goethe's aesthetic theory. As regards his philosophical thought, he did not fully agree with Reimarus, even though he had worked on the posthumous publication of his works. Lessing did not believe that a body of doctrine could be demonstrated rationally and universally, although it may have strictly natural truths. The absolute and final truth belongs only to God.

Lessing's attitude to the truth is evidenced by this famous quote: "If God had in his right hand all the truths, and in his left hand the only motivation to always aspire to the truth, with the possibility of erring always and eternally, and he were to tell me, 'Choose' I would humbly kneel to his left and say, 'Father, give me this! Pure truth is reserved only to Thee.'"

According to Lessing, we cannot despise revealed religions. The value of all revealed religions should be measured by the social consequences that they bring. His interpretation of Christianity, made from the perspective of the social and moral consequences it has produced, were more positive than those held by other deists. Despite this positive assessment, Lessing was very far from orthodoxy.

The German philosopher held a vision of human history where Christianity was just a phase. World history passes through three periods, corresponding to the stages of the psychological development of man.

The first stage, parallel to that of human children, is symbolized by the Old Testament.

The second stage is youth: this corresponds to the New Testament, which preaches the immortality of the soul and God as universal Father. At this stage of history, Christians added speculative theological elements that are not entirely negative, but need rationalization.

Finally, the third stage, parallel to psychological maturity, is the stage of the eternal Gospel, in which man will do what is good for the sake of good, and not for the sake of reward or punishment. Lessing presented this theory of history, but he partly re-proposed some elements taken from Joachim of Fiore in a work entitled *The Education of the Human Race*.

* * *

The Enlightenment represented the centrality of man, the supposed triumph of reason over faith, progress over tradition. Its prophets announced a future full of light, once the medieval darkness was defeated. But lights and shadows are always mixed in the history of mankind, and continued to be mixed in subsequent centuries. The Enlightened Man rediscovered some values that were hidden under customs that could be considered superstitious, but he also lost something of great value, by rejecting the supernatural and the transcendent.

<u>Sources</u>

Pierre Bayle, *Dizionario storico-critico* (Bari: Laterza, 1976).

Etienne Bonnot de Condillac, *Oeuvres philosophiques*, Georges Le Roy, ed. (Paris: Presses universitaires de France, 1947–1951).

Joseph Butler, *The Works of Bishop Butler*, John H. Bernard, ed., (London: Macmillan, 1900).

Samuel Clarke, *Works*, (London, 1738–1742).

Jean le Rond d'Alembert and Denis Diderot, eds., *Encyclopédie ou Dictionnaire raisonné des sciences, des arts et des métiers* (Paris, 1751–1772).

Denis Diderot, *Opere filosofiche* (Milano: Feltrinelli, 1963).

Claude-Adrien Helvétius, *Oeuvres* (Deux-Ponts: Sanson, 1784).

Edward Herbert of Cherbury, *Tractatus de veritate*, (London, 1633); *De causis errorum* (London, 1645); *De religione gentilium* (Amsterdam 1663–1670).

Francis Hutcheson, *Works* (Glasgow, 1772).

Julien Offrey de La Mettrie, *Opere filosofiche* (Bari: Laterza 1974).

Gotthold. Ephraim Lessing, *L'educazione del genere umano* (Bari: Laterza, 1957).

Moses Mendelssohn, *Werke* (Leipzig, 1843–1844).

Charles-Louis de Secondat Montesquieu, *Oeuvres*, Edouard Laboulaye ed. (Paris: Garnier, 1875–1879).

Isaac Newton, *Sir Isaac Newton's Mathematical Principles of Natural Philosophy and His System of the World*, (London: Cambridge, 1934).

Jean-Jaques Rousseau, *Oeuvres completes* (Paris: Firmin-Didot, 1910).

Anthony Ashley Cooper Shaftesbury, *Saggi morali* (Bari: Laterza, 1962).

Matthew Tindal, *Christianity as Old as Creation* (London, 1730).

John Toland, *Christianity not Mysterious* (London, 1696).

Voltaire, *Oeuvres de Voltaire*, M. Beuchot, ed. (Paris, 1828–1834).

Christian Wolff, *Logica tedesca* (Bologna: Patron, 1980).

PART FIVE

KANTIAN TRANSCENDENTAL PHILOSOPHY

The figure of Immanuel Kant emerged in the eighteenth century like that of a true giant. It seems that all previous philosophy was a preparation for Kantianism, and subsequent philosophy a dialogue with the philosopher of Königsberg. We cannot doubt the importance of the Kantian philosophical project.

Kant was faced with the two currents of thought that characterized seventeenth-century philosophy: rationalism and empiricism. He closely followed the development of physical science with the theory of Newton; he lived with the major exponents of the Enlightenment and he saw the fall of the *Ancien Régime,* after the events of 1789.

Kant's transcendental philosophy was an attempt to give a global response to the new problems that confronted the European man of the late eighteenth century. How can we harmonize the skepticism of Hume, Newtonian science and rationalist faith in the ability of reason? Will science and metaphysics still be possible after the principle of causality has been criticized? What can man know, and how?

If the criticisms of the empiricists against the rationalist were valid, wouldn't the proofs of the existence of God in the seventeenth-century metaphysical systems and morality, based on transcendence, be invalidated? These questions, which reach the depths of human aspirations—God, freedom, consciousness—will obtain responses in the work of Kant.

Although he took ideas from both empiricism and rationalism, Kant's system was original, systematic and revolutionary.

"The starry sky above me and the moral law within me" are Kant's two objects of admiration: knowledge of nature, although we can only know phenomena by pure theoretical reason and the categorical imperative as the moral law, known by practical reason. God, freedom and immortality are recovered after Hume's skeptical crisis, but only as postulates.

Post-Kantian thought was faced with the "scandal of the thing in itself," a reality that, while not knowable by reason, was regarded as necessary. Fichte, Schelling and Hegel would give different answers from the Kantian one, but they presupposed the thought of the Königsberg master.

a) Life and Works of Immanuel Kant (1724–1804)

Kant was born in Königsberg (at that time, East Prussia) in 1724. He obtained a very careful education from the moral point of view, and through his mother, he was formed in the spirit of pietistic Protestantism. From 1732 onwards he studied at the *Collegium Fridericianum*, whose rector was the theologian Schultz. But a very strict discipline and too many exercises of piety eventually moved Kant away from religious practice.

From 1740 on, Kant studied at the University of Königsberg. He learned the theories of Newton, and studied physics, mathematics and philosophy. In 1746 he finished his studies, writing the work *Thoughts on the True Estimation of Vital Forces* (*Gedanken von der wahren Schätzung der lebendigen Kräfte*).

Between 1746 and 1755, because of the death of his father, he worked as a tutor for several families to earn a living.

In 1755 he published *Universal Natural History and Theory of Heaven* (*Allgemeine Naturgeschichte und Theorie des Himmels*); he obtained his doctorate with a thesis *About Fire*, and he obtained his teaching habilitation with the thesis *A New Elucidation of the First Principles of Metaphysical Cognition* (*Neue Erhellung der ersten Grundsätze metaphysischer Erkenntnisse*).

The university professorship of Kant will not address philosophical issues only. He would also teach biology, geography and pedagogy. Between 1762 and 1763 he published four works, which foretell his mature philosophical system.

In 1770 he held the chair of Logic and Metaphysics at the University of Königsberg. In that year he published a dissertation *On the form and principles of the sensible and intelligible world*, which marks the beginning of his intellectual transformation. After the publication of his dissertation in 1770, came eleven years of deep meditation. The result of this period is the *Critique of Pure Reason* (*Kritik der reinen Vernunft*), published in 1781, that had a second edition in 1787, equally famous as the first.

Between the first and second edition of the *Critique of Pure Reason*, Kant published *Prolegomena to Any Future Metaphysics* (*Prolegomena zu einer jeden künftigen Metaphysik*, 1783) and *Groundwork of the Metaphysics of Morals* (*Grundlegung zur Metaphysik der Sitten*, 1785). In 1788 he published the *Critique of Practical Reason* (*Kritik der praktischen Vernunft*), and in 1790 he completed the trilogy with the *Critique of Judgment* (*Kritik der Urteilskraft*).

The only academic problem Kant encountered during his university career was the controversy that took place after the publication in 1793 of *Religion within the Limits of Reason Alone* (*Die Religion innerhalb der Grenzen der bloßen Vernunft*). Kant was accused of having opinions contrary to Holy Scriptures. He then decided not to talk about religion anymore, though he changed his mind after the death of King Frederick William II when the freedom of press was restored.

Kant devoted the last years of his life to political philosophy and philosophy of history. He witnessed the fall of the *Ancien Régime*, and was excited about the French Revolution, but he condemned its violent excesses. In this field he published in 1795 *Perpetual Peace* (*Zum ewigen Frieden*), and in 1797 the *Metaphysics of Morals* (*Metaphysik der Sitten*). In the same year he left university teaching and began a review of his philosophical system. The notes he made during this period have been collected and published under the title *Opus Postumum* and were published in 1920.

Kant, after eighty years of methodical life, dedicated to philosophical research and study, died at Königsberg, his hometown, in 1804.

b) The Sources of Kantian Thought

As mentioned above, Kant received various influences, though he was to be a profoundly original author.

Continental rationalism, especially the systems of Leibniz and Wolff, was a source of Kantian thought. But Kant, after a period of rationalist tendencies, would criticize these metaphysical systems that he qualified as dogmatic, that is, systems that would deduce all principles *a priori*, without recourse to experience.

Kant claimed that it was Hume who woke him from his "dogmatic slumber." However, Kant's embrace of empiricism was not total. Contrary to the assertion that experience is the only source of knowledge, Kant accepted, in his critical stage, an element which is *a priori*, given by pure reason for the sake of experience. Thus Kant was able to reject the skepticism of Hume and restore the principle of causality as a true foundation of scientific knowledge.

At the core of the Kantian system we can also find the influence of Newton. Kant believed that Newtonian physics combined the accuracy of mathematics with experimental knowledge. The method by which Newton laid the foundations of physical science should also serve to provide the foundations of metaphysics. The difference is that, in the first case, science deals only with the phenomena of experience, whereas in the case of metaphysics, the phenomena serve only as a starting point.

If Newton is a key to understanding Kant's epistemology and his attempt to lay new bases for metaphysics and science, when it comes to morals, the place of Newton is occupied by Rousseau.

According to the testimony of Kant himself, the Genevan made him discover that man was not only reason, but also feeling and freedom. As a result, the Kantian system, by the influence of Rousseau, will become a humanism based on the notion of autonomy. Specifically, this notion in Kant has a clear origin in Rousseau.

Besides the influences of Newton and Rousseau, it is important to highlight the religious element of his training and in particular, pietistic Lutheranism which emphasized the subjective aspect of faith and religious practice, sidelining the dogmatic-doctrinal content of the faith itself. In this sense, there is identification between morality and religion, in which the strictly religious elements are absorbed by morality.

In Kant there is another influence from Lutheranism: a pessimism that led him to recognize the radical nature and ubiquity of evil. However, Kant wanted to harmonize this element with his faith in human progress, typical of the Enlightenment of which he also was a part. The autonomy of reason with respect to any instance of authority, a key feature of the Enlightenment, was significantly present in his system.

With respect to the stages of development of Kantian thought, most scholars speak of two periods: the pre-critical period, which runs from 1746 to 1770, where we can see rationalist influences and later empiricist influences. The 1770 *Dissertatio* would mark the boundary between the first period and the second, called the critical period. There are some historians who speak of a third period, the post-critical, but it seems there are no marked differences in the latest production of Kant to justify a border that would separate this period from the critical period.

c) The Pre-Critical Period

In this first stage, we find in the works of Kant elements that we would now call scientific, along with other elements that are strictly philosophical. However, the primordial interest of Kant focused on the search for an adequate method for metaphysics. Therefore, the most significant arguments of this period, related to this methodological pursuit, deal with causality, existence and the essence of space.

1) Causality

Kant began his reflections on causality by analyzing previous rationalist tradition. According to Kant, Wolff considered the concepts of cause and reason as convertible. Our author, however, distinguished between logical reason, which is the beginning of knowledge, and real reason or cause, which is the principle of being. He also criticized the notion of *causa sui* and the ontological argument; he judged it as not demonstrative.

Subsequently, and still at the pre-critical period, Kant explained the non-analytical nature of causality and the real distinction between cause and effect. However, he did not find any explanation for the real derivation of the effect with respect to the cause, while at the same time he also recognized without any difficulty the logical derivation of one concept from another through conceptual analysis.

2) Existence

Contrary to the possibilistic metaphysics of Leibniz and Wolff, Kant believed that existence is not a complement of possibility, but an absolute position of the object, which is only known through experience, not through conceptual analysis.

3) Space

Kant at this stage presented different attitudes with regard to space. He started from an opinion that is halfway between Leibniz and Newton. Kant concurred with Leibniz, who said that space is a relationship between bodies, but Kant denied that it is of a merely ideal order and he affirmed the possibility of the interaction of substances. Thus, his notion is more similar to the Newtonian theory of space as absolute, immovable, immutable, and prior to the existence of bodies.

But in 1769, according to his own statement, he received "a great light" that would make him see space as a pure intuition. Space "is not something objective or real, not a substance, nor an accident, nor a relation, but subjective and ideal, which arises from the mind, according to a stable law, as a scheme coordinating everything we feel externally."[151]

This discovery was already included in the *Dissertatio* of 1770. In this work there is another important concept, announcing the critical period, the concept of phenomenon: "Whatever behaves as an object with respect to our senses is a phenomenon."[152] This statement about the phenomena as relative to sensitivity is linked to the differentiation between sensitivity and intellectual knowledge.

According to the Kant of 1770, the intellect knows things as they are, that is, it knows the noumena, the things-in-themselves.

d) The Constitution of Critical Philosophy: the Object and the Transcendental

At the beginning of the critical period, Kant asked about the basis of the relationship between the representation (all cognitive forms) and the object of knowledge. In the first place, we must note the replacement of the term *thing* or *entity* with the term *object*. The first term is, in a sense, something absolute. Object, however, always expresses a relation to the knowing subject.

---

151. Immanuel Kant, *Dissertatio de 1770*, 403.

152. 152. Kant, *Dissertatio de 1770*, 397.

The peculiarity of the Kantian attitude lies in this: in order to address the problem of knowledge he directed his attention to the subject and its cognitive powers. It is a reflective method that does not tend toward things, but rather to the cognitive mediation that enables the constitution of an object.

The central point, therefore, is not the possibility of the objects themselves, but the possibility of knowledge that is *a priori* with respect to experience. It is, more precisely, a retroflection, a reflection "looking back" towards the subject, a reflection about reflection, thinking about thinking itself, not forgetting that for Kant, thinking is always about objects and not about the void.

Kant did not ask only about what we know or how we know, but also about the very possibility of knowledge; in his response he established a process that is "looking back," which claims to be a process that is constitutive.

Kant achieves a Copernican revolution in the sense that the transcendental system is an attempt to constitute the objects starting from the subject. But Kant is not a rationalist like the philosophers of the previous tradition, because as we have seen, he rejected the *a priori* deduction of objects: his starting point was sensory experience.

But, since experience is a kind of knowledge, we must consider the mediation conducted by the intellect. In this sense, Kant is not an empiricist either, since he admitted a transcendence of sensory knowledge, consisting, as we shall see later, in the *a priori* forms and concepts of the intellect.

This revolutionary theory was treated in the first part of the *Critique of Pure Reason*. But before analyzing this work it is necessary to clarify the use of the word *transcendental*.

For Kant, transcendental does not mean the properties that derive necessarily from all being, as the classics had it: *verum, bonum, pulchrum*, etc. Nor does it mean the adjective transcendent. In the Kantian critical context transcendental is a property of knowledge, when dealing not with objects, but with our way of knowing *a priori*. Transcendental is the

Kantian method: it means the entirety of the internal laws of knowledge and is the condition of all experience. "Transcendental doesn't signify something that goes beyond all experience, but something that does indeed precede experience *a priori*, whose role is simply to make knowledge through experience possible."[153]

e) Analysis of the Critique of Pure Reason

1) Purpose of the Work

The *Critique of Pure Reason* has as its purpose to examine the faculty of reason in relation to knowledge that can be had outside our sensory experience. In other words, it is about verifying, according to Kant, the possibility of metaphysics as scientific knowledge. Pure Reason, in this context, means reason untainted by sense experience.

Kant, in a position analogous to that of Descartes, observed the progress of physical and mathematical sciences and he wondered whether metaphysical problems are caused by an incorrect methodology. In this sense, the *Critique* is a treatise about the method that metaphysics should follow. Kant was in an intellectual environment in which many had denied the possibility of metaphysics.

According to Kant, we must find out if there is any function in our knowledge that is able to reach the unconditional, that which transcends experience. And this is not only a theoretical quest: we seek the unconditional in order to provide a foundation for morality. Thus, the *Critique of Pure Reason* is a preliminary work—not only in a chronological sense—to the *Critique of Practical Reason*.

The whole of philosophy, according to Kant, should respond to three questions: What can I know? What should I do? What I am allowed to expect?

---

153. Immanuel Kant, *Prolegomena*, 373.

The scientific method *par excellence* for Kant is that of the physical and mathematical sciences. We see, then, a certain dogmatism at the moment of defining science. This dogmatism will ultimately prevent knowledge from going beyond sensory experience, closing the door to the possibility of metaphysics in the strict sense.

2) Synthetic a priori Judgments

The philosopher of Königsberg said that while all knowledge begins with experience, not all of our knowledge comes from experience. Starting from this statement, Kant distinguished between *empirical* or *a posteriori* knowledge, and *pure* or *a priori* knowledge.

Empirical knowledge is *a posteriori* with respect to experience. It is contingent and particular knowledge.

In contrast, pure knowledge is *a priori* with respect to experience, and gives us necessary and universal knowledge.

Having made these distinctions, Kant proceeded to classify judgments.

There are *synthetic* and *analytic* judgments. Synthetic judgments give new knowledge, in the sense that the subject of the judgment does not necessarily belong to the predicate, and since they come from experience, they are particular and contingent.

Analytic judgments, however, are necessary, since the relationship between subject and predicate is one of identity or belonging. They are *a priori* with respect to experience, but do not add any new knowledge.

Kant asked about the possibility of synthetic *a priori* judgments. That is, we have to verify the possibility of joining the necessity and universality of analytic judgments, with the increase of knowledge that synthetic judgments give. It is necessary, therefore, to find a judgment that is both synthetic (that is, it adds new knowledge) and *a priori* (and therefore universal and necessary).

According to the Prussian philosopher, mathematics and physics have made progress because they are based on synthetic *a priori* judgments. Kant will attempt to demonstrate this thesis in the first two parts of the *Critique of Pure Reason*, which he called *transcendental aesthetics* and *transcendental analytics*. But are synthetic *a priori* judgments, which provide a foundation for metaphysics, possible? This question will be answered in the third part of the *Critique*, called *transcendental dialectic*.

3) The Transcendental Aesthetic

Kant admitted two "trunks" of knowledge: sensibility and intellect. Through sensibility, objects are given to us while through the intellect, objects are thought of. Transcendental aesthetics is the study of the *a priori* elements of sensitive knowledge: "The science of all principles of *a priori* sensibility is what I call transcendental aesthetic."[154]

For Kant sensation is the pure modification or affection that the subject receives passively from the object. Sensibility is the faculty that receives sensations. Intuition is the immediate knowledge of the objects. Therefore, Kantian intuition is always a sensible intuition; it is not intellectual since objects are always sensible.

The object of sensible intuition is called *phenomenon*—appearance or manifestation—while the thing in itself—the *noumenon*—is unknowable.

In any phenomenon we can distinguish between matter, that comes from particular sensations—and as such, is always *a posteriori*,—and the form, that does not come from experience but rather from the subject, thus organizing the multiple sensory data by giving them definite relations. Insofar as they come from the subject they are *a priori*.

---

154. Immanuel Kant, *Critique of Pure Reason*, A298, B355.

Kant called the knowledge wherein sensations are concretely present *empirical intuition*; while he called *pure intuition* the form of the sensibility considered apart from matter. The pure intuitions or forms of sensibility are two: space and time. Space is the form of external sensibility and time of internal sensibility.

After these clarifications in terminology, it will be easier to understand the following text by Kant:

"I must first explain as clearly as I can my view about the basic constitution of sensible knowledge in general, so as to head off any misinterpretation of it. What I have wanted to say is this: All our intuition is nothing but the representation of appearance. The things we intuit are not in themselves what we intuit them as being, nor are they related, in themselves, in the way they appear to us to be related. If we strip off from the story our own mind, or even just the subjective character of our senses, then all the structure—all the inter-relations—of objects in space and time would disappear; indeed, space and time themselves would disappear; because as appearances, they can't exist in themselves but only in us. We know absolutely nothing about what objects are like in themselves, considered apart from all this receptiveness of our sensibility. All we know is our way of perceiving them, which is special to us and may not be the same for every being, though it is certainly the same for every human being. We aren't concerned with anything except this. Space and time are its pure forms, and sensation is its matter.

The first ones we can know *a priori*, that is, prior to any actual perception and are therefore called pure perceptions. The second however, is due to what in our knowledge is called *a posteriori*, that is, empirical intuition. The former are inherent to our sensibilities with absolute necessity, whatever our sensations may be, which may be very varied. Although we might be able to clarify our intuitions to the full, not for this would we be closer to the nature of the objects themselves. Since in that case, we would just come to know very well our mode of intuition, that is, our sensibility; but it is always subject to the conditions of space and time, originally inherent in the subject. The clearest knowledge of the phenomena of objects, which is the only thing we are given of the objects, would never make us know what they are in themselves."[155]

According to Kant, geometry and mathematics are based on pure intuitions of sensibility: they have necessity and universality insofar as they are *a priori*, and they are applied to the sensations that provide the matter of phenomena. This knowledge, as is clear from the text just quoted, is phenomenal: it does not penetrate the noumenal world of the things in themselves.

4) The Transcendental Analytic

1. *The Kantian Categories*
   At the end of the transcendental aesthetic we find the data provided by the senses and ordered by space and time, the pure forms of sensibility. Now the intellect must intervene. But whereas sensitivity is intuitive, the intellect is discursive.

   The concepts of the intellect, according to Kant, are functions. And the proper function of the concept is to unify and order the manifold under a common representation. In other words, the function of the intellect is to judge because, in the judgment, the unity of concepts is achieved. This is a further step in the constructive activity of the knower. To the ordering of the phenomena through the application of the pure forms of sensibility (space and time), is now added the unification performed by the pure concepts of the intellect.

---

155. Immanuel Kant, *Critique of Pure Reason*, A43, B60.

The transcendental analytic forms part of the transcendental logic, which is the study of the origins of the *a priori* concepts of the intellect. The analytic, in particular "explains the elements of pure knowledge of the intellect and the principles without which no object can be thought of absolutely."[156]

The unifying activity of the intellect develops according to twelve types of judgments. The syntheses that correspond to the forms of judgments are called categories, not to be confused with Aristotle's *leges entis* but rather, *leges mentis*. "The same function which gives unity to the various representations in a judgment, thus also gives unity to the simple synthesis of various representations (. . .) this unity is called *pure concept* (or category)."[157]

The forms of Judgment and the consequent Kantian categories are:

a) *Judgments of quantity:* universal, particular, singular; from which arise the categories: unit, plurality, totality.

b) *Judgments of quality:* affirmative, negative, infinite; from which arise the categories: reality, negation, limitation.

c) *Judgments of relation:* categorical, hypothetical, disjunctive; from which arise the categories: substance and accident, cause and effect, interaction between agent and patient.

d) *Judgments of modality:* problematic, assertoric, apodictic; from which arise the categories: possibility-impossibility, presence-absence, necessity-contingency.

---

156. Immanuel Kant, *Critique of Pure Reason*, A50, B74.

157. Immanuel Kant, *Critique of Pure Reason*, A79, B105.

158. Immanuel Kant, *Critique of Pure Reason*, A92, B124.

According to Kant, the categories "contain the basis for the possibility of all experience in general."[158] Similar to what happened with the pure forms of sensibility, *a priori* elements of intellect are what make knowledge possible. Without them, we could not refer to an object. The knowing subject through the discursive intellect, constitutes the very possibility of experience. The pure forms of sensibility—space and time—carry out a first step in the unifying process of knowledge. The categories further unify the sensible representations. But in the Kantian system, according to the method we have designated as retroflexive, the foundation of the unifying activity of the intellect is behind or beyond the pure categories: it's the *Ich denke* or transcendental subject.

5) *The Transcendental Subject or Ich denke*

The unifying element that is necessary for the unity of the object of experience, as we have just said, has to be found beyond the categories. The high point of the transcendental analytic is in the *Ich denke* (I think), also called the *transcendental apperception*.

The twelve categories presuppose an original supreme unity, which further carries out a unifying function. This unification is given by self-consciousness or *Ich denke*.

The *Ich denke* should not be understood as an empirical individual "I," as a psychological subject, but only as a structure of thought common to all empirical subjects: that by which any empirical subject is a thinking and conscious subject. In the words of Kant, "the various representations which are given in a certain intuition would not all together be my representations, if they did not all belong to a self-consciousness."[159]

The unification achieved by *Ich denke* or the transcendental subject is the highest point, and at the same time the basis of the constructive activity of the knower.

---

159. Immanuel Kant, *Critique of Pure Reason*, B134.

In the end, Kant came to tell us something very simple, but of deep consequences in philosophy: there is no object except for a subject.

For modern thought, this is a truism, but this truth is the essence of the modern philosophy of the subject. The Copernican revolution has been accomplished: the objects of knowledge are regulated by the subject and not the other way around. Objectivity comes from subjectivity.

The position of the object as an object matches the position of the subject as a subject. The unity of the object comes from the unity of consciousness, that is, in the "I think." That's why the "I think," viewed historically, is not only the center of Kantian thought, but also the summit of modern subjectivism.

The subject is no longer, as in Descartes, a mere starting point: I see things from the perspective of the I, but things are still things in themselves. The subject has become a starting point and center: my perspective constitutes the things. If Descartes historically signified the youth of modern subjectivism, Kant is its maturity. After him can only come the romantic thought of Fichte: the ego as self-positing."[160]

6) Analytic of Principles

Up to this point in our discussion, Kant tried to explain the cognitive process based on experience, and he arrived at the foundation of the unity of the object of experience, the transcendental subject. But at this stage, Kant ponders the way back to the phenomena, that is, how pure intellectual categories can be applied to the matter of sense knowledge.

---

160. See Eusebi Colomer, *El pensamiento alemán: de Kant a Heidegger* (Barcelona: Herder, 1986), 1.121.

Kant's answer to this problem is called the *transcendental schema*. The schema, or application of the categories to the matter of the phenomena, must lie in some element that is both sensible and pure, because it is a mediation between the pure categories and sensible objects. For the Prussian philosopher this mediator is *time*, which is both pure and sensitive. In the transcendental aesthetic, Kant spoke of *space* as a form of external sensibility, and of *time* as a form of inner sensibility. But the same externality, once the phenomena are known, becomes internal. Therefore, time as an *a priori* form of sensibility is the general condition according to which only the categories can be applied to an object.

There are as many schemes as categories. To give some examples, the scheme of the category substance is *permanence in time*; the scheme of cause is *temporal succession*; the scheme of action is *temporal simultaneity*.

Having explained the application of the categories to phenomena through the form of internal sensibility, Kant can already speak of nature as the order and connection of phenomena. All the principles derived from the categories represent the entirety of the *a priori* knowledge we have of nature.

Kant speaks of the metaphysics of nature as the study of the set of principles that constitute the conditions of natural science. As is clear, this is not classical metaphysics: it is the epistemology of Galilean-Newtonian science, which always remains in the field of phenomena, without ever reaching the noumenal core of reality.

7) *The Distinction between Phenomenon and Noumenon*

Kant thought that, with what we have explained so far, we have demonstrated the possibility of mathematics and physics. But the conclusion of the analytic method leads to a science that is purely phenomenal. We still have to solve the problem of *the thing itself*, the noumenon.

The thing itself is not an object of the senses. Noumenon means an intelligible being, since it is an object thought by the intellect. According to Kant, we can understand the noumenon in two ways: in a negative sense, it is the thing as such, abstracting from the way it can be known; in a positive sense, it would be the object of an intellectual intuition.

Kant continues that we can only think of noumena in the first sense, since there are no intellectual intuitions. But the concept of noumenon is problematic because when we consider sensible intuition as being limited only to the phenomena, we are tacitly admitting a noumenal substratum.

Furthermore, the concept of a thing in itself is not contradictory. Moreover, this concept is necessary so that sensible intuition does not extend to the thing itself, and thus we can limit the objective validity of sensible knowledge. The concept of noumenon is an inevitable limit concept that limits sensibility.

8) The Transcendental Dialectic

After analyzing the transcendental aesthetic and analytic, we now study the last part of the *Critique of Pure Reason*: the Transcendental Dialectic. After denying the possibility of noumenal knowledge, is there any room for metaphysics? Kant devoted this part of his Critique to respond to this question.

Kant, as we have said, affirmed the inability of going beyond sensory experience, if our aim is a rigorous knowledge. But reason always strives to exceed that limit and because of this, it falls into errors and illusions. Kant described the transcendental dialectic as follows:

"So the transcendental dialectic will content itself with exposing the illusion of transcendent judgments, while also keeping us from being deceived by it. It can't make the illusion actually disappear (as logical illusion does), because what we have here is a natural and inevitable illusion, trading on subjective principles that it foists on us as objective; whereas logical dialectic, in exposing deceptive inferences, has to deal merely with a failure to follow the rules—i.e. with an illusion artificially created by something imitating a valid inference. So there we have it: there's a natural and unavoidable dialectic of pure reason. It's not something that a bungler might get tangled in through ignorance, or something that a sophist has contrived so as to confuse thinking people. Rather, it is inseparable from human reason; even after its deceptiveness has been exposed, it will go on playing tricks with reason, continually tricking it into momentary aberrations that have to be corrected over and over again."[161]

For Kant therefore, these illusions are natural: we can defend ourselves from them, but we cannot remove them.

Kant used the term *reason* to designate the understanding that goes beyond the horizon of possible experience. But since this tendency is natural, Kant also used the term reason to designate the faculty of the unconditioned, in the sense that it manifests the demand for the absolute that exists in man.

Reason is the faculty of metaphysics, and its function is not that of the intellect, that is, to judge, but rather to reason by way of syllogisms.

There are three types of syllogisms: categorical, hypothetical and disjunctive. To these correspond three ideas: the psychological idea (soul), the cosmological idea (world) and the theological idea (God).

---

161. Colomer, *El pensamiento aleman: de Kant a Heidegger*, B354–355.

From these presuppositions, Kant developed the critique of rational psychology, rational cosmology and rational theology.

Let us review them briefly:

1. *Critique of Rational Psychology*: the transcendental illusion of reason makes one fall into paralogisms or defective syllogisms. This happens when the *Ich denke* is understood not as a purely formal activity, but as an object. When we think of the *Ich denke* as an object of intuition, we give it the category of substance. The idea of soul, object of rational psychology, is the result of this going beyond sensory experience. The basis of the *a priori* categories of the intellect is converted into a substance, about which we have no experience.

2. *Critique of Rational Cosmology*: the idea of the world is understood as ontological totality seen from the viewpoint of its ultimate noumenal causes. Kant spoke of the world as a metaphysical whole. The transcendental illusion makes us fall into antinomies, that is, thesis and antithesis that are simultaneously defensible at the level of pure reason, but have no support in experience, since we cannot have an experience of the world as a whole.

   The antinomies are the answers to the following questions: Is the world finite or infinite? Can it be resolved into simple parts or not? Is there necessary or free causality in the world? Does the world presuppose a necessary and absolute cause or not? Reason vacillates between the two opposites, because beyond experience, concepts work in a vacuum.

   According to Kant, the antinomies can be overcome when it is shown that the conflicts are just apparent, because the error lies in having applied the idea of absolute totality, of the metaphysical whole, to phenomena, when in reality it belongs to the noumenal world, about which we cannot have experience.

3. *Critique of Rational Theology*: the idea of God is configured as an ideal. For Kant, it is the only ideal strictly speaking, in the sense of a concept of a thing that is universal in itself, determined by itself and as representation of an individual. However, this ideal that reason presents us leaves us in total ignorance about the existence of a being that has such preeminence. Therefore, Kant considered it necessary to investigate the validity of the proofs of the existence of God.

Kant held that all proofs that have been given throughout history can be summarized in three basic types: ontological proofs, cosmological proofs and physical-teleological proofs. The first are based on the concept of the most perfect being, the second, on the concept of necessary being, and the third are based on the finality, beauty and order in the world.

Kant rejected the ontological proof, arguing that from a logical concept one cannot derive real existence. The proposition asserting the existence of a thing is not analytic but synthetic: existence is the real position of the thing. In this topic, Kant incorporated some of the elements that he developed in his pre-critical stage. There is no means by which we know the objects of pure thought. It would require an intellectual intuition which, according to Kantian presuppositions, is impossible.

Neither is the cosmological proof valid: the principle that leads us to infer a cause from the contingent has meaning only in the sensible world, but outside this world, it makes no sense since the principle of cause and effect is based on experience. Similarly, the physical-teleological proof suffers from the same problem: it goes beyond experience and therefore lacks a rigorous foundation.

The physical-teleological proof merges with the cosmological proof: it goes beyond experience.

9) The Regulative Use of the Ideas of Reason

After analyzing the different parts of the Critique of Pure Reason, we must now follow Kant in his conclusions: metaphysics as a science is impossible, because the *a priori* synthesis which would be at the base of this science—the ideas of soul, world and God—presupposes an intuitive intellect, and the transcendental dialectic has shown the errors and illusions of reason as a faculty of metaphysics.

However, the ideas of soul, world and God have a regulative use: they serve as schemes to put order into experience, as if all phenomena concerning man depended on a single principle, as if all the phenomena of nature unitarily depended on intelligible principles, as if all things depended on a supreme intelligence.

From the scientific point of view, we cannot go beyond sensory experience. Therefore, metaphysics is not possible as a science. We are left, however, with two metaphysical elements: the non-contradiction of the noumena and the regulative use of the ideas of reason. Through the practical use of reason, as we shall see, Kant will approach the world of noumena.

It should be added that when Kant spoke of metaphysics, he had in mind seventeenth-century rationalist metaphysics. His criticisms do not make a dent in classical metaphysics, which, unlike dogmatic metaphysics, begins with experience and uses abstraction to reach universal and necessary knowledge.

f) Kantian Morality

The *Critique of Pure Reason* answered the question about knowledge: what can we know? But now, the *Critique of Practical Reason* must answer the question about morals: what should we do? The Kantian moral response will be as revolutionary as his theory of knowledge.

1) Duty and the Categorical Imperative

Kantian morality is a morality of duty. Up until Kant, the basic concept of morality was the good, which was related to the ultimate end of man. But the philosopher of Königsberg believed that such a conception of morality is itself immoral.

Kant faced an empiricist conception of the good, understood as pleasure or interest. With respect to this doctrine, Kant's critique seems clear: the tendency towards the good is a selfish, hedonistic and utilitarian tendency. Kant's critique, however, loses force against rationalist morality, which understands good as an absolute that transcends the sensible; or against the classical position, which considers the moral good as the full realization of human nature understood in a teleological sense.

At any rate, according to Kant, the pursuit of happiness can never substantiate an obligation. If man seeks his own good, this means that he has a selfish tendency. And since this tendency is a fact of life and a natural necessity, a natural tendency that is necessary and not free cannot serve as a basis for moral obligation.

The Kantian opposition between freedom (the moral sphere) and Nature (the sphere of the necessary) becomes clear at this point: no tendency can be a source of morality, insofar as these tendencies fall within the ambit of nature, the sphere of the necessary, and not to the moral dimension of freedom.

The first revolutionary conclusion of his starting point is that the morality of human actions cannot be based on the matter of the action, that is, the goods or purposes towards which the action tends, but in the form, that is, the intention of the agent, taking into account whether this intention conforms to the duty dictated by reason.

Between the *Critique of Pure Reason* and the *Critique of Practical Reason*, Kant published *Groundwork of the Metaphysics of Morals*. In this work, our author asserted that the only thing that we can call good is a *good will*. What makes a will good is neither works nor the success that can be achieved, but the will's uprightness, which consists in the intention to act out of duty. It is not only to act in accordance with duty, but out of duty. An action done only by inclination is not moral, although materially it may conform with duty.

In the same work, Kant spoke of the only moral sense, which is respect; he identified it with the submission of the will to law, together with the inner conviction that obedience perfects us morally. Along with this unique subjective principle of morality, we find the main objective principle: duty. What is duty? It is a law that comes from reason *a priori* and that imposes itself to every rational being. It is a *factum rationis*, and is translated into consciousness through the *categorical imperative*.

Kant distinguished between the hypothetical imperative and the categorical imperative. The first determines the will only with the condition that it wants to achieve certain objectives: If you want to get good grades, you must study. The hypothetical imperative may be a rule of convenience, or a prudential advice. The categorical imperative, however, declares the action as objectively necessary in itself, without a relation to any end: the categorical imperative does not say, "if you want . . . you must"; but rather, "you must . . . because you must."

The categorical imperative is a practical law that applies unconditionally to all rational beings, because it is an objective and universally valid rule, independently of all subjective accidental conditions that may be found among men.

In the *Groundwork*, Kant presented three formulas of the categorical imperative:

Act as though the maxim of your action were to become, through your will, a universal law of nature.[162]

Act in such a way as to treat humanity, whether in your own person or in that of anyone else, always as an end and never merely as a means.[163]

To act only so that the will could regard itself as giving universal law through its maxim.[164]

By means of the third formulation the key concept of autonomy is introduced. Duty is not imposed from outside of the will, since it comes from the reason that constitutes man. To subject oneself to an external reason would be a *heteronomy* incompatible with the dignity of the human person. For Kant, the autonomy of the will is the sole principle of all moral law and its respective duties. Heteronomy cannot justify any obligation and is contrary to the morality of the will.

In Kantian moral theory, autonomy is closely related to freedom. Freedom is the independence that the will has with respect to the natural laws of the phenomena. In the negative sense it is independence; in the positive sense it is self-determination. The moral law is a law of liberty. First we know the law, duty, as *factum rationis;* then we infer freedom as its foundation: you must, therefore, you can.

---

162. Groundwork of the Metaphysics of Morals, Ak 4.421.
163. Groundwork of the Metaphysics of Morals, Ak 4.429.
164. Groundwork of the Metaphysics of Morals, Ak 4.434.

Kantian morality is configured as a formalist morality, one of duty, autonomous and universal. As can be
observed, there is a notable change of perspective between
the *Critique of Pure Reason* and the *Critique of Practical Reason*. The first criticized the tendency of reason to break
away from experience and work in the void: this is why
Kant criticized pure reason. But, in the second *Critique*,
Kant wanted to alert us regarding the tendency of reason
to be bound to experience in the field of morals. Therefore, he criticized not pure practical reason, but practical
reason as such, the reason that wants to base morality on
the sensible.

2) The Postulates of Practical Reason

In the *Critique of Practical Reason*, Kant reviewed the same
theme of the *Groundwork*, and added the theory of the postulates. The ideas of pure reason, those ideal demands that
are beyond reason, become postulates in the field of practical reason since they represent a noumenal world that cannot be known.

What is a postulate? Kant responds: Postulates are not
theoretical dogmas, but rather suppositions that are practi-
cally necessary; while they do not broaden our speculative
knowledge, they give objective reality to the ideas of speculative reason in general (by means of their reference to what
is practical), and authorize concepts, whose possibility we
could not otherwise venture to affirm.[165]

The thesis of the postulates is a demand of practical reason, because they are conditions for the moral life.

The affirmation of the postulates requires an act of practical faith. Faith, as such, adds nothing to our knowledge. It
is a free and voluntary affirmation. The three postulates of
practical reason are: the immortality of the soul, freedom
and the existence of God.

---

165. See Immanuel Kant, *Critique of Practical Reason*, Ak 5.240.

Freedom is a condition for moral life and, as we have seen, it is based on the law. Kant added that in the noumenal field, freedom can be understood as a cause. Thus, man belongs to the phenomenal world of necessity, and the noumenal world of free causality.

The existence of God is justified as follows: the moral law commands me to be virtuous, by virtue we mean the adequacy of my action to duty. Being virtuous makes me worthy of happiness. Being worthy of happiness and not becoming happy is absurd. Hence the need to postulate God as the fulfillment of happiness, which can never be found in this world.

The postulate of the immortality of the soul comes from the fact that the highest good, that is, the perfect conformity of the will to the moral law, is holiness. Since this goal requires an infinite process towards full conformity, it will be possible only if we assume an existence and personality of a rational being that lasts infinitely, and this is nothing other than the immortality of the soul.

At the end of the *Critique of Practical Reason* we face three moral realities that were the ideal demands of pure reason. In a certain sense, the noumenal world is recovered with the theory of the postulates. There is, therefore, supremacy of practical reason over theoretical reason, which manifests the moral purpose of the Kantian project. It is clear that this recovery is not of the epistemological order: the theory of knowledge of Kant never exceeds the barrier of possible experience.

g) The Critique of Judgment

The third Critique or the *Critique of Judgment* has, in the Kantian system, the task of mediating between the two first Critiques. With pure reason we can only know the phenomenal world, where necessity reigns; with practical reason, we come to the noumenal world of freedom, not theoretically, but through a practical perspective.

The foundation of the unity between the two worlds is a third faculty, judgment, which consists in thinking that the particular is contained in the universal. In other words, Kant sought, through reflective judgments, the hypothesis of the finality of nature, since judgment, by reflecting on the objects already constituted by pure reason, captures things such as the harmony of things with each other and with us. In the concept of finality, we can find the mediation between necessity and freedom: nature conceived teleologically agrees with moral finality.

According to Kant, the finality of nature can be grasped by reflecting on the beauty or the order of nature. The first reflection gives rise to an aesthetic judgment, and the second, to a teleological judgment. The aesthetic judgment is not theoretical, because it is based on a feeling of pleasure. All men possess this feeling, but we are dealing here with a subjective universality in the sense that everyone has his own feelings. Beauty is the form of the finality of an object, insofar as this is perceived without the representation of an end.[166]

The sentiment underlying the aesthetic judgment is a disinterested pleasure, produced by the harmony and order we perceive in the object itself and in relation to others. Kant distinguished between the beautiful and the sublime. Beauty is characterized by limitation, by determination. The sublime, on the contrary, is unlimited; it awakens in the subject a feeling of respect.

---

166. See Immanuel Kant, *Critique of Judgment*, Ak 5.223.

As regards teleological judgments, these manifest the irresistible tendency of the subject to consider nature in a teleological sense. To think of nature as teleological is a determination of the use of one's cognitive powers, but it says nothing about nature considered noumenally. Nor is it a new *a priori* principle that constitutes the possibility of objects. Teleological judgments are found, rather, in the field of the ideals of pure reason and the postulates of practical reason and act as links that unite the world of necessity to the world of freedom. At the end of the *Critique of Judgment*, Kant stated that the ultimate purpose of nature is the moral fulfillment of men.

i) Religion, Law, History

Some scholars of Kant speak of a fourth Critique, which would include the writings of Kant on religion, law and history. All these writings present a collection that is rather homogeneous and systematic and they represent another attempt by Kant to unite nature and freedom.

1) The Philosophy of Religion

For Kant, as we have seen, God is an ideal of theoretical reason, and a postulate of practical reason. In his most important work of philosophy of religion—*Religion within the Limits of Reason Alone* (*Die Religion innerhalb der Grenzen der bloßen Vernunft*)—and in other minor writings, we can find an identification between morals and religion. Morality is based on itself, and with it we arrive at the concept of God as law giver.

Along with the moralization of religion comes a rationalization of the same, as is well expressed by the title of the work referred to. Kant distinguished between pure religion, which has only rational content commanding us to follow an upright behavior guided by the categorical imperative, and historical religion which has both rational and non-rational elements, the latter of which can be superstitions.

For Kant, the role of historical religion, that is, religion based on an alleged divine revelation, serves as propaedeutic to pure religion. There is one God, and therefore only one religion, which is the rational religion. In this rationalist context, Kant conceived of Christ, above all, as the personification of the moral law.

Despite his moralization and rationalization of the philosophy of religion, there is one aspect of Kant's religious doctrine that presupposes the need for a redeemer: the doctrine of radical evil. There is an inclination to evil in man, resulting from the use of freedom. Along with this inclination there is also a predisposition of human nature to the good. Kant believed that the biblical account of original sin is a symbol representing evil in man.

To go from evil to good one has to undergo a radical conversion and achieve moral purity in one's intentions. Such purity is personified in Jesus. This doctrine of radical evil and the necessary conversion is perhaps the vestige of religion in Kant's autonomous humanist philosophy.

2) The Philosophy of Law and History

The issue of law appeared constantly in Kant's writings. In this area, his most important work is the *Metaphysics of Morals*.

Kant clearly distinguished between law and morality. The law concerns the external acts of man, while morality deals with the internal acts. Law, according to Kant, "is the set of conditions under which the will of one can be reconciled with the will of others, following the general law of freedom."[167]

The rule of law is found only within civil society, a stage that is posterior to the state of nature, which Kant conceived not as something historical but as a methodological hypothesis.

---

167. Immanuel Kant, *The Metaphysics of Morals*, Ak 6.230.

In the state of nature there already is a certain form of society, but the passing over to civil society brought with it a greater juridical security. The influence of Rousseau is evident and deep, both in Kantian doctrine on morality and politics. For Kant, as for Rousseau, man retains his freedom in the civil state, since he obeys only the laws to which he has given his consent, thus ensuring the autonomy of his will. Kant added a theory of a universal legal order in a paper entitled *Perpetual Peace* (*Zum ewigen Frieden*), in which he proposed a world republic governed by universal laws.

The Kantian concept of history has many elements from the Enlightenment. For Kant, history is a continuous process towards progress. The historical stages are seen as preparations for an improvement of the human species. There is a rational plan for nature, sometimes referred to by Kant as providence, where it seems that the decisive factor is the same intentionality of nature rather than human freedom.

The ultimate goal of history is man himself, not taken individually, but as a rational species.

* * *

A general assessment of the whole Kantian system is difficult, especially considering that Kant, in the last years of his life, decided to write a systematic work, which he never finished. The annotations of this work, which are fragmented and disjointed, were published in 1920 under the name of *Opus Postumum.*

Although we may say that these annotations do not present a different Kant, there are contradictions that can leave us perplexed. For example, according to some fragments, Kant speaks of God as transcendent to man, but there are others where he presents an immanent God, identified with the moral law.

Leaving aside the doubts that arise from the reading of *Opus Postumum,* we can see in Kant an attempt at universal systematization, only comparable in modern philosophy to the work of Hegel.

Kant studied the most important issues of human existence. The answers he gave are not definitive and we have the right not to share his starting point nor the conclusions of his system. But the philosophical-moral project of the thinker of Königsberg is a necessary reference for all subsequent thought, and is also a challenge for philosophers who wish to walk in ways different from Kant.

Sources

Immanuel Kant, *Gesammelte Schriften* (Berlin 1902–1942).

EPILOGUE

In philosophy, endings do not exist, or rather, all endings normally refer to a type of subdivision, which means that it is essentially relative. In this introductory course on the history of modern philosophy we have gone through the centuries in which philosophical speculation passed from an initial moment of differentiation with respect to medieval philosophy, to a development whose characteristics appear to be what we may by now call *classical*. If in the fifteenth century, we had found many philosophical and cultural elements that still belonged to the great medieval tradition, soon after we entered into the full maturity of modernity. Sometimes, the Renaissance period has been defined as opposed to the philosophy of the seventeenth and eighteenth centuries; like walking in the dark without a clear destination. Exaggerations aside, there is some truth to this statement: in contrast to the modern project, Renaissance philosophy is still poorly defined and is more linked to tradition. On the other hand, from Descartes and Bacon, modern philosophy begins to appear as a project. While the differences between thinkers and movements are many, there is no doubt that a great unity of vision covers both rationalist and empiricist philosophies; at the same time, a very fluid contact exists between these two philosophical currents. Moreover, culture becomes more and more marked by a new character: rationality, new conquests of freedom in various fields, political change, the birth of the scientific mentality, experimentalism, etc. These emerge strongly from the seventeenth century.

If we were to speak of a rupture or a distinction between what is medieval and what is modern, we should not only refer

246 A History of Modern Philosophy

strictly to the philosophical level, but also to the whole of philosophy, politics and art. In this conjunction of elements, philosophy sets the pace and takes the initiative in the new era. Although many elements from ancient and medieval tradition remained during the modern period, as we have seen, it is also clear that this tradition suffered substantial changes. In Descartes or Leibniz, to name two examples, we see philosophical concerns that were very much related to a philosophical tradition, but at the same time, these concerns were inspired by quite different interests from those of tradition. The new demand for evidence, the constant awareness of the capabilities of man and the constant measuring of reason and freedom with what man could or ought to do, formed part of a new force proper to modern thought. Empiricism is, in this sense, an example of the critical capacity to know. The same observation applies regarding the world of ethics and freedom. Kant provides a great synthesis of this modern development. Reason must know itself and judge itself; freedom must find the decisive justification of its own activity in itself: man has become the center of the world without exceptions. The philosophical interest is not directed toward the thing itself, but focuses on the capacity of man—or lack thereof—to attain it.

With Kant, the drama of modernity reaches, so to speak, a definitive configuration; it paved the way for a form of rationality and morality which became the culmination of many attempts done previously. But the drama takes form not so much in the consciousness that man begins to have with respect to his own possibilities, nor in his need to justify all his steps in the field of knowledge and praxis. Rather, the drama takes shape around the *losses* that this philosophical attitude implies. The rationality of Rationalism, that is, the manner of conceiving the very motion of reason and its scope, is a rationality separate from life. It is abstract. Man, in an attempt to criticize his own way of judging, has been locked in the lone consideration of that which he is capable of, without the possibility of going out of his own subjectivity. The ambit of freedom suffers a similar process: the modern man's increased awareness of his freedom and the vivacity of his perception of it, remains, in a sense, just in that: the pure perception of that liveliness and awareness.

From this point of view, freedom also becomes, paradoxically, something abstract, something that cannot be attained. All this leads to a profound contradiction: there is greater awareness of the means that man has at his disposal to conquer the world, knowledge, to achieve higher ethical standards; but at the same time, by not having gone beyond the mere consciousness of these means, he is prevented from reaching the real world: rationality and freedom are two ideals that are largely at risk of remaining as just that, ideals, that are contemplated and considered, but not lived. Man knows that he is free and to be freer, he has an inner law that can justify his own actions; he also knows that in order to guide reason critically, without the shadow of dogmas, he must submit everything to rational criticism.

But what is the purpose of all this? Both freedom and reason have withdrawn into themselves, they have entered a space that only they can occupy; they know their own laws, that is, their own subjective limits and possibilities. But all this has been done by an inward reflection, in which man sees himself in all his grandeur and at the same time, in the most complete solitude: reflection has separated man from the realization of rationality and freedom.

During the height of the time of Kant's critique, that is starting in 1770, some signs began to emerge of a first assessment and renewal of the modern consideration of freedom and rationality. At first, a cultural, literary and poetic movement, *Sturm und Drang*, developed criticizing the Enlightenment worldview. The first Romanticism, born from this cultural movement, goes further in its criticism. In the last decade of the eighteenth century, when Kant completed his philosophical project, a critique of the Kantian system and, more generally, of the Enlightenment culture, had already come about. These were the years of the young Hegel, Schelling and Fichte. Each in his own way tried to rethink the great modern issues with the aim of finding a solution to the drama that man had created after having reached a lively awareness of his own capacity and mission. These were also the years of the philosophical poetry of Schiller, Holderlin and Novalis; and of the *Systemprogramm*, the first explicit program of radical critique of Kantianism and the Enlightenment. The motto seems always to be the same: to reconcile thought with life, to rebuild or rediscover the unity that the Enlightenment had divided. The greatest in carrying out this project will undoubtedly be Hegel.

This emerging Romanticism coexisted with the last manifestations of the philosophy of the Enlightenment, taking up once more the philosophical theme begun during the time of Descartes, and in some cases, Renaissance topics. The rediscovery of the Middle Ages is, in this context, not so much the acceptance of a philosophical tradition in the strict sense, but rather an expression of a new love for what is almost unknown and has therefore a mysterious character. The tremendous clarity of the enlightened reason that had wanted to reduce mystery to a simple question of scientific ignorance now begins to doubt itself and to find areas that are beyond rational self-transparency.

Although historical periods serve to give some minimum parameters for understanding history, they do not exhaust it. We therefore find ourselves at the end of a period and, at the same time, before the emergence of critical movements against the period that has just ended. Modern philosophy does not, in fact, end with Kant nor with romantic philosophy: modern philosophy still continues alive today. We finish this book outlining the historical continuation of what has been proposed for consideration and study. Above all, we hope that this may serve as an incentive for the continuing search for the truth.

INDEX